# WRESTLING'S
# MADE MEN

★ ★ ★ ★ ★

# WRESTLING'S MADE MEN

## Breaking the WWE's Glass Ceiling

Scott Keith

**CITADEL PRESS**
Kensington Publishing Corp.
www.kensingtonbooks.com

CITADEL PRESS BOOKS are published by

Kensington Publishing Corp.
850 Third Avenue
New York, NY 10022

All Kensington titles, imprints, and distributed lines are available at special quantity discounts for bulk purchases for sales promotions, premiums, fund-raising, educational, or institutional use. Special book excerpts or customized printings can also be created to fit specific needs. For details, write or phone the office of the Kensington special sales manager: Kensington Publishing Corp., 850 Third Avenue, New York, NY 10022, attn: Special Sales Department; phone 1-800-221-2647.

CITADEL PRESS and the Citadel logo are Reg. U.S. Pat. & TM Off.

First printing: August 2006

10 9 8 7 6 5 4 3 2 1

Printed in the United States of America

Library of Congress Control Number: 2005938609

ISBN 0-8065-2771-4

"I'm not leaving the WWE for good, I'm not leaving wrestling for good.
When I'm ready to come back I will. It may be one month, it may be
one year, but when the time is right, I'll know and I will return and
be better than ever....I wouldn't think of returning any other way.
You won't see me doing any conventions or indie shots in the meantime.
If I'm going to be in the wrestling biz, it will be with the WWE. I'm a
member of the WWE family for the rest of my life...just like the
Mafia."

--CHRIS JERICHO

# CONTENTS

# INTRODUCTION

"Just when I thought I was out, they pull me back in!"
—MICHAEL CORLEONE, GODFATHER PART III

IN FEBRUARY 2000, at the No Way Out pay-per-view (PPV) show, former three-time World champion Mick Foley wrestled a match against then-current World Wrestling Federation (WWF) champion HHH, with his fifteen-year career on the line as a stipulation. And he lost. Most felt that it was inevitable, since Foley was riding high on the success of his first book, *Have a Nice Day*, at that point, and it was well known that he wanted to retire and write more books. However, six weeks later he was back on TV, wrestling in the main event of the sixteenth Wrestlemania to help the company's bottom line. Not many were surprised by that, either, because retirements in wrestling are a joke. However, many *were* surprised when four years later, after several best-selling books and millions of dollars in royalties, Foley returned to active competition to make a new star out of Randy Orton, since most assumed that this retirement, more than any other seen in wrestling before, would be the one that stuck. In the end, however, the basic truth came out again: Much like the mafia, once you're into wrestling, you're in until you die.

Yet despite what would seem to be a somewhat dire warning of failing health in later years and drug-related deaths too numerous to count at times, there's always another crop of young guys, sucked in by the cool factor of having thousands of people chanting their name, ready to come in and take the place of the "retiring" older generation. Whether or not that actually *happens* is another matter, but there's no shortage of people willing to give it a try. With the mafia, at least you know that you've got a good shot of someone getting whacked and opening up a new slot above you, but with wrestling people tend to hang on a lot longer than that.

There's a very strictly enforced hierarchy within the World Wrestling Entertainment (WWE), because once Vince McMahon "opens up the books" and declares you to be one of his guys, you're set there for life. Take for instance the case of Hulk Hogan, the biggest star of the '80s and still sadly attempting comebacks in 2003 with broken-down knees and hips, and almost all of his hair and muscle-tone gone. Although a comeback in 2002 initially worked well, generating excitement among the old-school fans in the audience hungry for nostalgia, every subsequent attempt by the WWE to make Hogan back into something worthwhile failed, leaving him spinning down the card until he ended his career in a silly masked-man gimmick as "Mr. America" and lost his final match on an episode of Smackdown before disappearing from the promotion again. Still, despite all evidence to the contrary in the last, oh, five years or so, should Hogan return again he'll get another shot at the top in a high-profile position, because he already made it over the top and no longer needs to

earn his spot there. Fair? Of course not, but that's life in the funny pages.

Contrast that with the story of Chris Benoit, long regarded as the best (and most unappreciated) wrestler in North America and never given a shot at the top due to typical WWE circular logic: You can't be a main eventer in the WWE until you've main evented in the WWE. So finally in January 2004, after years of teasing following his initial jump from World Championship Wrestling (WCW) in 2000, Benoit was given a win in the Royal Rumble match to earn a shot at the World title, and he won the title in dramatic fashion to seemingly kick off a new era for the promotion. This was the wrestling version of making someone an official part of the mafia—from that point on, the person is considered to be a main event talent and will be treated accordingly in future feuds and booking plans. Well, in theory. At any rate, while someone like Hogan got a free pass back to the main event based on achievements twenty years prior, Benoit had to work his way into the spot, which is itself a rarity in the sport. We'll examine his rise and see if it's too little, too late.

The other focus lies on the new generation of talent looking to break into wrestling's version of cosa nostra: the developmental stars from the Ohio

**BELOW: John Cena**

Valley Wrestling (OVW) who are starting to fill the time on WWE programming and have become a regular part of the promotion in surprisingly short time. Randy Orton, the guy who Mick Foley left retirement to turn into a star, is the highest on their list in terms of potential, but there are many others, including John Cena, Nick "Eugene" Dinsmore, the Basham Brothers, Shelton Benjamin, Charlie Haas, Batista and Muhammad Hassan, most of whom the promotion are seemingly grooming to be the next generation of superstars to carry the load. We'll take a look at them and how successful they've been thus far, and where they're liable to be in the future. We'll also take a look at the ones who *didn't* make it, like Brock Lesnar and Nathan Jones, and where they went wrong.

Finally, the book is a month-by-month, show-by-show examination of the dramatic shift in quality of their flagship show, RAW, and its secondary cousin on the talent side, Smackdown, and how they both got that way.

# ACKNOWLEDGMENTS

THIS BOOK, the fourth in what has become for me an increasingly improbable adventure, could not have happened without the support and help of a great many people.

First and foremost, my beautiful wife and best friend, Jodi, whom I forced to nag me incessantly until I had done one chapter a night, and gave me the support I needed to finish the book on time.

Thanks to my parents for their continued support over the years.

Thanks to my agent, Frank Scatoni, for continuing to make my dreams of writing a reality, and thanks to Richard Ember at Kensington Books for continuing to give me a chance to live out that dream.

Thanks to Mike Jenkinson, Steve Beveridge, Seth Mates, Murtz Jaffer, Blake Norton, and Mike De-George for their invaluable proofreading and early feedback. Although I still don't agree that the movie reviews were "filler."

Thanks to Zen, Huy, and Jodes for giving me a great wedding party and sending me into married life drunk enough to handle it.

And thanks, of course, to all the great fans who continue to buy the books and frequent my rantings on the Internet. Hopefully, this one doesn't disappoint, either.

Note: This book was written using Open Office 2.0, available for free at http://www.openoffice.org.

# WRESTLING'S MADE MEN

★ ★ ★ ★ ★

# APRIL 2003

```
* * * * * * BACKLASH * * * * * *
           FROM: Worcester, MA
           DATE: April 27, 2003
           ATTENDANCE: 10,000
           BUYRATE: 325,000 buys
ADVERTISED MAIN EVENT: The Rock v. Goldberg
```

## RESULTS:

Smackdown tag champions Shelton Benjamin & Charlie Haas
d. Eddie & Chavo Guerrero (15:03, ★★★)

Sean O'Haire d. Rikishi (4:52, -☆½)

RAW tag team champions Kane & Rob Van Dam
d. The Dudley Boys (13:01, ★½)

Jazz d. WWE Women's champion Trish Stratus (5:50, ★★½)

Big Show d. Rey Mysterio (3:45, DUD)

Smackdown World champion Brock Lesnar d. John Cena (15:11, ★½)

HHH, Chris Jericho & Ric Flair
d. Booker T, Kevin Nash, & Shawn Michaels (17:52, ★★½)

Goldberg d. Rock (13:04, ½★)

**OUR STORY BEGINS,** as all great ones do, with a big bald Jewish guy.

When we last left off, it was Wrestlemania XIX in Seattle, way back in 2003, and Steve Austin worked what would turn out to be his retirement match, against the Rock. Original plans for that event were a bit different, however, as Vince McMahon was trying to do a very un-Vince-ish thing and bring in an established name to push as his next big star and next big foil for son-in-law HHH. Namely, Bill Goldberg.

Normally, the modus operandi of the WWE's head cheese is to either develop talent internally and push them to the moon so they can justify their training system, or raid midlevel talent from the competition and also push them to the moon, usually to annoy Ted Turner. However, in the new world bereft of the WCW, there were no Ted Turners left to screw with, and thus everyone of value was already under contract. Unless, of course, they were so ludicrously rich that they had no real reason to continue any sort of serious employment in wrestling.

Goldberg was exactly that sort of fellow.

Back in 2000, just after the period when he was at his hottest as a draw, the WCW signed him to a contract that can only be adequately described as "iron-clad and very lucrative." The feeling from the WCW bean counters at the time was that, if worse came to worst, at least they have their biggest star locked up for the rest of his career and they could survive on his back. Well, Vince McMahon's purchase of the WCW in 2001 was pretty much worse coming to worst, and parent company Time-Warner was thus left with a big-name wrestler signed to a big-time contract and no wrestling promotion to use him in. However, because of the iron-clad nature of the contract, they had to continue paying him out (at a rate of what has been reported as being up to millions of dollars per year) because defaulting on it would incur a fate worse than Goldberg's patented Jackhammer—legal action at the hands of superagent Barry Bloom. However, buying it out completely would be prohibitively expensive and would have cost more than the selling price of the WCW, so Goldberg proceeded to sit at home and tend to his dogs for the next two years. Good deal if you can get it. However, by 2003 he only had a few months left, and from there it was a fairly simple matter for his people and Vince's people and Ted's people to get him out of the deal and bring him into the WWE. For yet another inflated amount of money, of course, but at least this contract was shorter.

This in itself was a pretty surprising turn of events to most people, because Vince has always been a very "What have you done for me in the past few minutes?" type of guy. However, if there's one thing he respects more than some guy marrying his daughter in exchange for power, it's money. The Rock championed the signing of Goldberg, and basically volunteered to be the guy to put him over from day one. The surprise of his signing and arrival was somewhat muted by all the video packages saying GOLDBERG IS COMING, however, which was strange considering how focused on the big surprise reaction the WWE usually is.

To take advantage of Goldberg's presumed popularity and build him up as the next big babyface for the company, Rock took one for the team and turned himself heel early in 2003, altering his image into that of a big Hollywood celebrity who thinks of himself as too big for wrestling. The part about being too big for wrestling of course hit closer to the truth than anyone behind the scenes probably would have liked, but it's said that the best characters in wrestling are the real person turned up to eleven anyway. Rock was also sporting a weird tribal tattoo across most of his shoulders and half of his torso, representing his roots and documenting his life to that point. Although easily covered up by makeup and shirts for future film roles, you have to think that awkward conversational pauses at parties would be the major problem with it. I mean, would you want to be around a guy who walks around going, "Hey, check out my armpit, that's where I won the World title for the first time"?

Having decided that Rock v. Goldberg at Backlash would now be promoted as the "biggest match in the history of our sport" (well, for that month at least), you'd think that they would do everything in their power to continue to make Goldberg look strong, and you'd be mostly wrong. In fact, their brilliant idea was to have him meet up with resident head-case Goldust and wear his long blond wig as a joke. And boy, when that buyrate came in, *everyone* was laughing, I tell ya. In fact, what was happening was that Rock was so over-the-top funny and cool, while ostensibly playing a big jerk, that everyone cheered him and wouldn't get behind Goldberg. Sure, people might have liked Goldberg, kinda, but not in the "We want this guy to shut up the major heel" way that draws money. In fact, putting him against Rock would prove to be a major mistake because the fans apparently didn't want to choose, and given the voice of the WWE for the past three years or some guy who was in WCW his whole career, they chose the home-grown talent.

The match itself proved to be a huge mistake on several fronts. As mentioned, the Rock's massive fan following over the years was out in full force for the Goldberg match, cheering him much louder and more enthusiastically than Goldberg's fans did. The match itself was far too long, booked to go fifteen minutes plus entrances, when nearly every decent match in Goldberg's career has been under ten minutes, and most under five. Rock, being the heel, took the lion's share of the offense, which is again a mistake considering that Goldberg's entire appeal is being the guy who plows through opposition and doesn't sell. The WWE seemingly had it in their brain that they would have to change him to fit the mold of their previous top baby-faces, guys like Hulk Hogan who would take a beating for a few minutes and then make the big comeback, instead of more dominant figures like Steve Austin and of course the Rock. Worst of all, Rock (who should and probably did know better) went out and fired off a bunch of spots that completely made Goldberg look like a chump. For example, playing possum long enough to sucker him into trying a spear, and then getting out of the way and making matador gestures to mock him. Another example was when he used Goldberg's own spear against him, then popped up and played to the crowd while Goldberg had to lie there and sell for him. The message was pretty clear in both cases: Rock was saying, without words, you are stupid for cheering this guy on when I'm much cooler than him. They didn't even do the spot with the Sharpshooter correctly, as the superpowerful Goldberg went for the ropes to break out of the move instead of the more visually impressive counter whereby he would power out of it. The faulty booking concluded with Goldberg taking the People's Elbow, which has long been one of the silliest spots in wrestling, and instead of popping up like the Rock would, he kicked out of the move after a two count. Little things like that annoy me as a fan, because it's really hard to get behind someone who is hyped as the next big thing and then booked to look that weak. Sure, Goldberg won the match, but he needed two spears to do it, and even then Rock had time to stop and do a comedy bit while selling the first spear. A bad match, and a bad start to Goldberg's WWE career, to be sure.

But whereas Goldberg had already been a main event star and thus was "juiced in" for life as a main eventer on the RAW roster, the Smackdown side of the card revealed an entirely different problem—that of John Cena. Originally brought up as an underdog rookie type of character, he quickly gained more face time by altering his persona into that of a goofy white rapper, ala Vanilla Ice. However, the WWE had high hopes for Cena, and certainly no one was going to take Vanilla Ice seriously as a credible, well, anything. Thus,

**BELOW: John Cena**

Cena began an interesting character change, as he suffered a knee injury during a match with Brock Lesnar earlier in the year and started doing much harder-edged promos to hype his return. Instead of Vanilla Ice, he started channeling Eminem for his interview style, making himself out to be a tough white kid from the streets who rapped out of anger, essentially forgoing the original direction of the character. The idea was to create the next big superstar heel on Smackdown, but the character ended up drifting in an entirely different direction. Brock Lesnar, for his part, had regained the Smackdown (WWE) title from Kurt Angle at Wrestlemania XIX and thus Cena was a natural springtime opponent for him. Since all the focus of Backlash would be resting on Rock v. Goldberg anyway, I guess they felt that they could take a chance by sticking the unproven Cena into a World title match against Lesnar. The feud did produce one bit of wrestling history, however, as Cena began mocking Lesnar's finisher, the F5 (which referred to the most destructive grade of tornado) by dubbing his own slam the "F-U," and the name has stuck to this day.

By this point, Brock was really floundering as a babyface, although in the ring he was one of my favorites by far. Combining cool power wrestling with unique mat wrestling, he was truly a hybrid not seen since Goldberg's glory days in the WCW, back when he gave a crap about what he was doing. Sadly, when it came time for the match, they were essentially left out there to die in front of a bored crowd, while all the booking gimmicks went to HHH's match. It was kind of sad that the previous month had featured Hulk Hogan v. Vince McMahon, with two guys who didn't need the heat or the help, being given multiple ref bumps, table breaking, ladders, and Roddy Piper in every effort to make it into a *** match. However, two guys like Brock and Cena, who needed to get over by any means to ensure the survival of the company, were left out

**ABOVE: Brock Lesnar**

there to die with a dull main event style match worked by two guys who weren't ready to carry a main event on their own. In fact, the main body of their match was taken up by a chinlock from Cena, which killed the crowd even worse. The WWE was banging the gong about getting fans to respond better to in-ring wrestling at this point to cut down on the number of dangerous spots performed during matches, which were (not coincidentally) the only thing that a large segment of the fanbase would cheer for. However, trying to retrain fans to like wrestling is one thing, but there's no "wrestling" involved in chinlocks and clotheslines for fifteen minutes, it's just the usual "main event style" offense that we've seen millions of times before. If you have nothing new to say with the match, it's not going to say anything new. The match, such as it was, had no real storyline to it, no psychology for the fans to follow and the finish was anticlimactic.

Probably the worst offender from this show as far as having guys who have been on top for too long already continuing to be there was the six-man match with HHH and his crew of suckups, which served two separate, yet equally important, functions:

1. **Provide a way for Booker T to continue pretending to challenge HHH after already blowing his one title shot at Wrestlemania.**
2. **Transition the feud to Kevin Nash, who had the advantages of being whiter, older, and HHH's friend, for a three-PPV series of matches.**

Booker T's match at Wrestlemania XIX is really a sore spot for a lot of people, and continues to be so, because the match was built up as Booker finally getting his big title shot at HHH after enduring weeks of racist interviews from the champion, and then having all of them proved correct when he couldn't, in fact, get the job done. He did get another title shot on RAW, and couldn't win *that* one either, even with tag team partner Shawn Michaels as the referee, which pretty much sealed his fate as far as ever being a serious main event wrestler again on RAW went.

ABOVE: Big Show, Brock Lesnar and Kurt Angle

Now, moving the feud from Booker to Kevin Nash would have been bad enough had they just left it at that, because Nash can stink up the ring with the best of them and was a couple of years past the point where being a cool guy can compensate. But they decided to do one of the strangest buildups I've seen for a match, playing on the assumed knowledge of HHH and Nash's backstage friendship. This was especially weird because the only time their friendship had ever been acknowledged was the infamous "MSG incident" in 1996, and other than that they had barely even been on the same show together, let alone ever teamed up or acknowledged each other's presence on TV. Kevin Nash is of course the most blatant example thus far of the "juiced in" philosophy of wrestling, and he even played a mafioso character early in his WCW tenure!

The buildup was even weirder because HHH won the match for his team by pinning Nash, which would seem to end the feud right there. But it didn't, no matter how much I wished that it would. In fact, this feud began a pattern for HHH's title reigns that continues to this day, as he was made the focus of the RAW brand for the entire summer, doing a three-PPV series against the same challenger despite none of the matches moving mountains at the box office. Backlash itself was no exception to that, drawing approximately 325,000 buys, which represented a major drop from the disappointing Wrestlemania XIX in terms of money and a bigger disappointment in terms of what people expected Goldberg's debut match to draw.

# 2 MAY 2003

**★ ★ ★ ★ JUDGMENT DAY ★ ★ ★ ★ ★**

FROM: Charlotte, NC
DATE: May 18, 2003
ATTENDANCE: 13,000
BUYRATE: 310,000 buys
ADVERTISED MAIN EVENT: HHH v. Kevin Nash

## RESULTS:

John Cena, Chuck Palumbo, & Johnny Stamboli
d. Chris Benoit, Rhyno, & Brian Kendrick (3:55, ¾★)

Sylvain Grenier & Renee Dupree d. Test & Scott Steiner (6:21, ½★)

Eddie Guerrero & Tajiri d. Smackdown tag team champions
Shelton Benjamin & Charlie Haas in a ladder match (14:21, ★★★)

Christian won the Intercontinental battle royale,
eliminating Booker T (11:48, no rating)

Mr. America (Hulk Hogan) d. Roddy Piper (4:43, -☆☆)

Kevin Nash d. RAW World champion HHH (DQ, 7:44, DUD)

Women's champion Jazz d. Trish Stratus,
Jacqueline, and Victoria in a four-way match (4:47, ¾★)

Smackdown World champion Brock Lesnar
d. Big Show in a stretcher match (15:27, ★★¼)

**SPEAKING OF PEOPLE** who have been hanging around too long and worn out their welcome, that brings us to May PPV, Judgment Day, and the epic PPV debut of Mr. America. In a sense, I'm actually kind of glad that I'm getting a chance to talk about him, because it allows me to talk about a few other things that are tangentially related and far more interesting.

The first thing we need to cover is Sean O'Haire, who got turned from a potentially major player into a two-bit second banana in one fell swoop and never recovered. A survivor of the miserably failed Invasion angle of 2001, O'Haire was sent to the training facilities of the OVW to relearn his craft (i.e., learning to wrestle "WWE style") and was given a rather impressive set of vignettes to reshape his character for the debut. In fact, once in the OVW he was so popular with the fans that he was made OVW champion, showing that he could excel whether using the WCW training formula or the WWE's own formula. The idea, which was quite brilliant in hindsight, was to make him the evil opposite of a motivational speaker, almost a de-motivational speaker. He was supposed to be representing a Satanic figure who encourages people to engage in sinful behavior, and was doing quite well with it. Here's an example of the sort of advice that his vignettes dished out:

*"Go ahead—do it.*
*You have sexual needs. Desires.*
*You want to.*
*You need to.*
*Do it for you.*
*When was the last time you did something*
*for you?*
*Of course it's just a physical thing, it's not*
*like you're going to leave your wife.*
*Let me put it this way: It'll make your rela-*
*tionship stronger in the end.*
*What she doesn't know, won't hurt her.*
*It'll make you appreciate your wife more.*
*In fact, you might even learn a few things.*
*And believe me, your wife will thank you*
*later.*
*But hey, I'm not telling you anything you*
*didn't already know."*

Now, this was actually getting him over as a kind of cult figure on the Internet (especially the catch-phrase) and stirring up a bit of well-earned controversy with the usual religious types who get upset whenever anyone dresses in black and expresses an opinion against the prevailing religion, so huzzah, right? Hell, he even looked like a Satanic version of Ty Pennington, so the women were all over him.

Then, in a strange decision that I suppose was done out of the need to try to make Sean a bigger star, he was suddenly paired with "Rowdy" Roddy Piper, who was his manager. Piper had made a rather shocking return at Wrestlemania, interfering in the Hogan v. Vince match that was promoted as the main event on all the posters. This was particularly shocking because Piper was such an outspoken flake in the months leading up to his return, going on any public media forum that would have him and speaking about the evils of steroids and Vince McMahon in general. He would take dates with "rival" promotions like the short-lived World Wrestling Alliance and the longer-lived National Wrestling Alliance–Total Nonstop Action (NWA-TNA) and cut rambling shoot interviews about Vince, basically promising never to return to the WWE no matter what. Well, apparently "no matter what" was simply a matter of enough money, because there he was again in 2003, luckily on a show (Smackdown) that was taped, allowing them to edit down the craziness in postproduction if need be.

Now, everyone with half a brain could see that Piper was only one live interview away from saying something stupid enough to get fired and that putting any kind of long-term faith in his ability to carry his

end of a feud was foolhardy, but still they chose to put him with O'Haire and try to get some sort of rub off him. Piper is, by the way, very much one of the best, and last remaining, examples of the mafia mentality of wrestling, as he was trained in the "old school" way and acted like the sport was real in just about every mainstream interview he ever did. Piper made a lot of money for Vince in the '80s, so he was in for life no matter how stupid he acted outside of the sport or what comments he might have made without thinking. But while Piper's devilish attitude might have worked well with O'Haire's devilish persona, say, fifteen years and a few hip surgeries earlier, the aging and overexposed Piper was now instant death for the cool factor of the younger and meaner O'Haire, who had both an edgy character and real street credibility thanks to his martial arts training.

Even worse, once O'Haire was paired up with Piper, his previous character completely fell by the wayside and he was turned from evil manipulator into another goth, tattooed bodyguard type. The independent scene is littered with big muscular guys covered in

tattoos, and it was the character O'Haire was playing that set him apart from the rest. So now, no longer allowed to talk for himself and backing up a senile old-timer, the O'Haire-Piper duo were programmed with the corniest possible combination of opponents: Fading superstar Hulk Hogan and then one-legged sideshow act Zach Gowen.

Hogan's 2003 run was, to say the least, a huge disappointment financially and creatively, as no one in any position of power in the WWE hierarchy wanted to lay down for his legdrop any longer, leaving only Vince McMahon to fight Hogan in a "dream" match at Wrestlemania. It was also littered with controversy from Hogan himself, as he had previously demanded another run with one of the versions of the World title before signing (he didn't win that battle) and then de-

**ABOVE: Sean O'Haire and Roddy Piper**

manded a bigger cut of the Wrestlemania purse than the smaller-than-usual $200,000 or so he earned for being third from the top (he lost that battle, too). By the time May came around, Hogan was clearly a mid-card comedy act at best, and to that end he latched onto the most unlikely ratings draw possible to that point: Zach Gowen.

Gowen, an amputee who wrestled with one leg and did fairly well at it, had long told a story about being a Make a Wish kid and having his dying wish be a meeting with Hulk Hogan. In fact, it was that story that got him signed by the NWA-TNA and from there the WWE. Great story, but one problem: When people actually checked into it, it turned out that he made the whole thing up and hadn't actually been in a position of dying or on the Make a Wish foundation's list. But that's okay, because this is wrestling, where lying better than the rest to get ahead just means you're smarter than the rest, and by the time anyone realized what the truth was he was already on TVs across America and presumably inspiring people. Personally, I wouldn't have been surprised if he had been lying about losing the leg and had just hopped around on one foot very convincingly all that time, but that probably would have been pushing it.

The whole feud illustrated the same problem that the WCW had with the same people: The fans were nostalgic for the idea of the '80s generation, not seeing the same guys again at fifty years old stinking up the ring together, or an even older guy (Vince) engaging in a war of words with both of them. So in the angle to really send that Hogan-Vince feud (in the works for twenty years, mind you) into the stratosphere, Vince simply sent Hogan home with pay. My god, what an evil bastard he is. And then to show they weren't *trying* at that point, we immediately got vignettes for the mysterious (but patriotic) Mr. America, a masked man with remarkably orange skin and an unnatural love for the USA. The joke was that everyone knew that Mr. America was Hulk Hogan, but the problem was exactly that: It was a joke. While comedy angles may have played well in the sticks in 1986 (when Hogan was doing the same shtick as "Hulk Machine" and Dusty Rhodes was doing it as "The Midnight Rider"), I'd like to think that the wrestling audience was a bit more mature in 2003. Or at least had seen enough of wrestling in the '80s to remember that the same gag had already been done. On the other hand, it did prove that Hogan's character is a smart guy, because the story line said that Vince was paying him his contract to sit at home, and then Smackdown General Manager Stephanie McMahon signed Mr. America to another, unbreakable contract, so really he was collecting two paychecks and doing none of the work.

Which brings me to Zach Gowen.

To build up for the thrilling Piper v. Mr. America showdown at the Judgment Day PPV, Piper and suddenly silent cronie Sean O'Haire attacked Mr. America, trying to claim a bounty from Vince McMahon, just because they hadn't quite recycled *every* two-bit hack booking idea from Dusty Rhodes yet. Gowen jumped out of the audience to make the save, but his leg fell off while he was getting beat up by O'Haire. No, really. Thus did Gowen debut in the WWE. But wait, it gets worse!

Mr. America, representing America, and Roddy Piper, representing the senile, had a match at the PPV. I tried to forget it, but the evidence is there on DVD on my shelf, so I'm kind of stuck in that regard. I'd say "at least it was short" but I think an obscure version of Einstein's theory of relativity applied and turned the five minutes that it lasted into the equivalent of traveling to another galaxy in a slow-moving rocket while watching the same match for 3,000 years on auto-repeat. There may be scientific precedent behind this phenomena, I'm not sure. I'm willing to accept government money to research it, however. My only requirement is a good pair of sunglasses to block out the glare from Piper's cadaver-like pasty white complexion these days, especially if he continues to wrestle without a shirt.

Gowen continued to chum around with Hogan like his creepy gay ringrat or something, until even Hogan realized that the Mr. America stuff wasn't going anywhere and he left, after losing a six-man match to Big Show that he felt he should have won. In the grand scheme of things, the character wasn't going anywhere anyway, so it was best that he left when he did. At the time, he was pretty pissed about it, though. Then, to continue the comedy of errors that was this period for the WWE, Roddy Piper went on an HBO special about drug use in sports and spilled his guts again, and was fired almost before it hit the airwaves. Piper is

smart enough and rich enough not to care about that sort of thing, but it left Sean O'Haire, who had sacrificed his entire character buildup in exchange for a shot at something bigger with Piper, in limbo. Of course, Piper and Hogan came back later at their whim, because they had already "made their bones" in the business and didn't need to worry about who they pissed off. O'Haire disappeared from TV at that point, after months of buildup, and was quietly fired a couple of months later. To this day I, and many others, don't understand why he was let go when lookalike slugs like Tyson Tomko were given prominent spots on TV. Best theories involve a backstage problem with wheelchair-bound Darren Drozdov and a bogus charge for assaulting a woman at a nightclub.

Over on the RAW side of things, the post-Wrestlemania period meant it was time to try out new talent, and the one that they were obviously highest on was a team called La Resistance. Originally comprised of rookies Sylvain Grenier and Rene Dupree, they had impressive xenophobic promos to build them up, portraying them as French invaders to capitalize on the hatred of France during the second Gulf War. Of course, France turned out to be right on that one, but I'll leave that sort of thing to Michael Moore. At any rate, the explosives in Iraq weren't the only bombs dropped, as Grenier and Dupree completely stunk up the ring from the get-go and it was immediately apparent what a horrible mistake they had made putting any faith in La Resistance being the team of the future. Of course, because Vince is never wrong, that meant an immediate and huge push of them to justify the weeks of buildup. Also, Grenier is the son of Pat Patterson's longtime golfing partner. Dupree actually had some small amount of potential as a heel, especially with his obnoxious "French dance" and preening. He had actually been another one, like O'Haire, who took the OVW by storm when he debuted and seemed to be the heel of the future for the company, but wasn't there long enough to actually learn anything useful. Grenier, however, has been on TV for two years now and is still almost as bad as he was when he debuted.

For those keeping track of the xenophobic tendencies in the WWE tag team division, by the way, 2003 saw Evil Mexicans, Evil Samoans, Evil Italians, Evil Homosexuals, and Evil Canadians, twice, and then of course Evil Frenchmen with the debut of La Resistance. In fact, they later relocated to Quebec, making the third set of Evil Canadians.

Finally, in what no one could ever suspect was a move that would ever lead to anything bigger, Eddie Guerrero and last-minute partner Tajiri (subbing for an injured Chavo Guerrero) defeated Charlie Haas and Shelton Benjamin to win the Smackdown version of the tag titles at Judgment Day. Most assumed it would be a quickie title reign and not lead to anything. And it wasn't supposed to. But it did, and no one inside or outside of the WWE could have possibly predicted it.

# 3 JUNE 2003

**JUNE 2003 PROVED** to be the start of a couple of interesting things for the promotion, on a PPV that wasn't expected to be a particularly big seller.

First up, the third exciting chapter in the saga that was HHH v. Kevin Nash was to be held in the dreaded Hell in a Cell match at Bad Blood, the first-ever RAW-only PPV. The problem was that Kevin Nash was completely broken down at that point and could barely elicit a reaction from the fans, let alone work a **** cage match with good friend HHH. So they did what all desperate bookers do: they brought in a ringer as the special referee. In this case, Mick Foley.

Foley had of course been retired since 2000, after losing to none other than HHH in none other than the Hell in a Cell match. So there was a certain symmetry to the move, I'll give them that. The problem was that expectations of the match quality were not high, to say the least, and personally I wondered if Foley would want to be associated with something likely to be, at best, embarrassingly bad. However, he had a book to promote, and you do what you have to do.

For his part, HHH once again attempted to reform the previously aborted Evolution group. The original idea, in late 2002, was that HHH would form his own version of the legendary Four Horsemen, with him as the leader and godlike omnipotent presence, of course. Early candidates for the slots not occupied by HHH and Ric Flair were Scott "Sick Boy" Vick and Mark Jindrak. Luckily, neither of those came to pass, and instead a loose grouping of HHH, Flair, Randy Orton, and Dave Batista was decided on. After being forgotten for a bit, the group came to light again in June 2003, as Flair turned heel on Shawn Michaels to set up their PPV match (shocking no one) and Orton helped HHH to win a match (HHH winning a match also shocked no one), leaving only Batista to formally rejoin the group a bit later. The big concept behind the group was that, like the Horsemen, the other three guys existed only to help HHH retain his title at all costs.

Interestingly enough, HHH in real life generally needed no help in keeping that title except for his own. For example, the third match between Nash and HHH wasn't even supposed to headline the PPV. From almost the moment he signed, the plan was to have Goldberg go through the Rock and then immediately segue into a June showdown against HHH and win the title, so as to pay off the investment as quickly as possible. HHH, apparently desperately in love with his own belt, begged off and had the match switched

to Summerslam instead, leaving Goldberg with literally nothing to do for a few months. To rub some salt into those wounds, Linda McMahon even went on a conference call with investors and publicly announced how disappointed the company was with Goldberg's first outing! But as for Nash, I'm guessing his hair-care regime was getting too out-of-control for him to afford any longer and he wanted another PPV payoff to finance his Conditioner of the Month club subscription, but that is of course baseless speculation on my part.

Luckily, with lots of blood and weapons and gimmicks, but ironically not much use of the cage itself, the HHH-Nash match was at least within the bounds of what I considered to be watchable, and has been called everything up to "pretty good" by some people. High praise indeed considering expectations going in. The match was overly long for a Nash match, unfortunately, at 21:01, but Big Kev at least did the job, so I can forgive them. But what that match really set up in the grand scheme of things was the rise of Randy Orton.

Randy is the son of Bob Orton Jr., who was best known for having an on-screen relationship with Roddy Piper in the '80s that was a little too close for most people's comfort, as well as having more nicknames than given names (at various times he was "The Bodyguard," "Ace," and "Cowboy," sometimes all three in the same ring introduction!) despite barely ever winning a match in his entire tenure with the company. His best-known gimmick was probably his arm, which was viciously broken by Hulk Hogan in 1985 and resulted in a cast being on his arm for the next fifteen years. Orton was introduced as the good-looking pretty boy babyface "hot new thing" wrestler that all the girls loved, and of course it immediately bombed and the backlash started quickly. Luckily for him, he suffered a shoulder injury early in his run with that lame character, much like the Rock had done in 1997 when a similar gimmick was dying a fast death. And amazingly, Vince McMahon actually seemed to learn something from that lesson, because Orton was repackaged while he was recovering, doing video packages playing up his "pretty boy" image and deliberately positioning him as a heel for his return. The icing on the cake was the "RNN" news updates, where he would provide fans with a running tally of his shoulder injury, expressed in percentage recovered, and delivered on a weekly basis. But with Mick Foley back in the company, even on a short-term basis, and Orton getting ready to put into a planned feud with another legend, Shawn Michaels, a new gimmick was added to his heel repertoire. After punking out Foley to end Mick's very short 2003 run, Randy Orton declared himself to be the Legend Killer and started going up the card from there.

But whereas Mick Foley knew when his time was up, and that it was best to put someone over and move along to something new, Steve Austin did not heed the same lesson. Thanks to years of merchandise sales and being the #1 star in the history of wrestling, Austin was wealthy many times over and had no need to ever work again if he so desired. After years of neck injuries, one final spinal problem removed him from the sport en-tirely after Wrestlemania XIX, and he was effectively retired as a result. Yet, like the guest at a party who won't take the hint to leave at 2:00 A.M., Steve still stuck around a bit longer. Apparently feeling that Eric Bischoff as the "general manager" of RAW wasn't enough dramatic tension, Austin was given the role of "co-GM" by the creative team, supposedly there to keep things fresh and exciting for the fans. (Another lesson that no one has learned in recent years is that burying the quality of your own TV show, on that very TV show, doesn't make fans want to keep watching it.) In reality, the new job title led to Austin being out there week after week emasculating Bischoff and what-ever heels were unlucky enough to get in his way. And Steve of course had no interest in using this new role to put over anyone but himself, as he instead engaged in silly wastes of PPV time like the "Redneck Tri-athlon" against Bischoff, which consisted of burping, pie-eating, and singing contests. This was doubly frus-trating to the fans, and myself, because the only role people want to see Austin in is that of no-nonsense asskicker, and while his now-limited mobility meant that he might occasionally beat the crap out of a heel, no one could give it back to him. And none of it helped ratings, either.

Austin's role as GM did, however, give one charac-ter a much-needed makeover, although whether it was for the better or worse in the long run is debatable. In the tradition of mismatched tag team partners, aimless midcarders Rob Van Dam and Kane, both victims of HHH in the past year to boot, had been essentially shunted into a tag team together and were making the best of it. After winning the tag team titles shortly after Wrestlemania, and getting "made" as a true superstar tag team by beating the aging Road Warriors in their last appearance on national TV before Hawk's death in 2003, the standard follow-through for the mismatched partners angle began, which is the "Can they trust each other?" story line. And since this is wrestling, you just knew one was going to turn on the other. Meanwhile, Batista had not yet been introduced as the final member of HHH's new Evolution stable, so there were several subplots involving HHH asking various people to join his group. His asking Mick Foley was the impetus for the Foley-Orton feud to begin, and the week after that he asked Kane to join the group. Austin, in the interest of seeing more excitement on the show, tried to get Kane all fired up and back to his old monster self again, and the result was Kane challenging HHH for the title, and putting his mask on the line as collateral should he lose.

Kane had worn the mask since his debut with the character in 1997, although a series of cosmetic changes to the gimmick over the years had stripped it down to the bare essentials. A full face mask had given way to a crab-shaped half-mask to make it easier for him to give interviews.

**RIGHT: Rob Van Dam**

A full body suit had given way to a standard set of wrestling tights. Keeping quiet all the time had given way to speaking with a voice box, and then just speaking normally. Interestingly enough, all these makeovers contradicted the original origin of the character, which stated that he was a burned and scarred freak underneath the protective covering he wore and he couldn't talk due to throat damage. But then if *that's* the most bothersome thing about the character changes over the years to you, count yourself lucky. A novel was released by the WWE to explain all the changes, and was about as good as you'd expect.

As expected, to pop a rating for the show that week, Kane lost the title match, and thus unmasked and turned heel on partner Rob Van Dam. Not at the same time, of course. Thus continued yet another annual WWE tradition: The repackaging and repushing of Kane as a crazed monster, which seems to happen every time they run out of ideas of what to do with

him. This time around was truly impressive in the over-the-top nature of Kane's push, however, as he not only screwed over Rob Van Dam's own chance to beat HHH, but then beat up Steve Austin over an innocent remark, and set Jim Ross on fire with a can of gasoline. You knew it was gasoline, see, because the can was helpfully marked "Gasoline" in big letters in the same way those money sacks in cartoons have dollar signs written on them. Now, I'm hardly one to complain about the silly nature of angles in wrestling and how they're not the least bit believable most of the time, but dousing someone in gas and then lighting them on fire kind of crosses the line for me as far as stupidity goes. Never mind that committing arson and assault on a live TV show would normally result in getting locked up for a very long time, regardless of whether Jim "pressed charges" or not.

Just because this sort of thing tended to bug me, I checked with a lawyer friend and got some clarification on the stuff surrounding the whole incident. The following is a paraphrased version of the explanation given by Jon Richardson:

First off, there's no such thing as "pressing charges." The district attorney (crown attorney in Canada) alone makes the decision as to whether or not charges are pressed. It generally only arises in domestic abuse cases where the wife files a complaint, then withdraws it because "she loves him so much." Because the whole case was a he said/she said in the first place, the loss of the complaining witness means that there's no way the case would win in court, so the charges are dropped by the prosecuting attorney. In this case, however, you don't need a complaining witness because there's clear evidence of what Kane did. Show the video to a jury and you have your case made. If JR didn't want to "press charges," he could even choose to testify for the defense, but the state would still have grounds to make a case and thus arrest Kane.

Now, the Stamford DA could have watched RAW in the first place and had Kane arrested without JR even filing a complaint. Outraged viewers could have called him demanding action. JR really doesn't even fit into this mess because it's a pretty open-and-shut case of aggravated assault.

Finally, house arrest. There's no such thing until after a trial when it can be imposed by a judge. Assuming Kane had been arrested, he'd need to be arraigned, where bail can be assigned, or Kane remanded. In either case, Kane would have to apply for special permission to leave Connecticut, as there's a pending action against him. He could use the excuse of potential loss of job if he doesn't travel to California, but the WWE could instead show that they have no plans for Kane at Monday's RAW and thus don't need him (and therefore permission would be denied). If the DA hasn't decided yet whether or not to charge Kane, then Kane wouldn't be in shackles (unless he enjoys that sort of thing and don't you know that story line is coming soon), though you'd think he'd be more wary of committing more assaults against well-known people, especially ones being carried out on national television where (presumably) the DA would be watching his actions.

I know you didn't ask, but I just love picking this stuff apart anyway.

The intention of all this was to make Kane into a main event star again, but the really brutal irony of the whole situation is that had he been booked to win the title from HHH instead of losing his millionth title match and thus causing the whole angle, they would have accomplished their entire goal with one match. Truly, however, the most repulsive part of the whole angle, and the thing that guarantees I will never forgive Kane no matter how many face turns he does, is that with Jim Ross "injured" due to attempted murder, I had to listen to Jonathan Coachman on commentary for a month.

Bastards.

# 4

# JULY 2003

## ★ ★ VENGEANCE (SMACKDOWN ONLY) ★ ★ ★

FROM: Denver, CO
DATE: July 27, 2003
ATTENDANCE: 9,500
BUYRATE: 325,000 buys
ADVERTISED MAIN EVENT: Brock Lesnar v. Kurt Angle v. Big Show

### RESULTS:

U.S. title tournament final: Eddie Guerrero
d. Chris Benoit (22:14, ★★★★)

Jamie Noble d. Billy Gunn (4:59, ★½)

APA win a "bar room brawl," Smackdown tag team champions
Shelton Benjamin & Charlie Haas
d. Rey Mysterio & Billy Kidman (14:52, ★★★★¼)

Sable d. Stephanie McMahon (6:23, ★)

Undertaker d. John Cena (16:01, ★★★½)

Vince McMahon d. Zach Gowen (14:01, ★★½)

Kurt Angle d. Smackdown World champion
Brock Lesnar & Big Show in a three-way match (17:29, ★★★★)

**GETTING OUT OF WRESTLING** is tough to do for most of the top-level stars involved in it. There are really only three feasible exits from the sport that don't involve getting fired:

1. Finding a source of income greater than the original position in wrestling. This is the route taken by the Rock and to a lesser degree Mick Foley, and it's the rarest one.
2. Death. Pretty obvious, and sadly one of the most common in the past few years.
3. Injury to the point where physical competition is no longer feasible. Again, sadly one of the more common exits from the sport in recent years, although not necessarily a permanent one.

One of the more popular departures from active competition in the ring is that of the retired wrestler turned road agent, which is not exactly leaving the sport but close enough that it warrants an honorable mention, I think.

Other paths within the business include finding someone dumb enough to invest in you and starting your own wrestling promotion (which is the path taken by Jeff Jarrett) or simply shifting your on-screen role and becoming a full-time manager (a route much less popular now that most interviews are scripted by writers and managers are no longer required).

The third alternative, serious injury, is by far the most "popular" route as of the modern era. In particular, spinal problems have plagued the new generation of wrestlers, after years of suplexes and piledrivers have worn down their necks to the point where eighty-year-old men have more stable vertebrae in their neck than many wrestlers do. Some prime examples of this:

- Steve Austin is the most obvious, as he was having the best year of his career to date in 1997 and was a rising superstar of the first order. However, a piledriver gone bad in a match with Owen Hart compressed his spine and nearly ended his career, and in fact should have ended it had Austin actually listened to his doctors. Instead, he came back and drew more money than anyone before him, including Hulk Hogan, while working the new "main event style" by combining in-the-crowd brawling with big moves to pop the crowd and booking gymnastics. He managed to extend his career another two years this way before surgery to fuse two of the vertebrae in his neck

was absolutely necessary, and thus he sat on the sidelines for most of 2000 while HHH and the Rock drew obscene amounts of money without him. In fact, had Austin been healthy, there's no telling what kind of money the WWF would have made that year. After a year-long recuperation and rehabilitation, Austin returned as what seemed to be a shadow of his former self and stumbled through the next two years of his career before retiring permanently due to the neck injuries in 2003.

- Chris Benoit was similarly having a big year in 2001, but a series of suplexes and diving headbutts, all delivered by himself, wore down his neck to the point where he also required the dreaded spinal fusion surgery. He missed the entire Invasion story line and returned to a mediocre push in 2002, although his fortunes would improve from there. Fortunately, the surgery has not seemed to impact his performances in the ring, which are as strong as ever, although he quickly reneged on a promise not to do the diving headbutts anymore.

- Edge seems to be the most hapless when it comes to major injuries at the worst possible time, as he has seemingly suffered career-ending mishaps in the ring whenever he's on the verge of his biggest pushes, and has luckily recovered fully from each of them. The most well-known example of that is (what else) the spinal-fusion surgery he endured in 2003 after years of beating his neck by spearing opponents and taking suplexes off ladders. In fact, initial fears from noted neck surgeon Dr. Lloyd Youngblood was that Edge would need four vertebrae fused instead of the usual two, which would have ended his career but saved him mobility later in life. Instead, Edge opted for only two in 2003 and essentially promised to have the rest done once his career was over. Oddly enough, he still uses the spear as a finisher.

• The most famous retirement and then comeback is that of Shawn Michaels, who I'm convinced is superhuman at this point. He not only suffered his own back injury in 1998, before any of the others did, but opted for full spinal fusion of the damaged vertebrae, which essentially ended his career. However, in what can only be termed a medical miracle, he returned four years later wrestling at what seemed to be 100 percent of his former capacity, with no loss of movement

or pain whatsoever. He has been more or less a full-time active wrestler since his return, looking none the worse except for the occasional minor injury. Shawn credits Jesus for the resurrection of his career, as he switched to a born-again Christian belief system in 2001, and it's hard to argue with the results.

So all this brings me to Kurt Angle, who had been one of the premier workers in the business from his debut in 1999 until early 2003, when he started suffering the dreaded warning signs of neck problems: numbness in the hands, shrunken muscles in the arms, and severe neck pain. Kurt had won the Smackdown version of the World title from Big Show in December 2002 and was building to an anticipated Wrestlemania title match against former amateur wrestling rival Brock Lesnar, and thus it was the worst possible time

**RIGHT: Kurt Angle and Big Show**

for him to be looking into career-ending neck surgery. He decided to delay it for as long as possible, completely staying out of the ring up to Wrestlemania, except for some quick shots on TV and the award-winning Match of the Year title defense against Chris Benoit at the 2003 Royal Rumble. Because really, a little thing like a bad neck should never stop you from delivering a ***** match, right?

**ABOVE: Chris Benoit and Kurt Angle**

Amazingly, Angle nearly did it again at Wrestlemania, putting on an amazing show against Lesnar that was only ruined somewhat by Lesnar badly botching a shooting star press off the top rope and nearly breaking his neck in the process. I had to deduct points from the match for it—it's a cold business, what can I say? At any rate, Angle then essentially said good-bye for a year and went off to have surgery.

And then something weird happened.

While making preparations with Dr. Youngblood (who, along with Dr. James "Tape it up and work through it" Andrews, must make most of their yearly salary off the WWE), Kurt's case was brought to the attention of an unknown surgeon named Dr. Jho by Scott Hall, a previous patient. Jho felt that he could bypass the usual spinal surgery and in fact have Kurt or anyone else back in the ring six to eight weeks after surgery. Instead of actually fusing the bones together,

Jho's method involved cleaning out bone spurs from the neck, which press down on nerves and thus cause the pain and muscle shrinkage associated with the neck problems. Since going with the standard surgery would involve losing a year of his career, and probably more, Angle opted for the experimental surgery instead. Everyone laughed.

Then, six weeks later, Kurt Angle returned better than ever, and won the World title back from Brock Lesnar at the Vengeance PPV in July to jumpstart their feud again. More desperate wrestlers went to see Dr. Jho quickly after that, such as road agent Steve Lombardi, but sadly his techniques were shown to be a combination of good luck and Kurt Angle being a freak of nature, because in the long run Angle's neck returned to its previously pained form again and he seems to be facing career-ending surgery any day now, with no miracle of escape possible this time around.

But back to Angle's return again.

In a rather odd move, it was felt that the returning Angle would be viewed as a babyface by the fans, so he went back to his 2001 form of waving the American flag and cheering on the troops, essentially becoming the white-bread babyface again that everyone hated so much in the first place. Even worse was the atrocious babyface persona that Brock Lesnar was putting forth, having changed into a smiling wuss since losing the WWE title in 2002. The story line had the two girly men bonding as athletes, acting like total dorks, and getting into pushup contests and other activities that were, to say the least, overtly gay. That wasn't the intention, but *man* was it the result. Thank god that the WWE came to their senses after Lesnar lost the title and changed him back into the kind of mean-spirited bully that turned him into a star in the first place, because I couldn't have taken another week of Brock and Kurt drinking milk together and smiling knowingly at one another. Not that there's anything wrong with that. Heck, *Brokeback Mountain* made over $100 million.

The Vengeance show, which was excellent and probably the best PPV of 2003, by the way, also saw the continuation of the odd story that was Eddie Guerrero. Eddie had teamed up with odd couple partner Tajiri in May to score an upset and win the Smackdown tag team titles, and then quickly turned on him in favor of his low-rider's well-being, because it was a really nice car and all. The problem was that Eddie's previous team, with nephew Chavo, had built him a

**ABOVE: Eddie Guerrero**

cult following with fans, who were entertained by their "Lie, cheat, and steal" philosophy and by Eddie's creative match finishes. Most of those finishes were planned out by Eddie himself and involved increasingly devious ways to trick challengers for the tag belts into getting themselves disqualified. For example, Eddie would hit them with a chair behind the referee's back, then put it in the hands of his opponent while feigning unconsciousness. Thus, the ref sees the other guy with the chair, calls for the DQ, Eddie wins. This was supposed to be vile and cause for hatred of him, but the fans, bored with the usual telegraphed finishes and cheap endings, ate it up and cheered Eddie all the louder for actually being *smarter* than everyone else. They respected him, you see, and didn't respect all the other guys who were booked to look like schmucks.

So by the time Eddie turned on his partner and supposedly turned heel, the fans had no interest in booing him for doing so. Whether he represented good or bad, he was entertaining and his matches didn't insult your intelligence, so the reactions were still positive and the cheers for him got louder. So at Vengeance he was involved in the finals for a tournament to resurrect the long-dead U.S. title (last seen being unified with the Intercontinental title at Survivor Series 2001), beating good friend Chris Benoit to win the belt. He cheated, of course, and won. He was not only devious and smart, but he was successful, and thus the fans got behind him even stronger.

This was even more apparent in Latino markets like California, as fans there were starved for someone to represent them on TV in a positive manner, and Eddie Guerrero fit the bill. And since California is such a large market, his increasing market value and ratings power did not go unnoticed.

# 5

# AUGUST 2003

**SUMMERSLAM (BOTH BRANDS)**

FROM: Phoenix, AZ
DATE: August 24, 2003
ATTENDANCE: 17,113
BUYRATE: 410,000 buys
ADVERTISED MAIN EVENT: Brock Lesnar v. Kurt Angle and
The Elimination Chamber II

**RESULTS:**

RAW tag team champions Sylvain Grenier & Renee Dupree
d. The Dudley Boyz (7:49, ✶½)

Undertaker d. A-Train (9:19, ✶)

Shane McMahon d. Eric Bischoff (10:33, ½✶)

U.S. champion Eddie Guerrero d. Rhyno, Tajiri, & Chris Benoit
in a four-way match (10:50, ✶✶✶)

Smackdown World champion Kurt Angle d. Brock Lesnar (21:19, ✶✶✶½)

Kane d. Rob Van Dam (12:51, ✶✶¼)

RAW World champion HHH d. Goldberg, Chris Jericho, Randy Orton
Kevin Nash, & Shawn Michaels in an
Elimination Chamber match (19:15, ✶✶✶)

**IN AUGUST,** Shane McMahon returned.

Stuff like that always bugs me because there's always such a big deal made about how he's getting thrown out of the company, like in November 2001 (the last time we saw him before this), and of course the stipulations are never adhered to. It becomes a vicious circle of the WWE never adhering to stipulations, so fans are conditioned never to believe them, so the WWE doesn't bother adhering to them, and so on. This was most ridiculously shown when Stephanie McMahon, also booted out of the company at the same time as Shane in the story lines, returned six weeks later to become the general manager of Smackdown.

I think what really bugged me about the whole Shane thing, however, wasn't the way in which he was brought back, or the blatant ignoring of the backstory, but that his entire purpose in being put on

TV was to provide Kane with a credible opponent.

Now, let's take a moment to summarize here. Kane, who's really big and has a character generally portrayed as being just this side of the Frankenstein monster, begins a story line where he *really* snaps and turns into a completely maniacal animal out to kill everyone in his path. Who better to stop his path of rage than twenty-something buffoonish son of the owner, Shane McMahon? A guy who actually has a theme song that goes "Here comes the money" and thus is supposed to be treated like a babyface. A guy who is more well known for bringing his high school pals into the business as "The Mean Street Posse" and thus flaunting the influence he wielded while portraying a spoiled rich kid. Just to make sure he was treated like a face, they made sure to have him beat up on monster supervillain Kane after a series of actual wrestlers couldn't get the job done.

The whole Kane story line was actually too silly for words for the most part, as they couldn't get their own internal logic straight and had him "under house arrest" despite Jim Ross never pressing charges. This led to Linda McMahon declaring that he somehow still had the "right to work" and thus he was ferried around the country, in chains mind you, by law en-

**ABOVE: Rob Van Dam and Val Venis**

forcement, who kept him under guard with laser-sighted Taser guns at all times. If I was Kane, I'd forgo the physical attacks and just go out and get a good lawyer. On the other hand, Martha Stewart was allowed to make a reality show while wearing an ankle bracelet, so I guess maybe Kane set the precedent for her.

The guy who really got screwed in the whole deal was Rob Van Dam, as his big blowoff match with former partner Kane at Summerslam, the second-biggest card of the year, was essentially moved onto the backburner while the silly feud that Kane was building with Shane McMahon was turning into the issue that the creative team was focusing on. Kane, to the shock of no one, squashed Van Dam like a bug at Summerslam. The problem was that Kane has traditionally shown a clear pattern when it's time for his yearly push:

1. He's stuck in the midcard so they make him a monster again to freshen up the character, which leads to . . .
2. He flails around in the midcard beating up midcarders for a while and by the time they decide . . .
3. . . . that it's time to shoot him up to the main event again, he's cooled off again and it's time to repeat the whole process again.

And this has been happening for close to ten years now, starting with Glen Jacobs's initial repackaging as Kane in 1997, so you'd think that someone would pick up on it at this point and realize that it's a lost cause.

Speaking of lost causes, Goldberg wasn't exactly burning up the ratings or buyrates after a few months in the company, but with the kind of money invested in him, they had no choice but to push him all the way to the top. So after an initial plan of Goldberg facing HHH in June, which was in turn changed to Summerslam in August, HHH pitched one last idea to keep the title on himself for a little longer: Switch the match again, from August to September. And this after they already announced a main event of HHH v. Goldberg for Summerslam.

In all fairness, HHH had a fairly bad groin injury and thus would have been forced to do a quick and decisive job to Goldberg and probably not look superhuman in the process, so you can see why he was hesitant to do the right thing at that point. Still, they needed *something* to main event Summerslam, with apparently Brock Lesnar v. Kurt Angle for the Smackdown World title not being important enough to warrant inclusion as the big match of the night. So the solution was the usual "throw everything at the wall" method, as they dragged the Elimination Chamber out of mothballs again.

You may remember the match from its debut at Survivor Series 2002, at a cost of $500,000. It's a giant circular cage enclosing the ring, with minicompartments inside holding four wrestlers, and two wrestlers in the ring. The first one was won by Shawn Michaels, giving him a brief run with HHH's RAW World title at the point when it was thought that his stay in the WWE would be even briefer. This time around the match was much more weak in terms of star power—it consisted of an injured HHH, plus challengers Goldberg, Chris Jericho, Kevin Nash, Shawn Michaels, and an odd addition in the form of Randy Orton. These days it wouldn't be a very big deal, but Orton had yet to even win the Intercontinental title at that point and was considered very much a work in progress, rather than someone legitimately ready for main eventing a major show. Kevin Nash was a particularly weak addition as well, because the match was well known to be his swan song with the promotion before he left to pursue his "movie career." To date, it has consisted of a minor cameo in *The Punisher* and playing an effeminate guard in Adam Sandler's remake of *The Longest Yard*, but if it keeps him out of wrestling, more power to him. HHH of course won a rather lackluster match by cheating egregiously after wrestling for all of a minute or so, and retained the title, living to defend it another day against Goldberg. Summerslam did a fairly strong buyrate, even without Goldberg winning the title, so maybe he was actually right to delay the title change, who knows.

Over on the Smackdown side of things, Brock Lesnar finally turned on "good friend" Kurt Angle to set up their big rematch, after months of homoerotic skits. However, that too was overshadowed by an even more epic feud: Vince McMahon and the returning Sable taking on Stephanie McMahon and Zach Gowen. Most people assumed that everyone involved would come to their collective senses and stop pushing the sideshow attraction as the main story line of the show, but *boy* were we proven wrong about that one. Thankfully, the new heel Brock Lesnar broke Zach's remaining leg to write him out of the story lines for a while. My own theory was that he was just trying to wish him *really* good luck.

Almost as silly as that joke was the debut of the Basham Brothers, who aren't really brothers. Well, not

**BELOW: Brock Lesnar**

many people promoted as relatives really are, so that wasn't the silly part. The silly part is that they were in the training system for months on end feuding with each other as Doug Basham and Damaja. Then, while working a dark match on a Smackdown taping as a tag team, they were put under masks so that they wouldn't be perceived as jobbers if they were called up soon after that. Smart enough, but the show was running short in the editing stage that week, so their dark match against Rey Mysterio and Billy Kidman was put into the show and they were dubbed "The Conquistadors" by the production staff as an inside joke for those who remembered the anonymous team from the '80s. However, apparently they worked together as a tag team well enough that those in talent relations actually decided to call them up as a tag team, thus ruining months of story line buildup for the people who actually bothered to pay attention to the OVW and their feud therein. So they debuted as the Basham Brothers, Doug and Danny, playing off an S&M gimmick to go with their black leather masks and tights from the dark match. This of course immediately failed to get over to any significant degree, despite the fact that both guys are tremendous wrestlers who could have been doing something fairly significant as singles, so naturally they were pushed hard as a team and won the tag titles multiple times. I suppose you could count them as a success despite themselves. At the very least, the gimmick wasn't any dumber than that given to Nick Dinsmore, who we'll get to later.

# 6 SEPTEMBER 2003

## ★ ★ ★ UNFORGIVEN (RAW ONLY) ★ ★ ★

FROM: Hershey, PA
DATE: September 21, 2003
ATTENDANCE: 10,347
BUYRATE: 300,000 buys
ADVERTISED MAIN EVENT: HHH v. Goldberg

### RESULTS:

The Dudley Boyz d. RAW tag team champions
Sylvain Grenier, Renee Dupree, & Rob Conway
in a tables match (10:16, ★½)

Test d. Scott Steiner (6:56, ½★)

Randy Orton d. Shawn Michaels (19:22, ★★¾)

Trish Stratus & Lita d. Gail Kim & Molly Holly (6:41, ★★½)

Kane d. Shane McMahon in a Last Man Standing match (19:54, ★½)

Intercontinental champion Christian
d. Rob Van Dam & Chris Jericho in a three-way match (19:03, ★¾)

Jonathan Coachman & Al Snow d. Jim Ross & Jerry Lawler (8:17, -☆☆)

Goldberg d. RAW World champion HHH (14:56, ★½)

**SO FINALLY, IN SEPTEMBER** it looked like things might change for the better. Or, at the very least, change, period. I'll take what I can get. First and foremost, this was a period for introducing new characters over the summer. Or, in this case, introducing a new one and repackaging an old one. This brings us back to La Resistance, the evil French tag team who were supposed to sweep over the landscape of wrestling and become the monster heel tag team to define the decade or something. In reality, while Rene Dupree improved fairly quickly, to the point where he was watchable in the ring by the summer, Sylvain Grenier was still terrible as ever, and these guys were supposed to be the tag team champions.

It clearly wasn't working, so in a move that was transparent even by the WWE's thin standards, OVW alumnus and solid wrestling technician Rob Conway was introduced in August as a serviceman who was actually a

French sympathizer, which would thus generate heel heat for betraying the troops, and also cash in on the French hatred covering the nation. I'm sure Vince McMahon was the kind of guy to order "freedom fries" at McDonalds, believe me. Vince never met a knee-jerk xenophobic trend that he didn't try to make a buck off of. Anyway, Conway was one of my favorite wrestlers out of the OVW, and I've long been predicting that he'll be much bigger than the stupid La Resistance gimmick allowed him. Smartly, they took the tag team titles off the newly created three-man unit at Unforgiven, because the gimmick was dying fast. Sadly enough, despite the slow death of the La Resistance concept even back in 2003, it took until 2005 to split up the team for good.

And then there's Rosey.

Introduced in 2002 as one-half of Three Minute Warning, the latest attempt to create the *definitive* evil Samoan tag team, they were hampered by being too evil for their own good, as Jamal was fired in early 2003 for assaulting a police officer while in a bar fight. You'd think this would be a perfectly good excuse to cut some more dead weight and dump Rosey along with him, but no. Instead, faux superhero Hurricane, whose only true power was the uncanny ability to lose every match he was in, announced a search for a new sidekick. The call was quickly answered by the aimless

ABOVE: Renee Dupree and Maven

Rosey, who was taught the fine art of rescuing cats from trees and was thus dubbed a superhero in training, or SHIT. And that's really about it as far as character depth goes, as they came up with that acronym and a goofy superhero costume and basically had another curtain-jerking tag team and nothing more. They of course went on to win the RAW version of the tag team titles in 2005 in a match treated as a fluke win and promptly disappeared from TV, as the writers had nothing to do with them, seemingly taking the belts with them. That shows you not only how little the promotion thinks of their own tag team division but also how decimated the ranks had to have been for Rosey and Hurricane to be the best remaining alternative to get the belts.

Over on Smackdown, however, it was less about introducing new faces than it was about the amazing comeback story of Eddie Guerrero. After a month or so of ostensibly playing a heel and yet getting bigger babyface reactions than anyone else on the show, even the brain surgeons of the creative team were able to stop fighting the crowds' reactions and just started booking him against heels instead. In fact, not only was Eddie one of the few organic, fan-created face turns in recent memory but he also helped to engineer a significant spike in UPN's viewership during his matches, as he became a legitimate ratings draw among the significant Latino population in the United States. This was all the more amazing considering the trials and tribulations that Eddie had to endure on his way back to the WWE.

His problems had begun in the WCW, as have the problems of so many before him. Married early in life and thrust into the national spotlight of the Monday Night Wars, Eddie's addictive personality caught up with him in the worst way. Years of drinking problems and painkiller addiction culminated in a brutal car accident after he drove to the store while half-asleep on liquor and pills, and he was declared dead at the scene by the police. His condition was luckily upgraded to "alive," and the general feeling was that he might walk again, but his career was over. However, he was not just an addict, but a stubborn one, and he returned six months ahead of

**RIGHT: The Hurricane and Maven**

schedule on a bad leg and ended up injuring it even more, requiring another round of painkillers and booze to deal with the pain. After an overdose and a trip to the hospital, he left the WCW and began his first stint with the WWF, reinventing himself as Chyna's boyfriend, and creating the Latino Heat persona. Sadly, the reinvigorating character change didn't help his personal life, as alcohol was still ruining his life, so his friends Chris Benoit and Dean Malenko "betrayed" him to the office and reported his lifestyle problems. A trip to rehab followed, writing him out of the promotion for much of 2001, and he lost his wife in the process, unable to accept a change in his life as drastic as giving up drinking. As 2001 ended, after successfully completing rehab, the depression from his divorce overcame him, and he went back to drinking. The result was hitting rock bottom with a DUI charge in December 2001.

However, in a rare happy ending for this type of

story, he went through one more rehab session, this time taking it seriously, and was fired by the WWF to send a message to future drug abusers in the promotion. The message was intended as much for Eddie as for anyone else, and he paid attention to it, working hard to not only rehabilitate his addictive nature outside of the ring but also to appear in smaller shows around the country to get himself back to the form that made him a superstar in the first place. This proved to the people who initially fired him, and still believed in him, that he could be trusted on the road again, and he was hired back in early 2002 on promising that he would stay sober for the rest of his life. As a nice bonus, he also got his wife back. Most people felt that he would happily inhabit the midcard and be thankful for it, but 2003 was showing that a reborn Eddie Guerrero was a force to be reckoned with. After winning the re-created U.S. title on Smackdown by defeating Chris Benoit in a tournament final in July, Eddie found himself becoming the most popular wrestler on the Smackdown roster, drawing huge fan reactions for his immensely creative cheating tactics, and by September he had undergone a de facto babyface turn without ever officially turning, and was now programmed in a minifeud with equally hot heel John Cena. This was compounded by a reunion with nephew Chavo Guerrero Jr., and resulted in the instantly hot babyface team regaining the Smackdown tag team titles from Charlie Haas and Shelton Benjamin in September 2003. Eddie was now a dual champion and the hottest act in the company, but

everyone assumed that it was as high as he could climb given his size limitations and ethnicity. We would be proven very wrong.

On the same episode of Smackdown where the Guerreros won the tag titles back, another title change occurred, one that would indirectly affect Eddie Guerrero's life a few months later. Fresh off a heel turn, newly motivated monster Brock Lesnar was ready to carry the big belt again, as Kurt Angle's dorky babyface persona was not carrying the Smackdown side the way they wanted and expected. So in a fairly bold move for a company that lives and dies by TV, the entire second hour of Smackdown was given to Angle and Lesnar's big blowoff match on September 18. It was to be a one-hour Iron Man match, the first guaranteed one-hour match in the WWE's television history and the first match of that kind of length since Sting met Ric Flair at the WCW's first Clash of the Champions show in 1988. The gamble didn't work in the ratings the way they wanted, with everyone essentially watching for the first few minutes of the match and then tuning out until the finish at the end of the hour, but it was certainly a good match and a refreshing change from the usual talk-heavy shows at the time. Brock won the match five falls to four, and despite the disjointed nature of the match itself, with commercial breaks inserted at awkward points, it was a candidate for the Match of the Year for 2003 and given a prestigious ***** rating by Wade Keller of the *Pro Wrestling Torch*. He was pretty much the only one, but I thought I'd mention it. I personally thought at the time that the

commercial breaks were just too annoying, and really we only saw about forty-five minutes of the match. While Brock was smart near the end, the psychology was just all over the place for most of the match, with Brock injuring his knee and then Angle doing an anklelock on the other leg. The last thirty minutes were tremendous, Match of the Year quality stuff, but the first thirty, with much of it spent by Brock outside the ring, were not, and it drags down the overall rating a lot. It also showed a problem with Brock's in-ring work around that time, which suggested something of a lack of motivation on his part, as he was stuck in feuds with the same people and was wrestling what appeared to be lazier matches. While he was battling injured ribs for much of the year, that didn't seem to entirely explain his motivational problems. As it would turn out, there was something going on, although we wouldn't find out what it was until a little later.

Of course, back on RAW the PPV ball was in their court for September, as they presented the *long* awaited one-on-one match between Goldberg and HHH after months of delays and buildup. The resulting buyrate

was higher than the September PPV usually scores, so the strategy was a smart one, but the match sucked. HHH, as is his habit, dictated the pace and timing of the match and forced Goldberg to wrestle a match far longer than was comfortable for him, stretching a five-minute story into a twenty-minute match in the process. In the end, HHH laid down and gave up his title to the challenger, but since everyone knew that Goldberg was in on a short-term deal, it was heavily anticipated that that would be the finish anyway, so that Goldberg couldn't possibly have any objections to returning the favor when it was time to leave. Plus, HHH's goal has long been matching idol Ric Flair's sixteen World titles, and you have to lose the belt fifteen times to get there. Unless you're Shawn Michaels, of course, in which case you just lie about knee injuries a bunch of times.

Speaking of Shawn, he was put into the rare position (for him) of using his rebuilt career and superstar name to attempt to create a new star, something that many people had been saying he should have been doing for years. At any rate, the project in question was of course Randy Orton, who was so high up their ladder of future prospects that there was even open talk from HHH backstage of main eventing the upcoming Wrestlemania against him. The idea was that Orton, as the hot young punk of HHH's Evolution group, would have had enough of HHH's leadership, and would recruit fellow "young" punk Batista and turf HHH out of the group, resulting in a babyface HHH chasing the arrogant new champion and his newer, punkier group of punks. However, with the Goldberg story line moved back so drastically, this left very little time to tell that story properly, and the backup plan for the upcoming Wrestlemania was put into place instead. I liked the backup plan much better anyway. Batista was brought into the group as planned, but just as a group member, not a co-conspirator. The Orton breakup was rescheduled for Wrestlemania XXI instead. Anyway, with that out, Randy "Legend Killer" Orton needed more legends to kill, and next up on that list was Shawn Michaels. There was some involvement from Maven here that was teasing Shawn into taking the Tough Enough winner under his wing, only to have him turn and join Orton's new Evolution group, but it all went by the wayside when the HHH-Orton feud was scrapped. Of course, because it's Shawn, the actual match was good enough to make

Orton look good, but the finish was indecisive enough to protect himself, as Shawn apparently had the pin, but fell victim to a set of brass knuckles for the real finish. Not that it mattered in the grand scheme of things because no one remembers that match except for a listing on the back of an Orton t-shirt. Actually, I think that's kind of a motto for the promotion as a whole during that period.

And finally, speaking of metaphors for the whole company, the Kane v. Shane McMahon "classic," which the world was waiting for I'm sure, was built up by a fabulously bad angle whereby Kane was sent backward in a big flaming dumpster full of garbage, to which Kane responded by attaching jumper cables to Shane's testicles and connecting them to a battery. I felt much the same way after watching the whole thing.

# 7  OCTOBER 2003

**REALLY, IN OCTOBER 2003,** the most important thing to happen in wrestling was not anything that occurred in the ring, but in a movie.

Long considered to be one of the better promos in wrestling, as evidenced by the millions of dollars he's made for the WWE, Rock revealed ambitions to become an actor in 2000 and actually took acting lessons around that time, which explains why his promos were suddenly so good. In fact, his natural charisma and good looks scored him a "featured" role in Stephen Sommers's *The Mummy Returns*, doing what was heavily advertised as a major role as *The Scorpion King* but ended up being little more than a quick cameo at the beginning and having his face stuck on a giant computer-generated scorpion at the end. However, that was enough to get his foot in the Hollywood door, and in the summer of 2002 Sommers took a chance on him by producing *The Scorpion King* as a spin-off from the *Mummy* series. Starring the Rock in the title role and directed by Chuck Russell, it was a moderate summer hit, with a very healthy international box office of $164 million and $94 million domestic, more than enough to make a profit for the studio. But how was the movie, you might ask? Overall, surprisingly good for the Rock's first effort.

A funny, over-the-top action sequence introduces Rock as superwarrior/assassin Mathayus, last of the Akkadians. Not to be confused with the Acadians, the guys who move to Louisiana and broil crawfish and stuff today. The Akkadians are apparently the most badass of the badass warriors of the world at the time, although not badass enough to keep from getting killed off to the point of being nearly extinct.

The introductory sequence leads into the pretentious, *Lord of the Rings*-ish backstory piece about how the villainous Memnon conquered the world and became king at some vaguely determined point around 3000 BC. And we dive right into the plot, as all the other kings are squabbling and Mathayus and his crew of assassins get hired to kill Memnon's mysterious sorceress, who uses movie logic to see the future and thus guarantee that Memnon's army can never be defeated. In a deleted scene, the screenplay waffles a bit and admits that she can't *always* see the future, so it's later emphasized that the symbolism of having her there is enough to motivate the men. Uh huh.

The movie jumps rather briskly into the thick of the plot, as we meet the comic sidekick and the bad guys kill off Mathayus's brother before he can even be *named*. That's how evil they are. And this is like ten minutes in, so if you got popcorn at the start of the movie, you're boned. And just as quickly, we learn that Mathayus has been sold out by the son of the king who

hired him in the first place, who has killed his father and taken his place at Memnon's side. You certainly can't complain about a slow pace in this one. The movie also tries to get "live free, die well" over as a catchphrase, but in all fairness having your throat slit and bleeding out is a pretty nasty way to go.

The sorceress, who we later learn is named Cassandra, works like a metaphysical CNN for Memnon, predicting victory for the rampaging hordes of evil. Maybe it's more like Fox News, come to think of it. So our heroes begin a Middle Ages buddy movie (One's an immortal assassin! One's a wacky horse thief!) and Mathayus breaks into the castle with the help of a kid, providing a nice moment ("I'll kill half, you kill half") and really showing some action star screen presence and charisma. There's also some really inventive (Mathayus using a gong as a shield) and funny (Mathayus meets the harem) action scenes in here, as the movie's tongue is firmly in cheek and it looks like an amusing action romp. Then, the tone suddenly does a 180, taking a more dramatic swing the other way as Mathayus kidnaps Cassandra (providing a PG-13 nude scene for Kelly Hu) and Stockholm Syndrome kicks in, giving him a love interest and relegating his former sidekick to the backburner.

Since Mathayus is essentially unkillable by the machinations of the movie (we know he lives to make *The Mummy Returns*, see) they try to bring him down to a human level with a poison arrow to the leg after a tremendously entertaining slaughter of Memnon's elite guard. It also allows Cassandra to play nurse, although you'd think that psychic powers would make diagnosing stuff easier than it appears. Now thoroughly pissed off, Mathayus and his band of weirdos go all Braveheart and recruit an army of misfit Nubians, as the tone switches *again*, which allows longtime wrestling fan Michael Clarke Duncan to no doubt live out a fantasy and work a match with the Rock.

There's also some perfunctory brushes with philosophy and the questions of destiny v. predestiny, but really if you want the definitive word on the subject, rent *Bill and Ted's Excellent Adventure*. During these discussions, Mathayus gets it on with Cassandra, and she loses all her powers according to prophecy. So that's what the hymen does.

So they begin their final siege on Memnon's castle, while Memnon plays parlor games to test Cassandra's powers (I don't think that's what she was expecting when he asked her to play Hide the Snake) and lots of uninteresting peripheral characters clog up the climax. We get swordfights with the Big Black Dude, the Amazon Queen, the Comedy Sidekick, the Wacky Scientist, and all the other people who are not the Rock and thus not given more than ten seconds to establish their character before moving into the big crowd scene at the end. Oddly, the film loses most of its charm here, breaking down into MTV-style edits and obnoxious slo-mo for "dramatic effect." Luckily, Memnon setting his swords on fire is offset by the coolness of Mathayus pulling an arrow out of his own back to strike the killing blow. And what movie set in ancient times is complete without a big pyrotechnic scene to blow everything up? No movie I wanna see!

Okay, stupidity of the premise and plot aside, *The Scorpion King* definitely had a certain charm to it, although the ridiculous shifting of tone from buddy comedy to sword-and-sorcery epic to historical drama keeps it from being a great, or even really good movie. I certainly enjoyed it as a popcorn movie, but repeated viewings lay the faults bare in all their ugly glory. Call it **1/2 for the movie.

*The Scorpion King* did really well at the box office, enough for the Rock's movie career to continue and for him to be given a shot at opening a movie on his own name rather than the *Mummy* name. So work commenced on *Helldorado*, which went through a series of name changes, landing at *Welcome to the Jungle* and then finally at *The Rundown* mere weeks before release in September 2003. Changing the name of the movie three times before release is generally considered a bad sign. Luckily, the charm of the movie and Rock's natural star quality carried the movie through its initial problems.

*The Rundown* is your basic action comedy, the kind really not seen since the '80s, a point that is immediately emphasized in a wink-wink moment via a cameo by Arnold Schwarzenegger as the movie opens. Rock's character is Beck, a "retrieval expert" who works for a bigtime hood and loan shark named Billy Walker and has a dream of starting his own restaurant someday. Of course, to do so and escape from the life of crime, he has to do one last job for his underworld boss.

That job proves to be retrieving Billy's son, Travis, from South America, who fancies himself to be an Indiana Jones type and is off looking for an ancient artifact. Billy wants him back home and offers Beck $250,000 to make it so. So off we go to El Dorado, somewhere in Brazil, a town run by Christopher Walken, playing Christopher Walken. The town is built on a gold mine, manned by slave labor that is created with the wonders of computer-generated imagery. I'm sure it was cheaper than hiring 200,000 extras to dig gold for 65 cents an hour, but I appreciate authenticity in my movies.

The movie kicks off properly with Beck finding Travis in a bar and quickly kicking the crap out of him to establish the relationship for the rest of the movie, but they quickly get shaken down by Walken's Hatcher character, because Travis may have actually found something of value after all. This leads to the main body of the film, as they head into the jungle to escape, and the movie becomes something of a buddy comedy, with lots of hilarious problems with urination and monkeys. It's also refreshing to see someone like Rock, who is almost a real-life action hero, so willing to let himself be humiliated and beat up by animals for the sake of the gag. It kind of stems from his personality while with the WWE as well, as he'd always be the first guy to let himself lose to someone underneath him in the name of making a new star out of them.

Speaking of hilarious, Walken delivers a classic monologue about the tooth fairy, which has carried this movie above the levels of standard action movie in some circles.

Beck and Travis cast their lot with native rebels after a crazy fight scene between Beck and a bunch of pygmies, and we learn that the innocuously hot bartender played by Rosario Dawson is in fact the leader of the rebels. This leads to another escape from a monologuing Walken and his crew, as Chris chews every inch of scenery he approaches. And thus it goes from chase movie to mystical quest movie, although they find their object of desire ("el gato," a golden cat) with way more ease than you'd expect for a loser like Travis. But hey, it keeps the plot moving along, so huzzah. Just as quickly, and off-camera, the bad guys steal the statue and kidnap the girl, so of course you know that Beck has to wage a one-man war against the forces of evil and kick some ass. And really, I'd be way more disappointed if he hadn't, because it pays off the "I don't like guns" tagline that had been driven into our minds for the whole movie. Interestingly, Beck doesn't stick around and join the rebels, as you might expect, because he's entirely about the business and actually does bring Travis home to daddy. Sort of.

As action movies go, *The Rundown* had a better narrative flow than *The Scorpion King* did, and certainly better fight scenes, but for whatever reason it didn't click at the box office and failed to turn Rock into the huge action star that Hollywood seemed to be predicting. Still, with both of his first movies making a profit, it was enough to put him into a continuing career as a leading man, if nothing else. The end result of Rock's adventures in Hollywood (besides giving Vince McMahon a free executive producer credit on his movies) was to essentially make Rock a full-time actor and part-time wrestler, and eventually eliminate the wrestling aspect completely. Aside from his brief stay in early 2003 for the shot against Goldberg, Rock was almost totally absent from TV, and wouldn't return again until Wrestlemania XX. He was now a Hollywood star first and foremost, escaping the world of wrestling in spectacular fashion and making the WWE look all the better in the process.

The flipside was the WWE themselves at that point, as October's PPV was headlined by the culmination of months of feuding between Vince McMahon and daughter Stephanie, in the form of a match that was promoted as the main event of the show. An "I Quit" match no less, thus ensuring that someone had to cry out in submission before the match could end. I tried doing so *before* the match, but sadly that tactic didn't work and it went on anyway. Vince won the match, of course, without Stephanie saying "I Quit" and as a result Stephanie was "fired" from the WWE. Again. However, as of two years later she shows no signs of returning to TV, thus marking one of the rare times that someone has actually been fired and not come back six weeks later. The shows leading up to No Mercy were ratings disasters and the show drew one of the lowest buyrates of the modern era, but I'm sure that had nothing to do with the main event. The match was also one of the most uncomfortable experiences seen in wrestling, as watching a father beat up his lookalike daughter has just too much creepy subtext to it for my liking. On the other hand, it was at least less uncomfortable than a previous match between Vince McMa-

**ABOVE: Big Show**

hon and Zach Gowen, which was best described as "about as good as a match between a senior citizen and a cripple could be."

The show also featured two booking decisions that, at the time, were considered bone-headed and strange—Big Show cleanly defeated U.S. champion Eddie Guerrero to win that belt, and one-legged wonder Zach Gowen cleanly defeated hot midcard act Matt Hardy on his way out of the company. Both results were considered odd at the time—the first one because Eddie was such a scorching hot act at that point and losing his title would seem to demean him, the second because Zach Gowen was considered on his way down the card—and in fact both results would change the careers of those on the losing end forever. We just didn't know how and why until much later.

## ★ ★ SURVIVOR SERIES (BOTH BRANDS) ★ ★

FROM: Dallas, TX
DATE: November 16, 2003
ATTENDANCE: 13,487
BUYRATE: 292,000
ADVERTISED MAIN EVENT: Vince McMahon v. Undertaker

### RESULTS:

John Cena, Chris Benoit, Kurt Angle, Bradshaw, & Hardcore Holly d. Big Show, Nathan Jones, Matt Morgan, Brock Lesnar, & A-Train in an elimination tag match (13:30, ★★½)

Women's champion Molly Holly d. Lita (6:49, ★½)

Kane d. Shane McMahon (13:29, ½★)

Smackdown tag team champions Doug & Danny Basham d. Eddie & Chavo Guerrero (7:32, ★★)

Mark Henry, Chris Jericho, Christian, Scott Steiner, & Randy Orton d. Shawn Michaels, Booker T, Bubba Dudley, D-Von Dudley, & Rob Van Dam in an elimination tag match (27:27, ★★★★)

Vince McMahon d. Undertaker in a Buried Alive match (11:59, DUD),

RAW World champion Goldberg d. HHH (11:41, ★½)

**SO LET'S TALK** about Steve Austin, shall we?

Austin's a guy who was always a personal favorite of mine, in the ring and out of it, until 2002. In a business populated by phonies and liars, Austin seemed like someone who was big enough to be above it all, generally played it straight all the time, and cared enough about his craft to take a stand when something didn't seem right to him. In fact, that's the legendary origin of his persona in the WWE—he was treated badly in the WCW, fired over the phone, and became the biggest name in wrestling as a form of revenge against the company that got rid of him in the first place.

By 2002, all that changed. With his career clearly on the downswing and asked to do a job for Brock Lesnar to make the younger man into a bigger star, Austin balked and essentially flaked out, leaving the company for a few weeks and forcing them to drastically realign their initial draft for RAW and Smackdown. While out of the spotlight, years of playing an over-the-top personality caught up with him, and his marriage disintegrated as a result, culminating in a humiliatingly public domestic abuse complaint by wife, Debra, in June 2002.

Austin pleaded no contest to assault in November 2002 and was sentenced to a year's probation and eighty hours of community service, but trouble continued to haunt him. In March 2003, he was again in trouble with the law, facing another complaint from new girlfriend, Tess Broussard, although in all fairness she later turned out to be a real nutjob and was revealed as a crazed stalker. Austin's retirement from wrestling in April 2003 and instant return as "co-general manager" of RAW were really indicative of the problems he was facing every time he left wrestling. He was apparently a guy who was so tuned into being "Stone Cold Steve Austin" twenty-four hours a day that when asked to step back for a while and let someone else have the spotlight, he was unable to and

**BELOW: Steve Austin**

needed to fashion newer and sillier ways to remain on TV.

I think that's the essential reason why it's so hard for many of the top stars in wrestling to let go, and Austin is certainly not unique in that regard. Friends of Austin reported that when sitting home awaiting trial in 2002, he was stir crazy and constantly drinking, more out of boredom than alcohol addiction. When someone with more money than he can spend is left to his own devices after years of being virtually imprisoned by the WWE system, it can be a shock, I suppose.

Sadly, by the end of 2003 Austin was no longer a wrestler who I could admire as a person, he was just another retiree clogging up the works for those underneath him. In a sense, he had become exactly what he hated most all those years before, when he was "making his bones" in the business and had to fight through the ranks of those above him who wouldn't let go, either. And it got worse, too. With Survivor Series on the horizon for November and no real money-drawing angles to promote for the show, they came up with one idea that seemed to reek of desperation but at least wouldn't hurt anyone on the active roster: Each of the GM on RAW would assemble a team, with Eric Bischoff recruiting Mark Henry, Chris Jericho, Christian, Scott Steiner, and Randy Orton and Steve Austin recruiting Shawn Michaels, Booker T, Bubba Dudley, D-Von Dudley, and Rob Van Dam. The losing GM gets fired from RAW and presumably disappears. The match came down to a three-on-one situation for Shawn Michaels, on the side of good, against Jericho,

Christian, and current enemy Randy Orton, and after some of the usual chicanery from the heels, Orton pinned Michaels decisively and thus sent Steve Austin packing from RAW.

Ah, most of us said at the time, good move, he needs a change anyway.

But then he came back.

With barely even enough time to digest his absence, Austin returned a few weeks later with a newer and sillier gimmick: "Sheriff" Steve Austin. To think of the once-great ass-kicking machine who drew millions of dollars in a cowboy hat and tin badge, riding to the ring on an ATV, was such a ridiculous notion and the character such a pointless addition to the show that even HHH called him out on live TV and mocked the new gimmick. Thankfully, Austin essentially disappeared from TV soon after and reduced his appearances to yearly cameos at Wrestlemania, but it was too late to salvage the respect that I once had for him as someone who would stand up for his convictions and not be made to look stupid in the name of another fifteen minutes of fame.

On the other hand, there were other people who would have killed for even a couple of minutes of Austin's fifteen at that time. The problem stemmed from a change in talent relations, as longtime second banana in the company Jim Ross wanted his role scaled back, so he gave up his job as vice president of Talent Relations (i.e., the guy who decides who gets hired and fired and brought up from the OVW) and turned it over to John "Johnny Ace" Laurinaitis, for-

mer Dynamic Dude and flagbearer for the Bushwhackers. Whereas JR's thing was an overwhelming desire for big bruising tough guys who could back it up in the ring (generally those he referred to as "hoss" in his TV commentary, like Kane or Brock Lesnar, were favorites of his), John's tastes ran toward people who *looked* like wrestlers, period. The belief being that they could always train someone to work in the ring later, but there was less of a chance of someone who looked like Mick Foley becoming a big TV star, I guess. The fact that Mick Foley *did* become a big TV star is exactly the sort of logic that guys like John hate, though. Here's another bit of logic that John would hate, too: Back in his Dynamic Dude days with the WCW, Johnny Ace was a scrawny jobber turned pretty boy wrestler, who looked more like a surfer bum than a wrestler, and certainly not the chiseled bodybuilder type he seems to prefer in his current position. In fact, when he went to Japan in the '90s to re-create his whole persona for a new audience, he quickly learned that the Japanese had no tolerance for giant muscle-bound clods with no real ring experience. He was forced by the unforgiving Japanese crowds to hone his style into something where he could win them over on his own merits rather than on a prepackaged "look." Thus, his own experience in the business would seem to suggest that he'd be much more forgiving of those who didn't fit the traditional wrestler mold and less tolerant of those without the attributes to make their own name in the ring like he did. No wonder he has trouble getting along with people.

So now you've got, as a result of Laurinaitis's new edicts, in short order, Nathan Jones, Matt Morgan, and John Heidenreich running around TV.

All three guys have three important things in common: They're really tall, very well built, and all are absolutely god-awful in the ring. In fact, Nathan Jones is such a special case that he managed to stink up not one, but *two* different shots at being a main event player because he was so absolutely terrible at everything he did. An Australian wrestler long under contract to the WWE but unable to wrestle outside his native continent due to visa issues (i.e., being a convicted felon), Jones debuted in the WWE in early 2003 after a series of well-done vignettes promoting him as the next coming of Hannibal Lecter. He had been legitimately in prison in his younger years and was considered mean and nasty enough to have some credibility as a tough guy, but when he actually stepped into the ring after weeks of buildup it was so embarrassing to watch that the decision was made to retool the character on the spot. He immediately became a "protégé" of the Undertaker and was portrayed as someone still learning the fundamentals of wrestling. Yes, that was his *character*. He hit rock bottom with the fans when they showed a much different vignette than his "crazy prison man" ones, as he was now reduced to being taught to run the ropes in humiliating fashion and treated like a drooling idiot by his mentor. And then they booked a tag match with Jones and Undertaker against Big Show and A-Train for Wrestlemania, but lost all faith in the idea of put-

ting Jones out there to die in the biggest show of the year and just made it a handicap match instead at the last minute. Jones was thankfully taken off TV and sent down to the OVW again for seasoning.

And then he came back.

This time, his gimmick was "big bald guy who stands around and looks tough," as he acted as backup muscle for Paul Heyman, who replaced Stephanie McMahon on TV as the GM of Smackdown. And Nathan couldn't even do that right, stinking up the ring in a couple of squashes and then flaking out while on tour of Australia in November, claiming that all the travel and flying was too much for him. He remained home in Australia, and then reappeared briefly in the public eye with a quick performance in *Troy* as a victim of Brad Pitt. Thankfully, his wrestling days appear to be over. However, I have to stop and relate the story of his lactating nipples before we never mention him again. Although later exposed as a probable hoax, the kiss of death for his badass image in the locker room came after stories started circulating among former bodybuilding colleagues of Jones, who let slip that steroid abuse in the '80s had led to Nathan leaking fluids from places Mother Nature never intended men to give fluids. I mean, really, who *cares* if it's true or not? You can't buy material like that to mock someone with.

Then there's Matt Morgan.

After dropping out of the Tough Enough TV show due to injuries, he was almost immediately signed to a developmental deal with the WWE because of his size and muscular look. Everyone agreed that he had limitless potential for being a future star in the business, maybe three or four years down the road. So of course he was called up to the main roster about two months into his training, because the writing team had taken a trip to the training facility to scout new talent and were starstruck by his size. And he, too, was horrible in the ring and was mercifully sent back down very quickly into his run. He reappeared, to the shock of no one, in 2005, with a new stuttering gimmick and another push up the ladder and nothing to back it up with in the ring.

Probably the worst of the bunch, and that's saying something pretty significant, is John Heidenreich. Initially called up in the fall of 2003, his gimmick was that he couldn't get a job with the promotion and spoke to someone off-screen named "Little Johnny," who was presumably the brains behind his brawn. Thankfully, we never found out what the payoff was supposed to be (I'd rather not trust the WWE to show me "Little Johnny," if you know what I mean) and he was banished to the OVW, but he returned in 2004, and if you guessed that he returned with a bigger push than before and a new gimmick, you're right.

Interestingly, his originally planned gimmick would have been that of a Nazi war criminal frozen in ice and revived in the modern day, ala Captain America in the comics. But that gimmick, and other equally whacked notions (like an alien invader from Pluto and Booker T: Voodoo Priest) were the brainchild of crazed Smackdown writer Dan Madigan, who had a brief stay in the promotion in 2004 before moving onto the WWE films division. Indeed, I almost would have been more intrigued by the idea of an unfrozen super-soldier than what we got: A poetry-reading psychopath who feuded with the Undertaker for months on end. These days, Heidenreich still reads poetry and has added the habit of pulling young girls from the audience and asking them to be his friend, then leading them in a goose step around the ring while his fascist music plays.

Well, that's much better, obviously. What parent wouldn't want their young child to be "friends" with a big, sweaty, tattooed, Aryan monster?

But while pushing big guys to undeserved roles was a relatively minor problem, the bigger one was showing itself in the form of the main event side of Smackdown at that point. Case in point, the "main event" of Survivor Series, which ended up being Vince McMahon v. Undertaker as a result of the Brock Lesnar–Kurt Angle Iron Man match. After the title change, I was left wondering why they even switched the title from Kurt Angle to Brock Lesnar. What grand plan couldn't have been fulfilled with the title still on Kurt that was fulfilled by Brock getting it? Brock v. Undertaker, part 3, at No Mercy in October 2003, a PPV that was headlined by Vince against his daughter and drew flies? It actually was, however, a bizarre form of backward booking—Vince wants to feud with Undertaker, so he decides that the best way is to cost him a match for the title, but Angle is the champion and they don't want a face v. face match and they don't want to turn Angle, so they switch the belt to Brock in a poorly rated match, have him beat Undertaker to retain the WWE title after doing a million jobs in the month preceding, make sure he needs help from the entire locker room to do so, and then Vince gets to beat Undertaker at Survivor Series and put him out for the long term, something that no other worker had ever been allowed to do before in story line form. Thus, everyone in the main event looks like shit and no one cares about any of them. Using parity to establish a new group of main event stars is one thing, making the entire core group in the uppercard look like a bunch of pantywastes while the focus is on the owner and his daughter is another entirely.

In fact, the mind-bogglingly stupid grand plan for the whole thing, if you can believe it, was revealed when Kane helped Vince defeat Undertaker, which then set up Kane v. Undertaker in an "interpromotional" match at Wrestlemania XX. Except of course that Undertaker was "buried alive" to lose the match of the same name, and thus was dead. No, really, he was actually promoted as being dead, which I guess was supposed to make his eventual resurrection just in time for the PPV all the more exciting. But they of course don't do murder angles, according to Vince.

So let's review: Kurt Angle is the World champion in August, loses the title to Brock Lesnar on TV in September because they want to headline the October PPV with Lesnar against Undertaker, so that Vince can screw Undertaker out of the title and thus set up Vince v. Undertaker at Survivor Series, and in turn Kane

ABOVE: Chris Benoit and Brock Lesnar

screws Undertaker out of that win and "kills" him with the end goal being a match between Kane and Undertaker, something like the three millionth between them and the second one at Wrestlemania alone, fourth or fifth from the top of the card. Who says they don't book in advance? I feel like I'm doing a twisted version of that *Connections* show on PBS at this point, but I really wanted to hammer home the point that if the story line involves Vince McMahon, then by god he'll move heaven and earth to bend everyone else's stories around his own until all roads lead to him, and he collects a yearly salary of about $750,000 as a performer, above and beyond what he makes as owner. Meanwhile, Zach Gowen and Brian "Spanky" Kendrick were quietly fired around the same time as all this went on, for cost-cutting reasons. Combined salary: Less than $100,000 a year. Yup, I bet that sure helped the bottom line that quarter.

# DECEMBER 2003

★ ★ ★ ★ ★ **ARMAGEDDON (RAW)** ★ ★ ★ ★ ★

FROM: Orlando, FL
DATE: December 14, 2003
ATTENDANCE: 9,000
BUYRATE: 230,000
ADVERTISED MAIN EVENT: Goldberg v. HHH v. Kane

## RESULTS:

Booker T d. Mark Henry (9:21, ★¼)

Randy Orton d. Intercontinental champion Rob Van Dam (17:59, ★★)

Christian & Chris Jericho d. Lita & Trish Stratus (6:41, ★★½)

Shawn Michaels d. Batista (12:19, ★★¼)

Batista & Ric Flair d. RAW World tag team champions
the Dudley Boyz, Test & Scott Steiner, Garrison Cade & Mark Jindrak,
Val Venis & Lance Storm,

Hurricane & Rosey, and La Resistance in a "Tag Team Turmoil" match to
win the titles (no rating)

WWE Women's champion Molly Holly d. Ivory (4:24, ¾★)

HHH d. RAW World champion Goldberg & Kane (19:29, ★¼)

**CHRISTMAS OF 2003** pretty much gave me the lump of coal in my proverbial stocking, as Goldberg's contract was coming to a close and he dropped the title back to HHH. The match sucked and there was peripheral involvement from Kane as the third participant, but it wasn't really interesting and everyone knew the result going in, so forget about it, it's not important.

Really, in the aftermath of Survivor Series on RAW, December was about one thing first and foremost: Love, and lots of it.

First up, in the move that would ruin his career, Matt Hardy left Smackdown for RAW in November. John Laurinaitis was less than enthused with having the very outspoken Hardy constantly making character suggestions and offering his thoughts on how to improve house show attendance, and they often butted heads backstage on

Smackdown. Plus, being on the B-show meant that wrestling's most sickeningly cute couple, Matt and Lita, could not be all over each other twenty-four hours a day, as they were destined to be. So after whining sufficiently to the powers that be, off to RAW Matt went without much of an explanation, leaving his poor MF'er #1* Shannon Moore all alone on Smackdown to get beat up by people bigger than him—that is, everyone.

The problem here was that Matt had gone from teen scream pretty boy sensation to slyly ironic cult sensation by creating his "Matt Hardy Version 1.0" character. Each entrance would be preceded by "Matt Facts" in lieu of the usual boring weight and hometown stats (samples: "Matt is better looking than Christian," "Matt tans wearing only a sock") and he began cultivating a persona that was half David Koresh and half Steve Jobs. It was pretty cool stuff and the Smackdown writers, especially Paul Heyman, completely got the character and let him have pretty much free reign over his character direction. Once he got to RAW, however, he was immediately put into an angle where he turned on real-life fiancée Lita in his first appearance after teasing a marriage proposal. This was really quite ridiculous because it made one of two assumptions about the people watching the show:

1. **They know that Matt and Lita are a long-term couple in real life, in which they'll know that the turn wasn't "real" anyway and won't believe it.**

2. **They don't know that Matt and Lita are a couple, in which case they'll be wondering why Matt would be proposing to Lita out of nowhere in the first place.**

Either way, the move didn't make much sense, and it sure didn't help Matt's growing cult celebrity status, as he immediately got lost in the shuffle of RAW's bigger and more star-loaded roster and became just another midcarder clogging up Sunday Night Heat. Really, though, he's the one who asked to go there, so it's tough to feel too bad for him about that. But man, did he ever get screwed over later, which makes joining the show to be with Lita all the more ironic. More on that later.

Lita had another on-screen love connection at that point, however, which made it tough to insert Matt into the mix on-screen. It was actually quite an interesting story line, as Chris Jericho had been milking his obnoxious heel character for going on two years at that point and was growing stale with it. So in a bit of a change for him, he started going after Women's champion Trish Stratus, except in a nice way.

By the way, I just want to say for the record that despite my general disdain for the women's division in the WWE and the vapid eye-candy they normally throw out there, Trish Stratus is easily the most talented Women's champion, probably in the history of North American wrestling, and she could easily be World champion overall if she were a man. Whereas

* MF: "Mattitude Fan"

Chyna was physically bigger than all the other women and thus imposed herself into the men's side of things despite nonexistent in-ring skills and brutal interviews, Trish has both an impossibly smooth style in the ring and acting talent on the microphone unsurpassed by anyone in the sport outside of maybe the Rock. I have seriously never heard a promo from her where I didn't believe every word she said and didn't buy it as simply the natural extension of her regular personality. Not only that, she has invented two moves that no one on the men's side even thought of trying: the handstand rana and the Matrix dodge. The "handstand rana" is my own pet name for one of her signature moves, when she catches an opponent sitting on the top rope by doing a handstand in the corner and snapping them down with a headscissors. It's visually impressive and looks like it would actually work—two key components of a great wrestling move. The Matrix dodge, with the name of course coming from the trademark slow-motion camera moves in the movie of the same name, which Trish mimics by arching backward into a bridge from a standing position to duck a kick or punch. Most of the men in the sport aren't even flexible enough to attempt that, with the exception of TNA's Elix Skipper, who has taken the move for his own. Plus, she's proudly Canadian. Case closed.

Anyway, the women's division at that point was a million different combinations of Trish v. Lita v. Molly Holly v. Victoria, all recycled again and again, and taking Trish and Lita away from it for a while was no big deal, to be sure. So a silly, high school romance-type story line was begun with Jericho shyly putting the moves on Trish, and Trish being all kerfluffled about the bad boy really being a good boy deep inside, and it was really charming and cute stuff. Plus, as mentioned, Trish is an incredibly talented actress within the confines of wrestling's dramatic limits, so it was much more believable than if it was, say, Test wooing Stephanie McMahon like in 1999. In fact, Test is such a wooden personality that he couldn't even believably play Stacy Keibler's boyfriend on TV, a role he inhabited on-screen for much of 2003, and in real life for several months before that! So the acting in this story line was refreshingly nonsucky. To add to Jericho's "aw shucks" romance of Trish, longtime treadmill-stuck midcarder Christian tried his hand at making time with Lita, and is again so charming and talented an actor within wrestling's confines that he was able to overcome Lita's notoriously stilted delivery of her lines and make it an interesting few weeks of television.

Sadly, they immediately went for the cheap sitcom payoff by having the boys reveal (on camera, of course) that they were just betting each other to see who could score first, but after some humiliation to punish them for their transgressions, the story line picked up again with Jericho seemingly still in love with Trish, but for real. Simple as it sounds, this bit of cliché Hollywood tripe got some real heat going behind Jericho's character, and he began building friction with Christian, with Trish in the middle of it. Of course, it couldn't last forever, but it was the start of a real upswing for Christian's career, as his slimy jerk character and smarmy remarks started building him a bigger cult following.

On Smackdown, a couple of pretty special things started happening, amid a ton of crap. Crap is more my milieu, so we'll start there.

First up was the inexplicable push of Bob "Hardcore" Holly. I use the word "inexplicable," even though if you put yourself into the mind-set of those doing the pushing, it becomes really quite explicable. Basically, Brock Lesnar needed a challenger for a few months to stall before Wrestlemania and a planned interpromotional showdown with Goldberg (they exchanged words at the mixed-brand Survivor Series show to plant those seeds) and they didn't want to waste someone good, so they built up Hardcore Holly as a challenger, bitter (as usual) over an injury sustained at the hands of Brock months earlier, which had put Holly on the shelf until then. Brock, still a raw rookie in 2002, had been wrestling Holly in a Smackdown match that was intended to make Brock look better, by beating up on a veteran worker. Standard operating procedure. However, Holly (a noted grump and "tough guy" backstage) decided that Brock Lesnar wasn't actually the badass that he portrayed on TV and opted to demonstrate that on national TV by sandbagging him on a powerbomb. "Sandbagging" is when one wrestler shifts his center of gravity and basically goes dead weight instead of assist-

ABOVE: Christian and Shelton Benjamin

ing the other wrestler with the move, like they're supposed to do. The idea was to make Brock look weaker, but in fact Brock powered Holly into the air, without help from him, and then dropped the shocked Holly on his head because he wasn't getting cooperation, breaking one of the bones in his neck as a result.

As a pleasant side effect, no one ever questioned Brock's credentials again.

Now, this sort of thing should really be beneath (above?) guys like Bob Holly and especially John "Bradshaw" Leyfield, another noted bully backstage. And you certainly wouldn't think of guys like that as positive role models for new wrestlers, but that was exactly the situation for Tough Enough III, which featured a recovering Holly as one of the trainers for the new recruits. One of the trainees, eventual co-winner Matt Cappotelli, was a lightweight who Holly apparently felt wasn't protecting himself well enough in the ring. So he decided to teach him a lesson: While demonstrating trust in your opponent to the other students, and using Cappotelli as the unlucky example, Holly started a routine lockup maneuver in the corner and then viciously kicked the rookie square in the face while he was unprotected, knocking him silly and nearly causing serious injury to him. His justification: Wrestling is a rough business and you have to learn to deal with guys who rough you up for fun. However, the kids were under strict watch of the trainers, and thus were unable to fight back anyway, so Cappotelli was not only unable to protect himself, but unable to launch any kind of counterattack against the sickening double-cross from Holly. Even worse, this was barely even played into an angle in the WWE, as Cappotelli was not called up to the main WWE roster after winning until the incident had been all but forgotten by the fanbase. It was a big angle in the OVW, but it could have been much bigger played on the national stage. And then, as a cosmic slap in the face to everyone, they stuck Cappotelli in the ring with Holly on a house show in the middle of nowhere to get him ready to debut on TV, and Holly injured him *again* while taking liberties with him. To date, Cappotelli has not shown up on WWE TV again, and really can you blame him?

**RIGHT: Brock Lesnar and Billy Gunn**

My point in all of this is that Holly's bitching about the injury suffered against Lesnar (both the injury and the bitching were both very much real) looked even more hypocritical and whiny after his treatment of someone smaller and less experienced than himself, as is often the case when a bully talks shit to everyone and then gets his neck broken while trying to back up his big talk. Even worse, Holly followed up the incident by doing the same thing later on to hot new talent Carlito, thus stalling his push, too. Lesnar would essentially destroy him and win the eventual match handily, so I felt better about the whole thing in the long run. Of course, when we get to the rebirth of Bradshaw, I can't promise the same thing.

I would also be remiss in not mention the very short stay in the WWE for Ernest "The Cat" Miller. As another sign that no one who works in the talent relations office actually watches wrestling, Miller was brought into the WWE on the recommendation of

good friend and karate partner Eric Bischoff, and Vince essentially signed him and put him on TV, sight unseen. He even gave Miller a bizarre form of the rub by dancing with him during his debut. The only problem is that the fans booed the crap out of Miller, and he was supposed to be a babyface. They quickly and desperately retooled him into his arrogant James Brown wannabe character from the WCW, but it was far too little, way too late, and Miller was fired a little over a month into his tenure. Around the same time, fellow dancing black entertainer Rodney Mack and wife Jazz, the former of whom was brought up from his first match through the WWE system, were both fired for

**BELOW: Jazz**

cost-cutting reasons despite being given no reasonable opportunity to find a voice for themselves. Had someone actually taken ten minutes to ask who Ernest Miller was and what his reputation was before hiring him, they could have just saved themselves the money and left, say, Mack and Jazz employed. Oddly enough, the firing of a third black employee a couple of months later would have much bigger story line repercussions, although it sure didn't seem like it at the time.

Finally, in a story line move that just seemed like another angle to fill time between PPVs, Chris Benoit lost his first title match in forever to Brock Lesnar, passing out to the newly adopted "Brock Lock" submission move and thus blowing his big shot at the title. This was of course nothing new to Benoit fans, long accustomed to having him come close to stardom and losing out in the end, but this one had a different twist. When it was over, heel GM Paul Heyman promised that Benoit would never, ever get another title shot as long as Lesnar was champion. And since heels in wrestling always deliver the opposite of what they promise, this made people think that another shot would be forthcoming after Brock disposed of Bob Holly at the Royal Rumble PPV. And to really hammer that point home, Heyman rigged the numbers drawing for the Rumble match itself, ensuring that Chris Benoit would enter at #1 and thus would have no chance to win. At all.

After all, no one had ever started the hour-long match at #1 and be there at the end, let alone win.

That, of course, was about to change.

## ROYAL RUMBLE (BOTH BRANDS) ★ ★ ★

FROM: Philadelphia, PA
DATE: January 24, 2004
ATTENDANCE: 17,289
BUYRATE: 600,000
ADVERTISED MAIN EVENT: Royal Rumble match

### RESULTS:

RAW World tag team champions Batista & Ric Flair
d. the Dudley Boyz (4:22, DUD)

WWE Cruiserweight champion Rey Mysterio d. Jamie Noble (3:12, ½★)

Eddie Guerrero d. Chavo Guerrero (8:03, ★★)

Smackdown World champion Brock Lesnar d. Hardcore Holly (6:30, ¾★)

RAW World champion HHH draws with Shawn Michaels (22:45, ★★¾)

Chris Benoit wins Royal Rumble (61:37, ★★★★)

**SO WE'RE AT THE** end of 2003, which means it's a good time to stop and examine the matches that I deem to be the ten best of that year.

10. Wrestlemania XIX—Shawn Michaels d. Chris Jericho (22:34, rollup ➡ pin, ★★★★). I had quite a few matches clocking in at ★★★★ this year, actually, but one of the best of them was Jericho v. Michaels, which signaled a career revival for HBK, even if the wrong guy went over here. I'm happy to be proven wrong about his career longevity after coming out of retirement. I found the match to be not as fast paced as I was expecting at times, but I think that came from them not being booked in the main event and thus not wanting to completely steal the thunder from others on the show. History has indeed shown that Jericho should have gone over, as Shawn replaced his habit of faking career-ending injuries with a habit of going over in the big matches, or losing the big match and then getting his win back a week later on RAW.

9. Smackdown, September 18—Smackdown World title, Iron Man match: Brock Lesnar d. Kurt An-

gle (60:00, Brock wins five falls to four, ★★★★¼). Here we move into the ★★★★¼ range, and I had this one as the "worst" of the ★★★★¼ matches because it had the potential to be sooooo much better and just wasn't, for whatever reason. Still, the effort and work were there, and I can respect two guys killing each other for sixty minutes. Wade Keller was nuts to give this ★★★★★, however. I covered this one pretty extensively earlier in the book, of course.

ABOVE: Rey Mysterio and Jamie Noble

8. Vengeance 2003—Smackdown tag titles: Charlie Haas and Shelton Benjamin d. Rey Mysterio and Billy Kidman (14:52, Benjamin clothesline ➞ pin Mysterio, ★★★★¼). This is a forgotten classic from 2003, as Haas and Benjamin really came into their own as tag champions and the Filthy Animals meshed so well as a team that Kidman's heel turn was jettisoned completely because the matches were so great with him as a face. Sadly, injuries would derail the push of Haas and Benjamin and the Mysterio and Kidman team would be shot down for no reason I could ever discern, but this match stands as a testament to what could have been.

7. NWA-TNA, September 3—Super X Semifinal: Juventud Guerrera d. Teddy Hart (9:58, Juvy Driver ➞ pin, ★★★★¼). I find it interesting that the TNA weighed in so heavily in this list. This is the shortest match of the list, but the craziest and one of the most innovative. Sadly, Teddy Hart flushed his career down the toilet with his behavior, but Juvy basically went out and decided to earn himself a job with this one. He didn't get one with the TNA, but showed up in the WWE two years later, if that counts. Teddy also turned up in

the WWE doing a couple of TV jobs during a Canadian tour, but it was too little, too late for his career.

6. NWA-TNA, August 13—NWA World title: AJ Styles d. Low-Ki (14:54, baseball bat ⟶ pin, ✶✶✶✶¼). This is one that I thought was gonna elevate both guys, but the TNA treated it as just another match and forgot about it the next week, in favor of the Jeff Jarrett Show. Their loss. Like much of the TNA during this period, I don't really remember much about this one specifically outside of some awesome *Matrix*-like martial arts sequences from Low-Ki, but I sure must have liked it if I put it at #6 for the year.

5. NWA-TNA, August 20—Ultimate X match: Michael Shane d. Frankie Kazarian and Chris Sabin (13:46, Shane grabs belt to win, ✶✶✶✶¼). I put this one above Low-Ki v. Styles because it was both exciting and innovated a new style of match, and had a long-lasting effect on the promotion. Essentially, the Ultimate X match was in the same style as a WWE ladder match, but instead of a ladder to be used as a weapon, the match featured a pair of cables suspended above the ring in the shape of an X. The belt is hung in the point where they cross, and the guys have to climb the cables and

grab the belt to win. Many crazy spots resulted, and it was a hell of a match.

4. NWA-TNA, September 3—Super X Finals: Chris Sabin d. Juventud Guerrera (14:42, *Back to the Future* ⟶ pin, ✶✶✶✶½). Welcome to ✶✶✶✶½ territory, which is some pretty lofty company. This one just rocked, with nonstop action and crazy stuff all around. Sadly, Sabin never took off as a major star like I thought he would, perhaps because he was lacking in personality or size.

3. NWA-TNA, June 25—NWA World tag title cage: America's Most Wanted (Chris Harris and James Storm) d. Triple X (Elix Skipper and Christopher Daniels) (17:49, Death Sentence ⟶ pin Skipper, ✶✶✶✶½). I thought this was gonna break Harris and Storm wide open and get them a job with the WWE, but they chose to stay with TNA instead for whatever reason. Normally, I admire loyalty, but in this case they should have sent the tape to Pat Patterson and camped out in the Brisco Brothers Bodyshop until they got a contract. Still, this was the TNA's first ever cage match, and everyone involved took the time to make sure it was done *right*. This is another famous case of a match where I was later retroactively taken to task by

some of my readership for "overrating" it, but considering how famous this match is and what it did for the reputation of the NWA-TNA as a strong wrestling show, I'll stand by my initial feelings. Besides, the match had buckets of blood and stands as one of the few wrestling matches of the modern era to have me literally standing on my couch and yelling at the TV with excitement, so I think it warrants a spot here.

2.  RAW, December 29—RAW World title: HHH d. Shawn Michaels (29:13, Shawn pins himself by accident, ✶✶✶¾). I took some heat for supposedly overrating the match, but there have been very few matches in recent years to make me watch with wide-eyed enthusiasm and shout with delight at the near-falls while forgetting that I'm supposed to hate the product. This match did that, and I loved it, so if I'm being too positive about it, *good*. The finish was even a brilliant payoff in itself, as Shawn Michaels had gotten into the sloppy habit of laying back too far while pinning people, thus technically having his own shoulders down for the pin. After a couple of months of that, this match finally acknowledged the trend and saw Eric Bischoff personally reverse the ini-

tial decision (Shawn winning the World title from HHH) because in fact his own shoulders were down, and a tie goes to the champion. Sadly, the rematch at Royal Rumble 2004 couldn't touch this one.

1.  Royal Rumble 2003—Smackdown World title: Kurt Angle d. Chris Benoit (19:47, heel hook ⟶ submission, ✶✶✶¾). What more needs to be said about this one? Clearly the best match of the year, and one of the rare cases where a match in January was so good and so overwhelmingly better than everything else that it survived in the minds of viewers until the voting in November. *That* is a Match of a Year, truly.

As for the WWE, they celebrated the end of 2003 by going to Iraq to entertain the troops. Now, I hesitate to go here again because this is the sort of topic that makes people think I'm just trying to be "edgy" and "controversial" for the sake of it, but you're this far in anyway, so hang in there with me.

Now, as much as I think that if a bunch of guys want to get all dressed up and kill people, it's entirely their choice, I had two problems with the whole "Christmas in Iraq" deal:

1.  I'm Canadian.
2.  I watch wrestling for wrestling, not political statements from Vince McMahon.

It honestly wasn't so bad even during the first Gulf War in 1991, because at least Vince's blatant exploitation of that war involved in-ring activities. This time around, not only were we treated to having the announcers practically come out and declare their support for George W. Bush's actions, but later in 2004 the WWE actually had correspondents at the Republican National Convention! Supporting the troops is one thing, but Vince couldn't (or wouldn't) stop with that simple sentiment, instead constantly hammering the viewers with right-wing propaganda and portraying anyone on his shows who spoke against "the brave fighting men of the armed forces" as minions of Satan himself. But of course this is wrestling, artform for the lowest common denominator, so instead of any thoughtful reasons for why the soldiers were heroes, the entire argument was reduced to mindless "love it or leave it"-type jingoistic rhetoric, shoved down our throats with all the subtlety of Bush invading a sovereign nation with live coverage on Fox News. And of course the whole circus of nationalism wouldn't be complete without Vince taking center stage in Iraq and congratulating himself for his patriotism. The original "Smackdown Your Vote" campaign in 2000 was at least nonpartisan and just about encouraging younger viewers to vote for whoever they wanted—Vince's propaganda campaign during the war reduced the whole exercise to a paid political announcement. It also leads me to wonder how sending troops overseas to invade a nation who quite clearly did not have any "weapons of mass destruction" is "defending freedom,"

but I think I've alienated enough readers at this point, so we'll just move on.

One person who definitely was on the side of the troops was Kurt Angle, the preeminent patriot of the WWE, and yet he was such a masterful promo artist at that point that even while spouting the company line, he still managed to sound insincere, and turned himself heel as a result. This was done to give the rapidly rising Eddie Guerrero a main event foil later on in 2004, and Angle started playing mindgames with him via Eddie's nephew, Chavo, attempting to get into both of their heads. This was really awesome stuff, because not only it was an interesting character piece for both guys but also the inevitable match was bound to be awesome.

Speaking of awesome, that brings me to Chris Benoit. Whereas for most of 2003 he was mired in the midcard of Smackdown, I was assured by people who knew such things that there were plans for him at the upcoming Wrestlemania. Benoit's previous biggest push had been in 2000, when the WCW's management strife and rampant injuries in the main event combined to give him the WCW World title. Benoit was so moved by their gesture that he tossed the belt in the garbage during a meeting with the president of the company the next day, and he jumped to the WWF soon after for better money and more respect. Unfortunately, that title victory was erased from the record books out of spite for his decision, but then the whole company was erased from the record books a year later, so who got the last laugh there, huh? After three years of yo-yoing up and down the middle of the card with the WWF and the WWE, Benoit was given that oh-so-clichéd story line of feuding with the figurehead of the show, in this case Paul Heyman, and being held down by management. Although in this case the parallel to real life was uncannily true. Long considered too small, or not good enough of a talker, or not believable as a main eventer, Benoit was thus never given a chance to be a main eventer. It's the vicious circle of the WWE booking strategy: You can't be a main eventer until you main event, and you can't main event until you're a main eventer.

So finally, at Royal Rumble 2004, someone decided to bite the bullet and push Benoit to the top. He entered the match at #1 and eliminated Bradshaw, Mark Henry, Rhyno, Matt Morgan, A-Train, Ernest Miller, and then miraculously Big Show to win the match. You'll note that with the exception of a comedy elimination of Miller, all the guys that Benoit tossed were much bigger than him, as I think they made a distinct effort to show him handling people who he was supposed to be "too small" to deal with. With that win, Benoit earned a title shot at Brock Lesnar at Wrestlemania XX, and I still think it was the greatest Royal Rumble match ever, a ***** classic in every way. The great thing about the win is that it not only gave him a title shot at the biggest show of the year in the main event of the show, but a title shot where historically every person to earn that shot won the title as a result. Had I stopped watching wrestling right there,

that moment would have ranked with my all-time favorite moments of my entire life, but luckily I kept watching for the payoff two months later.

The other major issue to get moved along at the Rumble was that of Mick Foley and Randy Orton. Orton entered the match at #2, having won the Intercontinental title from Rob Van Dam in December, and was booked strongly throughout the match, until Sheriff Austin introduced a wrinkle to him. The previous month on RAW, Orton had challenged a returning Foley to one match for all the proverbial marbles, winner take all, people get fired if they lose, etc. However, because it was a RAW near the end of the year, a time when ratings are traditionally down, they did a bait-and-switch where Foley did a head-scratching payoff and walked out of the match, thus saving the big payoff for later. The big payoff proved to be at the Rumble, as Steve Austin personally beat up Test to remove him from the match, and brought Mick Foley back into active competition as an opponent for Orton. They brawled out of the ring together to eliminate each other, and the feud was now on for real leading up to Wrestlemania. This was *huge* for Orton, as Foley of course has a reputation for sacrificing himself to make others look better, and this would prove to be no exception to that reputation.

It almost makes me wanna skip past the next chapter and get to the big payoffs at Wrestlemania, but there's one little thing that happened in February that I want to talk about first.

# 11

# FEBRUARY 2004

FROM: San Francisco, CA
DATE: February 14, 2004
ATTENDANCE: 11,000
BUYRATE: 250,000 buys
ADVERTISED MAIN EVENT: Brock Lesnar v. Eddie Guerrero

## RESULTS:

Smackdown tag team champions Scotty 2 Hotty & Rikishi
d. The Basham Brothers & Shaniqua (8:16, ✮½)

Jamie Noble d. Nidia (4:25, DUD)

Charlie Haas & Shelton Benjamin d. Faarooq & Bradshaw (7:19, ✮¼)

Hardcore Holly d. Rhyno (9:54, ✮¾)

Chavo Guerrero d. WWE Cruiserweight champion
Rey Mysterio (17:21, ✮✮✮¼)

Kurt Angle d. John Cena & Big Show (12:17, ✮✮¾)

Eddie Guerrero d. Smackdown World champion
Brock Lesnar (30:06, ✮✮✮✮½)

**AFTER WINNING** the Royal Rumble and guaranteeing himself a title shot at Brock Lesnar at Wrestlemania, Chris Benoit (the TV character) made a decision that kind of threw everyone for a loop. Since the Rumble stipulations (supposedly) didn't dictate that the winning wrestler had to challenge the champion of the show he was actually part of, Chris jumped to RAW the night after the Rumble and challenged HHH instead. This actually opened up several more interesting possibilities for Wrestlemania, even with Benoit getting sucked into the HHH Zone as a result of that booking decision.

First up, it was the worst kept secret in wrestling by February that Brock Lesnar v. Bill Goldberg would be a featured match at Wrestlemania, and that Goldberg's contract was coming due and he wanted out. In fact, he wasn't even on TV past December outside of the Royal Rumble, since they literally had nothing left for him to do after dropping the title back to HHH at Armageddon. So once all that was established, the feeling from fans on-line seemed to be that it would have to be a title match to really matter, and that Lesnar would go over in a big way to really establish him as the star of the future and use Goldberg's name for one last rub. That scenario seemed to leave Benoit out of the loop, so the logical move was to put him on RAW and have him go after HHH instead. However, even that was not without problems, as HHH was embroiled in yet another never ending feud with Shawn Michaels over that title. In fact, on the very show where Benoit debuted to challenge for Wrestlemania, Shawn laid him out and "stole" the contract from him, signing his own name in Benoit's place.

Now, of course this is wrestling so you have to accept that the legal system works a bit differently and beating someone up and then signing your name in his place is a perfectly valid way to change a contract. Other examples of this twisted legality include stealing a championship belt and declaring yourself the champion as a result, hitting someone in the face with a chair and not getting arrested for assault because the referee was unconscious at the time, and others.

**BELOW: Brock Lesnar and Billy Gunn**

Wrestling, in fact, is dominated by two ironclad rules of thumb:

1. **Possession is nine-tenths of the law**
2. **You can't call what you can't see**

This leads me to wonder what would happen if the rules of wrestling worked in the real world. For instance, if you're about to rob a bank and a policeman bursts in to stop you, can you then knock the policeman unconscious and rob the bank while he's out, free of prosecution (despite a million cameras watching your every move) because he can't call what he didn't see? Or if Bill Gates was about to sign a big merger deal with a smaller company, could you burst into the boardroom and hit him with a keyboard, allowing you to steal his company out from underneath him? Actually, I think that would be pretty funny, come to think of it.

At any rate, Benoit's triumphant jump to RAW and mingling with the main eventers was somewhat tempered by the fact that the other two essentially treated him like an afterthought distracting them from the importance of "their" big match at Wrestlemania, and just to muddy up the waters a bit more, the match was changed into HHH v. Chris Benoit v. Shawn Michaels for the title. In a bizarre and irritating move designed to really make Benoit look like the underdog, they even had Shawn beat him cleanly on TV leading up to Wrestlemania, which seemed to kill any chance he had at being viewed as a big-time player by the notoriously fickle New York crowd that would be populating the show. This annoyed me at the time, but I got over it.

Speaking of getting over, Eddie Guerrero's comeback was about to become complete. Although Eddie's popularity had noticeably cooled off since getting squashed by Big Show to lose the U.S. title back in October, he was still doing the miraculous feat of (gasp) drawing money at house shows, because fans wanted to actually pay money to see his act! Well, this kind of radical departure in thinking for the WWE took some time to sink in, so Eddie's push was delayed a bit, until after the Royal Rumble and a subpar match against nephew Chavo to split up that team and thus send Eddie on his own for good.

With No Way Out, the February PPV that traditionally doesn't draw very well anyway, in San Francisco, they decided to finally move Eddie into the main event with a title match against Brock Lesnar. The story line justification for the match was Eddie winning a #1 contender battle royale (which has since become the hackneyed plot device of choice for the writers when they can't find any better way to justify a title match), eliminating Kurt Angle to win the thing. This had the bonus side effect of setting up another match for Wrestlemania. Keeping in mind that no result is for sure until it actually happens, actually watching the match was a pretty harrowing experience, since deep down no one *really* expected them to actually pull the trigger on the Eddie push. But amazingly they did, as they were given thirty minutes and Eddie used his cheating tactics to win the match and the title. The ef-

fectiveness was undermined somewhat by the announcers harping on the size difference and essentially declaring Guerrero to be a fluke challenger for the whole match, which somewhat contradicted the buildup, which had Eddie winning matches and even pinning Lesnar in a tag match leading up to the PPV. In fact, truth be told, the real time to push Eddie to the top was *before* he lost the U.S. title to Big Show, when he was at his hottest and a legitimate draw all over North America. It's not like the extra few months with the title did anything for Lesnar anyway, although given what became known later about Eddie's feelings on being champion, perhaps holding off was a good idea.

It was also around this time when the WWE really started making better use of their unbelievably extensive video library, with the eventual goal being a twenty-four-hour-a-day wrestling channel to fully utilize all the footage they owned. And in fact as a result of years of buying out the competition and shrewd business deals, Vince McMahon now owned the collective libraries of the WWF, WWE, WCW, NWA, American Wrestling Association, Extreme Championship Wrestling (ECW), and much of World Class. This of course is a wrestling geek's wet dream, which is probably why their DVD sales started shooting up so high at the end of 2003. Specifically, several releases made good use of the library and demonstrated exactly what potential that amount of history could hold. The first was *Bloodbath: Wrestling's Most Incredible Steel Cage Matches*, which admittedly sounds like the title of a DVD in the $5 bin at Wal-Mart, but in fact was a fairly comprehensive history of what was once wrestling's most rare and bloody gimmick match. The key here was that rather than the usual fluff piece produced by the forward-thinking in-house crew, the DVD featured an assortment of matches from different places and times and truly highlighted the differences between the cage

**ABOVE: Lance Storm and Rob Van Dam**

match as an artform. Okay, that sounds silly, but it sold like gangbusters due to the extensive DVD extras in the form of uncut legendary matches like Magnum TA v. Tully Blanchard and the Rock N Roll Express v. the Andersons and even rarities like a Shawn Michaels v. Marty Jannetty showdown from 1993.

What that DVD truly set the stage for was the Holy Grail of wrestling: *The Ultimate Ric Flair Collection*. A three-disc epic spanning more than twenty years in the sport, they pulled matches from everywhere imaginable to chronicle Flair's journey from rookie in the '70s to larger-than-life superstar in the '80s all the way until his brief WWF run in 1992. It also stands as one of my favorite wrestling DVDs ever, featuring a stunning array of ***** matches collected on one set and enough rare TV footage to choke a horse. It actually sold so well off the initial pressing that retailers were unable to keep up with demand; it also signaled a drastic change in the way that future WWE DVD releases

were marketed: direct-to-geek merchandising was born. Not only was there an audience out there clamoring for historical matches in digital format but also there was a *lot* of them. With money.

Soon, just about every subject worthy of a DVD would be covered with extensive extras and footage. The pushes of Chris Benoit and Eddie Guerrero were mirrored by spectacular DVDs that brought together footage from Japan, the ECW, the WCW, and the WWE in seamless fashion (although with commentary by clueless Todd Grisham to balance things out), while a Rob Van Dam DVD featured many of his important matches from the ECW. It was truly becoming the digital era for the WWE, where every important happening was archived and released on DVD two weeks later, along with a second disc of extras.

And then, in March, everything led up to Wrestlemania XX.

# 12

# MARCH 2004

## ★ ★ WRESTLEMANIA XX (BOTH BRANDS) ★ ★

FROM: New York City, NY
DATE: March 14, 2004
ATTENDANCE: 20,000
BUYRATE: 900,000 buys
ADVERTISED MAIN EVENT: Numerous

### RESULTS:

John Cena d. U.S. champion Big Show (9:13, ✹)

RAW World tag team champions Booker T & Rob Van Dam
d. the Dudley Boyz, La Resistance, & Mark Jindrak
and Garrison Cade (7:49, ✹¼)

Christian d. Chris Jericho (14:51, ✹✹✹½)

Ric Flair, Batista, & Intercontinental champion Randy Orton
d. the Rock & Mick Foley (17:02, ✹✹✹✹¼)

Sable & Torrie Wilson d. Jackie Gayda & Stacy Keibler (2:31, DUD)

WWE Cruiserweight champion Chavo Guerrero wins
the "Cruiserweight open" (10:27, ✹½)

Goldberg d. Brock Lesnar (13:41, ½✹)

Smackdown World tag team champions Scotty 2 Hotty & Rikishi
d. Faarooq & Bradshaw, the Basham Brothers, & Shelton Benjamin
and Charlie Haas (6:00, ½✹)

WWE Women's champion Victoria d. Molly Holly (4:53, ✹½)

Smackdown World champion Eddie Guerrero d. Kurt Angle (21:32, ✹✹✹✹½)

Undertaker d. Kane (7:45, ¼✹)

Chris Benoit d. RAW World champion HHH & Shawn Michaels (24:46, ✹✹✹✹)

**IT HAS BEEN SAID** that there are no two sports more fixated with roman numerals than football and wrestling, and by that standard there was no bigger show in the history of the promotion than Wrestlemania XX, the twentieth edition of the biggest show of the year and an all-important multiple of ten.

As you can tell by the running commentaries I've been doing for all of the feuds, everything during the year builds up to this show, and in particular the WWE put all their promotional guns behind it to make sure that everyone on the planet knew that this one would be huge. In fact, the card was so loaded that it almost lost focus from a promotional standpoint, leaving the fact that it was the twentieth edition of the show to carry the hype job. Judging by the money drawn by the show, they should push the number 20 to the top.

Which is not to say that the show wasn't loaded from top to bottom with the proverbial "main event in any arena in the country," to quote the late Gorilla Monsoon. Of course, he used to say that about matches like Brooklyn Brawler v. Red Rooster while they were opening a show in front of 400 people, but here it truly fit. So here then, match by match, is Wrestlemania XX, the biggest show of the year.

**U.S. Title Match** *Big Show v. John Cena* **This was an odd choice for an opener, although Cena**

**BELOW: John Cena**

was becoming an increasingly hot babyface act on Smackdown by this time and was obviously the guy they were getting ready to hand the proverbial "ball" to. Those who succeed are said to "take the ball and run with it," again drawing parallels with football, and Cena was certainly lined up downfield waiting to take a pass from the quarterback at this point. Big Show had essentially done nothing with the U.S. title since winning it from Eddie Guerrero in October, which was all the more tragic because it nearly killed off the hottest act in the company when they changed the title. In fact, Show had only one recorded title defense in the five months that he held the belt—a win over Billy Gunn on Smackdown that was possibly the worst match of 2004. Still, Show knew how to work a crowd as a heel and Cena was a rising babyface, so the crowd was insanely hot for this, despite them stinking up the joint with a terrible opener. The highlight for me was listening to Michael Cole read from what had to be "Metaphors for the Insane," as he compared Big Show's punches to blows from typewriters and frying pans, as though we lived in a Tex Avery cartoon or something. Cena won clean (well, semiclean) with a pair of brass knuckles and the F-U slam at 9:13. This put the U.S. title onto Cena, where it would reside more or less for the entirety of the next year, as he was groomed for bigger things in 2004.

RAW Tag Titles: *Booker T and Rob Van Dam v. La Resistance v. Garrison Cade and Mark Jindrak v. the Dudley Boyz* This was something of a Wrestlemania tradition, as they threw as many people into a match as they could to maximize the paydays. Booker T and RVD were a thrown-together tag team who had won the belts from Ric Flair and Batista in what was, at best, a lateral career move. By this time, La Resistance were one step away from being jobbers, and the "hot young rookie sensation" team of Cade and Jindrak weren't much better than that, either. Cade is something of a weird case, but not isolated at all, in that his real and professional name before being called up was Lance Cade. However, with Lance Storm already on the roster, management felt that two Lances would confuse viewers (no, honestly) and so they changed his name to Garrison, which pretty much sealed his fate as a jobber right there. Finally, the Dudley Boyz were beyond stale at this point and were ready to leave RAW, having exhausted their act long before. Thus, the logical choice was a fairly easy and convincing win for the defending champions in another lackluster match, as RVD pinned Conway following his frog splash at 7:49. This uninspiring win gave the champions such momentum that they promptly dropped the belts back to Evolution the very next week on RAW and then left the show to feud with each other on Smackdown.

*Christian v. Chris Jericho* The first truly intriguing matchup of the night and the first one with a serious backstory behind it. Jericho had of course been chasing Trish Stratus for months as a result of a bet with best friend and former tag team championship partner Christian, but found himself increasingly falling in love with her for real (see chapter 9). Christian, who struck out decisively with Lita on his side of things, swore off women and tried slapping some sense into Jericho to get him to do the same. His reasoning was in the same vein as modern-day philosopher Will Smith, because girls ain't nothing but trouble. Finally, because he had no choice but to smarten him up, Christian challenged him outright to a match for Wrestlemania, and you knew the finish would involve Trish Stratus. Christian defeated Jericho at 14:51 after Trish's interference "accidentally" backfired and caused Jericho to get rolled up for the pin, and that set the stage for the postmatch story, as Trish turned on Jericho and played tonsil hockey with Christian to pay off the months-long story line. Virtuous babyface Trish was reborn as Evil Slutty Trish, and both heel and face characters were money for her, as Trish became the Women's champion again soon after and basically retired the title and the entire division by being so far above it all. Christian also started gaining momentum as a result of the turn, becoming more of a cult figure by the day. The match itself would have stolen the show on any other PPV, clocking it in at an impressive ✶✶✶½ rating from myself and borrowing heavily from another Wrestlemania classic, 1987's Ricky Steamboat v. Randy Savage epic.

*The Rock and Mick Foley v. Randy Orton, Batista, and Ric Flair* This was of course the first payoff in the continuing build of Randy Orton into superstar status, as his feud with retired hardcore legend Mick Foley was red hot, so much so that they were able to shift the Rock into the feud as a special guest star without him appearing at all out of place. The idea was that Foley, who came out of retirement to seek revenge on the obnoxious young star, was constantly being triple-teamed by Evolution, and thus needed a partner to even things up for his big shot at Orton. And since he's had no bigger partner than the Rock, he, too, came out of semiretirement in Hollywood to help out his buddy Mick. The problem with this match, if you can call it "a problem" with a straight face, is that it was insanely entertaining and again would have been the show-stealing masterpiece on any other PPV. To put it into perspective, the match was loosely booked as a comedy showcase for Rock and Ric Flair, thus detracting somewhat from the more serious issue behind the Orton-Foley portions, but if you can find a match with more downright fun moments than this one, good luck. Flair in particular was juiced up by the energized New

York crowd, as they chanted his name when he was on the apron and cheered him as a hero when he was in the ring. Rock, too, was extremely amped up for the match and engaged in sequences with Flair that will probably go down in history. Most notable was a spot late in the match where Rock was disabled by a Batista spinebuster, and Flair decided to try his own version of the People's Elbow. The crowd gave that attempt one of the loudest babyface reactions I've ever heard for a comedy spot, but their elation would be short lived, as Mick Foley did the right thing and ate an RKO from Randy Orton to get pinned at 17:02. This was without a doubt one of my favorite tag matches of the past few years, although certainly not technically great or anything. Still, with nonstop entertainment and a real sense of fun that was lacking for most of 2003, it earned a bigtime ✶✶✶✶¼ rating from me, thus placing it among the best matches of the year. Oddly enough, at the time Batista was a definite fifth wheel in the equation, just a big musclehead out there to collect his payday and not get in the way of the real wrestlers. By the next Wrestlemania, his fortunes would be vastly different. Just goes to show how quickly things can change when someone gets hot.

*Sable and Torrie Wilson v. Jackie and Stacy Keibler* This was a pointless RAW v. Smackdown interpromotional match, there only to plug Sable and Torrie's joint *Playboy* spread. It was merci-

fully short, as Torrie pinned Jackie at 2:31. The funny thing is that the story line involved them fighting over who got to do the *Playboy* spread, when in fact it was only Sable and Torrie doing a second one together because Jackie and Stacy had essentially refused to do it in real life.

Cruiserweight Open: *Chavo Guerrero v. the World* In another "get everyone we can onto the card" match, this one saw Cruiserweight champion Chavo Guerrero, who was experiencing something of a career upswing of his own thanks to the managerial techniques of father Chavo Guerrero Sr. (or "Chavo Classic" as the marketing machine dubbed him), facing a variety of opponents in a big clusterfuck of one-minute matches strung together. Chavo pinned Rey Mysterio at 10:27 of the

whole mess to retain the title. That feud would continue a while longer, however. This one was notable only for Ultimo Dragon, living out his dream of wrestling in Madison Square Garden at a Wrestlemania, slipping on the entranceway, and falling on his face on the way to the ring.

*Brock Lesnar v. Goldberg* This was immensely fascinating as both a match and a social experiment. The build to the match had started months previous, with the two behemoths exchanging words at Survivor Series, and then Brock cost Goldberg the Royal Rumble to further the issue. Goldberg retaliated by costing Brock his Smackdown World title against Eddie Guerrero, and soon the match was on. To really add to the tension, Steve Austin was added as the guest referee, and since Goldberg was leaving the promotion, unable to come to an agreement for

RIGHT: Spike Dudley, Chavo, and Funaki

an extension, the result seemed pretty cut and dried.

And then something completely unexpected happened, as Brock suddenly announced to shocked friends and co-workers that he was quitting the promotion after Wrestlemania to become a full-time NFL football player. And by suddenly I mean that even the writers weren't told until days before the show by Vince, who casually mentioned it in typical Vince fashion. Specifically, Brock was trying to make it with his hometown Minnesota Vikings, assuming he could make the team. Given that Brock was a wrestling champion in college and had never ventured into professional football, or professional sports of any kind for that matter, this had people immediately skeptical of his intentions and thinking that it was some kind of elaborate work from the WWE. Well, it wasn't, as the legitimate press picked up on the story, and suddenly Brock was the most hated guy in the arena when he made his way down to the ring for his match. However, this really threw off the cynical New Yorkers, because they were all ready to boo the crap out of Goldberg for being Goldberg and for leaving.

So suddenly they had *two* people to jeer mercilessly, and boy did they ever. This might be the only match where fans booed every single move from both guys and gave the referee the only positive reaction for the entire match. Even stranger was the reaction from the people involved, as neither Brock nor Goldberg were equipped to deal with the crowd essentially shitting all over their match, as they engaged in a long stalling session to start, trying to figure out their strategy. As it turned out, it didn't matter, because the fans viciously turned on the match from the first lockup, giving heel heat not to the participants, but to the very match itself. A very loud and embarrassing chant of "This match sucks" was even edited out of the DVD release, as the fans gave them no chance to recover and win them over. Even worse, Brock and Goldberg tried to ignore the crowd, which only made the fans angrier at the match. Goldberg pinned Lesnar, in what was a total 180 from original booking plans, at 13:41 with his standard spear and jackhammer, but Austin sent them both packing with stunners, drawing the only positive reaction from the crowd for the entire match. This was such a trainwreck of epic proportions that I was almost tempted to put it on my "Best of 2004" list in a stroke of bitter irony. I gave it ½✶, but mere star ratings cannot express the surreal feeling I got watching this.

The Brock Lesnar story continued getting funnier by the day, as he failed to make the team after a series of tryouts and buried wrestling in all the interviews he gave about his experience with the WWE. It was definitely an air of someone better than the sport that had made him a star . . . until he failed to catch on with any of the football teams on the roster and he was released as a free agent again, at which point he attempted a legal battle, instead. His tactic was to sue the WWE for signing him to a contract that restricted his ability to wrestle for competitors, specifically Japanese wrestling promotions and mixed martial arts promotions. Of course, he signed the contract himself and negotiated it himself, and the no-compete clause was put into the contract because he wanted to then breach the contract and compete with the WWE in the form of being a football player. This is the one instance where I sided with the WWE's team of lawyers instead of whatever hapless sucker they were pummeling in court. Brock got everything he deserved for his childish behavior. He couldn't find work anywhere outside of wrestling and he couldn't work within wrestling because he was so arrogant that he signed away his rights to do so to get away from the WWE, and he paid the price for it. Some argued that preventing Brock from working for another promotion was infringing on his "right to work," but that's silly. Brock had every right to work at whatever job he wanted . . . as long as it wasn't wrestling. He could be Brock Lesnar: Chartered Accountant if he wanted, but like many of the stories of wrestlers unable to find their calling outside of our so-called sport, wrestling was all he knew. I don't feel the least bit sorry for him. His legal challenge is still ongoing.

**Smackdown Tag Team Titles:** *Scotty 2 Hotty and Rikishi v. the Basham Brothers v. Shelton Benjamin and Charlie Haas v. Faarooq and Bradshaw* This was an uninteresting tag team title match thrown together at the last minute, which proved more interesting for the fates of some of the people involved. First, the result, unimportant as it was, was that Rikishi pinned Danny Basham to retain the titles at 6:00. The match itself was a total time filler, but it proved to be the last match for the venerable Acolytes Protection Agency, as Ron "Faarooq" Simmons was having troubles controlling his alcoholism and was fired as part of the same zero-tolerance message delivered via Eddie Guerrero. This left Bradshaw, career midcarder at best, with another shot at another push, but this time he would find himself in a much more unfamiliar role by the time the next Wrestlemania rolled around. This match also marked the swan song for the World's Greatest Tag Team, as Shelton Benjamin was sent to RAW soon after. Haas replaced him with Rico and won the tag titles from the champions, Scotty and Rikishi, a month after this match. Rikishi was fired soon after and Scotty disappeared. The match got ½✶ from me.

**Women's Title** *Victoria v. Molly Holly* This was an oddball stipulation match, as heel challenger put her hair on the line in exchange for a shot at the title, which had everyone thinking she'd win. Well, think again, as Molly quickly lost a forgettable match at 4:53 and then shaved herself bald. The new gimmick did nothing for her and she quit the promotion a few months later.

Smackdown World Title: *Eddie Guerrero v. Kurt Angle* This was of course the payoff for Eddie's big comeback and title victory, as Angle had turned heel on him and spent months playing mindgames with him. Angle then won a three-way match against Big Show and John Cena at the No Way Out PPV in February to earn the title shot here, and he made the most of it. The result was a spectacular match between two guys at the top of their game and featured some of the most unique ring psychology seen in ages. The story being told was that an arrogant Angle was too aggressive in attacking Eddie's legs, and thus Eddie set a trap for him by loosening his boot and letting it slip off to escape the deadly ankle-lock submission move. He then quickly cradled Angle for the winning pin at 21:32 to retain the title. This was notable because the match broke free of the now-traditional "main event style" of wrestling, with guys reversing each others' finishers ad nauseum, and introduced some more intelligence into the story line, specifically Eddie outsmarting Angle. Very few weak spots and almost entirely strong ones left this as a ✷✷✷✷½ classic and the perfect match to send the crowd home with on any other show, ever.

*Undertaker v. Kane* Yet another match advertised on equal footing with the other main events, as Kane had done the ultimate heel deed and "killed" Undertaker at Survivor Series. Undertaker returned from the grave to haunt Kane on RAW with bad pyrotechnics and lots of spontaneously combusting crucifixes. The real drama to the match was not who would win or how good the match would be, but what Undertaker's new outfit would look like, as he had long been rumored to be returning to the "old school" look from the '90s, replacing the biker look he had taken in 2000. Well, no such luck, as his "new" look was just a mixture of zombie Undertaker with cowboy Undertaker—Sergio Leone does *Dawn of the Dead,* in essence. Undertaker also brought Paul Bearer with him in one of those comebacks that no one wanted to see. Undertaker disposed of Kane at 7:45 with the tombstone to end yet another failed Kane push and begin yet another failed Undertaker push. It was a bad match, which I put at ½✷ because I'm a generous guy.

RAW World Title: *HHH v. Shawn Michaels v. Chris Benoit* Although Benoit was treated like an afterthought by the writers and other participants in the match, the crowd was clearly behind him for this entire match. To call the match itself a pleasant surprise would be a gross understatement, as I gave it my second ✷✷✷✷ rating of the year and immediately nominated it as the greatest three-way match in the history of wrestling. Which isn't saying much because the three-way matches preceding it have pretty much all sucked. This one found a way to tell a more compelling story, however, thanks to the talents of everyone involved, as Benoit played the sympathy card with the crowd and Shawn sold the hell out of everything, as he often does. The finish appeared to be Benoit getting destroyed on the floor, thus leaving Shawn and HHH to decide the match, but that false finish led to an even more compelling finish, as Benoit fought his way out of his own pool of blood and got rid of Shawn Michaels, then reversed HHH's deadly Pedigree into his own, equally deadly crossface submission hold, and HHH tapped at 24:46 to make Chris Benoit the World heavyweight champion, fair and square, for the first time in his career. This was truly the pinnacle of Benoit's career, even if it came three years too late to make him into a major superstar and probably the happiest moment of my life as a wrestling fan. After enduring years of snide remarks by detractors of Benoit because he was too small or too short and would never be a star, this was truly his last laugh.

The evening was topped off perfectly, as Smackdown World champion Eddie Guerrero and RAW World champion Chris Benoit celebrated together in the ring, marking what seemed to be the start of a new era for the promotion, with new faces on top and a new style for the main event. Things were looking good for the WWE.

Sadly, it was not to last. But then it never does. Unless you're HHH.

# 13

# APRIL 2004

**★ ★ ★ ★ ★ BACKLASH (RAW) ★ ★ ★ ★ ★**

FROM: Edmonton, AB
DATE: April 18, 2004
ATTENDANCE: 9,000
BUYRATE: 300,000
ADVERTISED MAIN EVENT: Chris Benoit v. HHH v. Shawn Michaels.

## RESULTS:

Shelton Benjamin d. Ric Flair (9:32, ★★)

Coach d. Tajiri (6:26, ★¼)

Chris Jericho d. Christian & Trish Stratus (11:13, ★★★)

WWE Women's champion Victoria d. Lita (7:22, ½★)

Intercontinental champion Randy Orton d. Mick Foley (23:04, ★★★★)

Hurricane & Rosey d. La Resistance (5:01, DUD)

Edge d. Kane (6:25, ¾★)

RAW World champion Chris Benoit d. HHH & Shawn Michaels (30:09, ★★★★¾)

**THE THEME OF THE WWE** in 2004, and this book in general, is change, and that's what April proved to bring. Sure, it was change enforced by the owner of the promotion with a rigged lottery draw, but by god, it was change nonetheless.

The period immediately following Wrestlemania is traditionally a "shaking things up" time, when the feuds that are going to define the year are laid out, and new people are brought into the promotion and given their characters in hopes of getting them over. It's the wrestling equivalent of a shakedown cruise, I guess. However, determining the fate of a promotion by a glorified game of bingo has always struck me as both hideously stupid, and yet strangely appropriate for the subject matter.

I am of course referring to the "draft lottery," which Vince McMahon announced the night after Wrestlemania XX. The idea is that the name of everyone on the roster goes into a pair of hampers, one filled with RAW names and the other with Smackdown names. No one, including the people making the picks, are exempt from being picked, and each show gets to pick six people from the other show via a "blind" draw that was of course completely predetermined in real life. The results of the lottery were as follows:

- Going to RAW: Shelton Benjamin, Nidia, Rhyno, Tajiri, Edge, and Paul Heyman
- Going to Smackdown: Rene Dupree, Rob Van Dam, Teddy Long, Mark Jindrak, Spike Dudley, and HHH

Now, immediately the point of the thing was undermined, because HHH was "traded" back to RAW in exchange for the Dudley Boyz and Booker T (three

**BELOW: Rodney Mack**

guesses who pitched that plot development) and Paul Heyman quit as general manager of Smackdown rather than work for Bischoff. Teddy Long became the GM later in the year after a bizarre period with Kurt Angle in charge and remains there to this day.

Long was actually kind of an interesting case, as he was more well known for his days in the WCW as a manager after being hired by the WWE in the late '90s to resume his refereeing career. When floundering midcarder Rodney Mack was brought to RAW in 2002, a semiretired Long was called literally with only hours' notice and asked to come in as his manager, with no set plan as to where the angle would be going. Long managed Mack for a thoroughly insulting series of squashes that he dubbed the "White Boy Challenge," basically perpetuating the usual stereotypes that wrestling makes about black men, but while Mack failed to set the world on fire with his in-ring performances, Long was strangely entertaining while doing an outspoken, Reverend Al Sharpton–type character. Although Long failed to energize the careers of either Mack or longtime failed push recipient D-Lo Brown with this approach, he earned himself a steady paycheck with the company and was legitimately liked by fans enough that they accepted him as the figurehead of Smackdown when put into that position.

The only move among those made at the draft lottery that made any difference was that of Shelton Benjamin, who was a legitimate rising star caught in the tag team treadmill of Smackdown. He was immediately given a huge singles push after coming to RAW, even getting to beat HHH in his debut match, and stands as one of the few guys allowed to really make an impact after debuting. Well, re-debuting in his case, I guess.

Speaking of re-debuting, Tough Enough 3 winner John Hennigan (i.e., the one not mauled by Hardcore Holly) suddenly arrived on RAW about this time, presenting himself to Eric Bischoff as a potential toadie. However, a fairly interesting idea for a character was cut off after a few weeks of a running gag where his last name changed every week (from Johnny Spade to Blaze and finally to Nitro), and he disappeared for nearly a year before resurfacing with the tag team known as MNM on Smackdown, with no mention of his past identity. The gimmick of the changing names was actually based on the TV show *WKRP in Cincinnati*, which featured Howard Hesseman as Dr. Johnny Fever, the latest in a never ending series of DJ names he could no longer keep track of.

The parade of repackaging continued with La Resistance, as Dupree's departure for Smackdown left Sylvain Grenier and Rob Conway as the evil French representatives, and then to confuse matters further they started billing them as being from Quebec instead of France. This was actually part of a strange period, where the WWE didn't want any of its top babyfaces getting booed for being Canadian, perhaps because anti-Canadian sentiment was running so high that particular week in Vince's weird fantasy world, so everyone on the roster normally hailing from Canada suddenly became repatriated Americans. Chris Benoit

moved from Edmonton to Atlanta, Chris Jericho from Winnipeg to Manhasset, and Edge from Toronto to Miami, although he quickly moved back once a heel turn was on the horizon. This bit of silliness not only became a WWE policy for a while, but then it moved one notch up the goofiness ladder and broke as something of a minor scandal among the Canadian sports media. We take wrestling far more seriously up here, trust me. The end result was people actually being outraged about where wrestlers were announced as being from. This was apparently such a hot-button topic that ring announcements for Chris Benoit started sounding like "originally from Edmonton, Alberta, but now residing in Atlanta, Georgia, eating lunch in Omaha, Nebraska, and thinking about buying a house in Minnesota" as they added layers of hometowns so that no one would be offended by it. Some people felt that Canadians were overreacting to the whole thing, but smart money says that actually taking time out of your day to worry about changing someone's fake hometown to avoid adverse crowd reactions is a far bigger waste of time from people who should know far better. The whole thing also made the reactions of the fans at Summerslam in Toronto later in the year all the more entertaining.

Another entertaining act, although it didn't seem that way initially, was Eugene. Long a part of the developmental system under his real name, Nick Dinsmore, his longtime "gimmick," if you can call it that, was that he was a great wrestler who could outwrestle people in wrestling matches. Sounds pretty out there,

I know. Apparently, however, having that kind of character for someone who works for the World *Wrestling* Entertainment was too much of a stretch for the WWE, so they came up with a couple of new ideas for him. First of all, he made a brief cameo appearance as a jobber in mid-2003, playing the long-forgotten gimmick of Doink the Clown for the goofy barroom brawl "match" at Vengeance, and then doing a quick job to Chris Benoit to send him back to the OVW again. As thrilled as hardcore OVW followers were about that development, that was nothing compared to the winning gimmick they devised for him following his return to the big leagues in 2004: Eugene Dinsmore, Eric Bischoff's retarded nephew. Yes, bastions of political correctness that they were, they had Dinsmore mussing up his hair and wearing a jacket inside out, playing someone with mental problems who spent his entire life watching wrestling on TV. The gag was that well-mannered gentleman William Regal would be charged with guarding and protecting him against hurting himself. However, the character suddenly found additional layers when Regal decided to train him to wrestle to humor him and found out that he was actually an idiot savant who could mimic any wrestler he ever watched. This had loads of potential for opening shows for years to come, with Eugene playing a different classic wrestler each time and probably selling buttloads of merchandise to boot, but of course they fucked it up by the summertime, and we'll get to that later.

The result of all the reshuffling on RAW was a Backlash card that seemed to be carried by two matches: a rematch of the three-way main event from Wrestlemania, and the long-awaited one-on-one match between Randy Orton and Mick Foley to settle things man on man, once and for all. The Orton match was especially important, because this was the year where they were going to strap the proverbial rocket to his ass and take aim at the moon with him, and Foley needed to do a hell of a job in convincing the world that Orton was a superstar. And in fact the match did exactly that. It not only told a story, with Orton surviving the assault of the Hardcore Legend for twenty minutes, but it also provided one of the most visceral experiences for viewers since the dying days of the ECW. The hardcore match as a genre had been essentially beaten into the ground since the late '90s, and luckily a three-year (or so) break from them had left them once again fresh for use in bigtime blowoff matches like this one. Although Orton's initial weapon (a barbed-wire two by four) was kind of sad, he more than made up for it by taking a sick backdrop onto a pile of thumbtacks in a memorable spot, and even having his crotch abused by various weapons wielded by Foley. Recovering with an RKO onto a barbed-wire baseball bat, however, Orton got the pin and immediately established himself as a name player. This was seemingly (and was planned to be) setting up Orton's eventual split from Evolution and feud with HHH for Wrestlemania XXI, but plans changed.

The other major match for Backlash saw Chris Benoit's first PPV title defense, in a rematch against

HHH and Shawn Michaels. And, not surprisingly, another classic three-way that changed up the finish slightly, seeing Shawn tapping to Benoit's Sharpshooter after thirty minutes of intense action. The match was actually something of a tribute to the infamous Montreal finish, as it was in Alberta (home province of Bret Hart) and featured Earl Hebner refereeing. Shawn Michaels, in fact, has been a hated enemy of Canada ever since 1997 and is constantly booed by Canadian crowds. There's a strange relationship between the WWE and Canada with regards to those reactions, because the on-air commentary from Jim Ross and Jerry Lawler constantly harps on Canadian fans for "not letting go" of Montreal, and yet the WWE makes sure to pull out the Montreal finish every few months to cash in on it yet again. And this was yet another example of it, as midway through the match Shawn put Benoit into a Sharpshooter, mimicking the famous Survivor Series finish, and the crowd picked up on it, literally bringing the match to a halt with chants of "You screwed Bret" at Shawn louder than it probably would have been had they done the match in Montreal. Being in the crowd, I was kind of proud to be part of that, since Shawn seemed legitimately flustered and it's always fun to annoy him. The finish of the match was, I supposed,

**RIGHT: Val Venis**

intended as an apology of sorts, as Shawn was the one to tap to the Sharpshooter instead, but no doubt the Montreal finish will be hauled out of the mothballs next time Bret Hart has a spat with Vince in the papers.

And just when I thought a road trip couldn't get any weirder, it does. The Backlash PPV was in Edmonton, and as per tradition they headed three hours down the highway to tape RAW in Calgary the next night, so I ended up there for that, too.

We picked up the tickets from the will-call about half an hour before RAW went on the air and immediately braced for disappointment when we were in the 201 section this time. However, a guy who was (supposedly) comped by Val Venis the night before was sitting in the grass outside the Saddledome and offered to trade ours for his in section 109, because he had to get rid of them to fill seats. So right off the bat, good stuff.

So it turns out that the seats were in basically the

same place as the PPV—right beside the hard camera, in the "comp section," this time to the left and behind the lighting control guy.

Sidenote: You get all sorts of interesting views when sitting behind the tech guys, like the *script*, for instance. Over the course of the two evenings I was able to check out actual WWE scripts, complete with fancy cover page and everything, and yes, it's all written down there. You can also see the lighting guy using a layout of the Saddledome to check which buttons to push to blacken which parts of the arena. Very neat stuff for tech-heads like myself.

Okay, so back to the main story, and I should set this up a little bit. Rather than the usual crew, I went to this one with my friend Zenon and his friend Dave. If you've ever seen *Trailer Park Boys*, you've seen Dave. He wore a trucker hat and an Iron Maiden shirt to the show, and he was primarily concerned with seeing the "rasslin" aspect of the show, which was something of a warning sign right off the bat for us because it's a TV taping and not conducive to long entertaining matches.

So as noted, we're in the comp section, and once again we're sitting right by who else but Shane McMahon. This time his date is Nidia instead of Chuck Palumbo, as it was the night before, which is a step up in the looks department if nothing else. Zenon thinks it's a good time to get a picture with him after the show

as a keepsake, so we decide to ask him after the show is over.

Now, the Saddledome was mostly blocked off because of the hockey game the night before—there were maybe 6,000 people there and all of the upper deck was taped off—and the crowd was pretty distracted by the impending game. So there was kind of a nervous mood all night. Dave, in particular, was anxious because he was promised fireworks, and they immediately raised his ire by skipping them and going right to the show. He complains loudly.

The night progresses with a lot of talk and commercial breaks, because it's TV and that's what you're getting into, and Dave gets drunker and more restless. The show might have come off really good on TV, but I was pretty distracted by the tech guys and Dave, so I could never get into it live. So by the millionth commercial break, Dave gets really loud, proclaiming that the show sucks and he's tired of sitting through commercial breaks and there's only been a few minutes of wrestling—so Shane McMahon turns around and gives him $100 (U.S.) to shut up and go home. We took a picture of the bill and Shane just to make sure it was documented, but sadly it didn't turn out.

Needless to say, we didn't ask for the picture after all.

## ★ ★ JUDGMENT DAY(SMACKDOWN) ★ ★ ★

FROM: Los Angeles, CA
DATE: May 17, 2004
ATTENDANCE: 18,722
BUYRATE: 250,000 buys
ADVERTISED MAIN EVENT: Eddie Guerrero v. JBL

### RESULTS:

Rob Van Dam & Rey Mysterio d. the Dudley Boyz (15:19, ★★★)

Torrie Wilson d. Dawn Marie (6:17, DUD)

Mordecai d. Scotty 2 Hotty (3:01, DUD)

Smackdown World tag team champions Rico & Charlie Haas
d. Billy Gunn & Bob Holly (10:25, ★½)

Chavo Guerrero d. WWE Cruiserweight champion Jacqueline (4:48, DUD)

US champion John Cena d. Rene Dupree (9:55, ★★¼)

Undertaker d. Booker T (11:25, ★)

JBL d. Smackdown World champion Eddie Guerrero (DQ, 23:13, ★★½)

## A BRIEF HISTORY OF BRADSHAW

By May 2004, longtime tag team wrestler John "Bradshaw" Leyfield had been left as a single again by the firing of partner Ron "Faarooq" Simmons, and a singles push seemed inevitable whether we wanted it or not, much like Peter Frampton doing another comeback concert. Bradshaw held many of the attributes that Vince McMahon values in someone inhabiting the main event—among them a full head of hair, an imposing physique, and a definite "tough guy" image—but after eight years in the promotion and many trips up and down the card, few would suspect that his political leanings would be the force that pushed him over the top and into the highest position on the card.

Bradshaw actually started impressively as an independent wrestler, doing a cowboy gimmick as John Hawk before joining the WWF in 1996 and getting retooled as Justin "Hawk" Bradshaw, a kind of love child of Stan Hansen and journeyman southern wrestler "Wild" Bill Irwin. Although initial trips up the card failed due to a combination of in-ring limitations and lack of personality outside of it, he was repackaged by the Vince Russo regime more than a few times in an effort to cash in on his redneck appeal and sheer size. From Justin Bradshaw in 1996 he became Blackjack Bradshaw in 1998, switching from one '60s icon in Stan Hansen to another in Blackjack Lanza. A partnership with a similarly repackaged Barry Windham failed miserably, as did their breakup angle and subequent feud. Amazingly, jet black hair and a porn star moustache didn't set his career on fire, and he experienced a brief renaissance as a tough guy in 1998, making it all the way to the finals of the Brawl for All tournament before losing to Bart Gunn and getting knocked on his ass in the process. By 1999, with a brief run as Terry Funk's sometime protégé and enemy quickly forgotten, he was stuck in a bodyguard role for Don "The Jackal" Callis during a period when it seemed like his career was in a permanent downward spiral, and it was there that he suddenly found his calling. When Callis left the promotion and the new team of Bradshaw and Faarooq needed a new boss, they became "Acolytes" for the Undertaker and suddenly found themselves as dominating tag team champions in 1999, with an actual purpose and character motivation.

The next tweaking of the character, and the one that arguably brought him the most career success to that point, came when the team split off from Undertaker and starting selling "protection" services to other wrestlers. Thus, the Acolyte Protection Agency was born, and it was quickly shortened to APA and plastered on t-shirts everywhere. The easy humor of the duo and laid-back attitude of their backstage skits, with surrealistic humor like an "office" comprised of a solitary door right out of Bugs Bunny cartoons, elevated them to something of a cult following, as they became kind of a working man's asskicking team. However, the act eventually wore out its welcome, as many do, and injuries to Simmons left Bradshaw as a single again in 2002. This time, he was given a variety of short-lived attempts to elevate him, from a run as European and then Hardcore champion to a rather sad attempt to rebrand him as Steve Austin's best friend and tag team partner. However, the same problem presented itself each time: while people liked the backstage skits of him drinking beer and insulting those who represented the upper class, they didn't buy him in the role of main eventer and wouldn't support him there. So when Faarooq returned in 2003, back to the APA they went.

However, on the sidelines of his activities as beer-drinking everyman, John Leyfield the real person started becoming known on the talk show circuit for being more intelligent than the average wrestler and for being more gifted at picking successful stocks than some professional analysts were. He even wrote a book on his financial strategies called *Have More Money*

All photos by
Edward O'Brian

Funaki gets slammed by Spike Dudley. While Spike didn't escape the horrific talent cuts of 2005, Funaki did, marking perhaps the only time that the short Japanese wrestler wasn't the first one on the firing line.

Chris Jericho and Chris Benoit hang out on the ring apron during a six-man match. Benoit, thought to be one of the prime candidates for elevation in 2004, ended up losing matches to Orlando Jordan after moving to Smackdown, while Jericho feuded with John Cena over who was a better singer. The jury's still out on who got the better deal.

The former Three Minute Warning beats up on Rico aa house show. Interesting to note that Jamal (left) and Rico (middle) were two victims of previous talent cuts in 2004, but went on to be tag team champions together in Japan after their firings. Rosey (right) also became a tag champion in the WWE. I never would have expected any of that to happen.

Lance Storm holds Rhyno in his half crab finisher. Storm actually got so sick of the political BS surrounding his new role as trainer in 2005 that he quit the company entirely, wrestling one last match at the ECW One Night Stand PPV before leaving. Meanwhile, the target of his frustration, JBL, wrestled in 17 straight PPV main events. Go figure.

The Hurricane, who won the tag team titles with joke partner Rosey in 2005 and still holds them as of this writing, probably because they haven't been booked on TV in weeks and the creative team forgot they were champions.

I was going to write a joke about JBL here, but he threatened to beat me up and rape me in the shower if I did.

Jackie Gayda, co-winner of the second Tough Enough competition, married boyfriend Charlie Haas in 2004 after her move to Smackdown. As a wedding present, the WWE fired both of them. . . . Oh, and gave them silverware, probably.

Christian built up a cult following for himself in 2004 and 2005, moving himself up through the midcard by sheer force of will. He had a catchphrase, a good finisher, and an imposing bodyguard, so of course he was moved to Smackdown in 2005 and never approached the main event again.

Randy Orton, after a big main event win. Just wanted to have that one for posterity because it didn't happen very often.

Roddy Piper, at an independent show in 2003, holds a pair of coconuts, demonstrating how big his balls had to be in order to go on HBO and trash the WWE's drug policies while he was still employed by them.

Steven Richards, longtime nobody in the WWE, actually got a career revival as part of the Blue World Order in 2005. It stemmed from friend Brian "Blue Meanie" Heffron getting roughed up by (who else) JBL and thus earning not only Heffron a job with the WWE but Richards and Mike "Simon Dean" Bucci a career reprieve as his backup. Most think that had the incident not occurred, Richards and Simon Dean would have been on the chopping block like everyone else in 2005.

Kane, in 2003, just before losing the mask to HHH. I think he should have kept it on, not because of marketing reasons or creative control, but because he's really ugly.

Rene Dupree, another one of those "can't miss" prospects who did nothing but miss. How do you say "He's a really god-awful worker" in French, again?

Val Venis signs signs autographs for fans at a festival. Apparently they couldn't get someone more prestigious—like Spike Dudley—booked in time.

This is a mask from the Machines angle of 1986, which is photographic evidence that Hogan's Mr. America angle was in fact 17 years old in 2003 and thus safe to steal again.

Sean O'Haire swan dives onto his opponent at an indy show, simulating his own career free fall in 2003. Wrestling can truly be art.

Kurt Angle, survivor of multiple surgeries and a walking medical miracle for still being able to wrestle ✶✶✶✶✶ matches today, was rewarded by being booked to lose his Olympic medals to Eugene in 2005. There's a lesson here somewhere, I think.

Tazz and Michael Cole, the Smackdown announcing duo, who alternate between "funny and insightful" and "irritatingly stupid." At either end of the spectrum, they're still better than Jerry Lawler.

I was going to write a joke about Bob Holly here, but he threatened to beat me up and end my career early if I did.

Chris Candido, in one of his last appearances before his death in 2004. Rest in peace.

John Cena, who makes millions of dollars a year in merchandising, but still wears Scooby-Doo underwear like a big dork. No wonder kids love him.

Rena "Sable" Mero returned in 2003, to the shock of everyone, having last been heard from in the courtroom during a lengthy legal battle with the WWE. Showing that money and a total lack of integrity can overcome any obstacle, the WWE hired her back and she immediately began dating Brock Lesnar, only to leave again with him in 2004. I wouldn't bet against seeing her again.

Chris Benoit applies the Sharpshooter to Brock Lesnar in early 2004. Given what happened with Brock, I think they probably would have had him put Benoit over at Wrestlemania instead of HHH, but hindsight is 20/20 and all that.

Later, Brock press-slams Benoit, showing that truly he is big and Benoit is small. Thanks, Brock.

I just like this shot of Brock further suplexing the crap out of Benoit because it shows the kind of innovation and spirit that Brock had before his NFL dreams turned him into a big jerk.

In conclusion, I think Billy Gunn's tights say everything about Brock that needs to be said.

Chavo Guerrero, who was enjoying a successful run in the Cruiserweight division in 2004, was moved to RAW in 2005 as "Kerwin White," with the catchphrase "If it's not white, it's not right." I think the gimmick will play great in the South, but otherwise I don't see why they're keeping him around.

Paul London charges into the ring, another case where he won a title in 2005 (the Cruiserweight title) and still holds it months later because the entire division was fired and no one remembers he's champion.

Charlie Haas and Shelton Benjamin were two of the brightest talents on the Smackdown side of things as "The World's Greatest Tag Team" in 2003-2004, and in fact were so good that they were immediately split up and Haas was fired in 2005 because they couldn't think of anything to do with him. Um, gee, let me think — how about wrestling Shelton Benjamin, his former partner? Nah, that's just crazy.

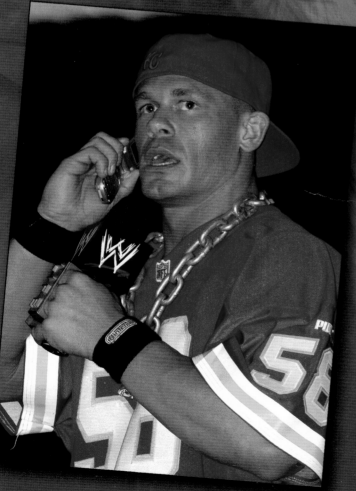

John Cena, so merchandise conscious that he has actually taken up selling his CD and belt replicas direct over the phone during slow points in his matches.

Eddie Guerrero, in a truly rare sight: Smiling and holding the WWE title. We wouldn't see either of those for a while in 2004.

And we finish with Sean O'Haire, superkicking the Abyss. Sometimes life really IS a kick in the head.

*Now*, which ironically flopped and didn't make him any. Vince McMahon has long cashed in on wrestlers who cash in on their natural personalities in the ring, with Steve Austin being the best example, and when the APA was split up for good in 2004, a new character was created by Bradshaw, and JBL was born.

Essentially playing a twenty-first-century retread of the famous Million Dollar Man character established by Ted Dibiase in the '80s, JBL was everything that fans hated about George W. Bush—an outspoken Republican who preached about his self-made wealth and rallied against immigration, he seemed to personify the increasingly conservative public image put forth by Vince McMahon himself. And there's no one that Vince likes to push better than himself, so with a few lengthy promos and a stretch limousine (with bullhorns on the front, despite JBL being from New York now) added to his repertoire, JBL was a natural foil for working-class hero and new Smackdown champion Eddie Guerrero. However, and this is the distinction that has eluded Vince since day one of the interminable JBL push in 2004, someone who is a main event character is not necessarily someone who should be a main eventer. After eight years as a career midcarder, people simply did not accept the newly created JBL as anything but a new coat of paint on the same old Bradshaw. However, the common feeling was that JBL was simply a stop-gap opponent for Eddie Guerrero at the May PPV while Kurt Angle recovered from his latest neck problems long enough to return to form and challenge Guerrero again.

**ABOVE: JBL**

That perception flew out the window when JBL was booked in a twenty-minute bloodbath against Guerrero at the PPV, as Eddie bled all over the ring in a stunning one-man performance and nearly carried JBL to the best match of his life. Opinions are sharply divided on it: some enjoyed the story told by the match and the old-school mentality involved in the buildup, with a very southern-style heel in the form of JBL doing things like assaulting Eddie's mother to make it into a personal issue and then drawing out the feud with a tough DQ win; others such as myself just couldn't buy the challenger as a serious threat to the hottest act in the company and were bored by the main body of the match enough that the blood couldn't save it as entertainment. Either way, JBL was on the rise, and a spot on CNBC as a financial commentator seemed to be the start of mainstream acceptance for the character and the person. By the next month, however, opinions would swing drastically in the other direction and alter the fate of Smackdown for a long time to come.

Another person who was about to get hit in the face with fate was Matt Hardy, who I've mentioned earlier as coming close to a career-changing moment. Matt's off-screen relationship with Amy "Lita" Dumas wasn't exactly a big secret or anything, and neither was his reasoning for wanting to be shifted from Smackdown to RAW in 2003. Life on the road without the woman in his life was wearing on him, and he wanted to strengthen the relationship by being on the same show. For months the creative team had avoided having the two interact, but by April 2004 Matt's charac-

**BELOW: JBL**

ter was floundering so badly as a midcard heel that it seemed something big was needed to freshen him up.

While Matt's cult status as a heel was understood by the Smackdown writers, the RAW team never seemed to get a grasp on what made the V1 character tick, and so they reverted him to the last character that worked for him: teen heartthrob. This went hand in hand with the latest attempt to rehabilitate Kane after his Wrestlemania loss to Undertaker, as Kane was once again ready to be a monster on the rampage who showed no mercy, blah blah blah. So in a simple and time-honored face turn, Kane decided to vent his frustrations on Lita, and former coward heel Matt Hardy stood up for his woman and got beat up as a result. Suddenly, he was thrust into a higher-profile feud than he had been in for many months, but at a pretty big cost. The idea was that Kane was not only a monster but also a monster in the sack who wanted some action from Lita. And hey, who could resist a guy who can break the laws of thermodynamics? Admittedly, Kane hadn't been involved with anyone, story line–wise, since his failed fling with Tori in 1999, so I guess he was due for some more nookie. Things progressed downward pretty quickly, however, as Kane offered to spare the life of Matt Hardy in exchange for sex from Lita, which was stupid on two essential levels:

1. **It made Lita look like a slut.**
2. **It made Matt Hardy look like a pansy for needing his girlfriend to protect him.**

No one respects a man who needs his woman to fight for him, and especially a man who doesn't flip out and do something desperate when a zombie freak goes after his fiancée. Never mind that having to watch both Kane and Lita try to act at the same time is like in *Ghostbusters* when they kept warning about crossing the streams. That would be bad.

Speaking of nothing good coming from it, there were some pretty oddball attempts at creating new stars from OVW imports and new signings over on Smackdown. Most notorious among these was the case of Kevin Fertig, a longtime member of the OVW roster who was called up and given the thoroughly uninspiring gimmick of Mordecai, a religious zealot who quotes from his own bible and wants to convert heathens. Now, for those who watch any wrestling at all outside of the WWE, this is a gimmick that you'll run across about eighteen times a week on a given independent show, because *everyone* seems to do it while trying to be the next Raven, and they all suck at it. Hell, even Raven makes a lousy Raven these days. Compounding the problem was that the promo videos for Mordecai made him out to be a fairly imposing physical specimen, and when he debuted he looked more like the lovechild of Scott Steiner and Pai Mei from *Kill Bill*. And about a foot shorter than either one. Even worse, he stunk up his debut match against Scotty 2 Hotty at the Judgment Day PPV and failed to draw any kind of crowd reaction whatsoever. After another shot on PPV, which he botched again, he was sent back to the OVW as a matter of courtesy, I suppose, before getting the axe permanently in 2005.

Another bizarre choice for a huge push was Kenzo Suzuki. Brought into the promotion in 2004 for god

knows what reason, even after appearing on PPV previously with the NWA-TNA and sleepwalking through a match with Perry Saturn that is most generously described as a steaming pile of turds, they still had big plans for the guy. The post-Wrestlemania promos, which were aimed at getting him over as a character on the RAW side, renamed him "Hirohito" after the Japanese emperor and emphasized how much Japan hated the United States for the whole atomic bomb thing. Now, how this even made it past creative control is beyond me (well, actually, no, it's not, but I like to pretend sometimes, so I can sleep at night), but needless to say when people in Japan actually saw the promos, well, insulted is not even the word for it. Imagine if you will the Japanese bringing in some loudmouthed American and naming him "Abraham Lincoln" and then having him talk about his hatred of the Japanese people for Pearl Harbor to draw heat, and you have the kind of idea of what this new character looked like to officials in Japan. So the whole thing was scrapped, and the most incredible tidbit to come out of the aborted push was that "Hirohito" was actually planned to be a summer main event opponent for Chris Benoit and given a monster push on RAW. To distance him from the previous gimmick, Suzuki was moved to Smackdown before he even debuted and then was given his own name instead, where he immediately crashed and burned from the moment he stepped foot in the ring. He, too, was fired in 2005.

Over on RAW, however, things were looking much more interesting as we headed into the summer . . .

# 15 JUNE 2004

**RESULTS:**

Chris Benoit & Edge
d. RAW World tag team champions La Resistance (DQ, 10:11, ★★½)

Chris Jericho d. Tyson Tomko (6:04, ★★¼)

Intercontinental champion Randy Orton
d. Shelton Benjamin (15:04, ★★★½)

Trish Stratus d. WWE Women's champion
Victoria, Lita, & Gail Kim (4:44, ★¼)

Eugene d. Coach (7:36, ★)

RAW World champion Chris Benoit d. Kane (18:12, ★★★¾)

HHH d. Shawn Michaels (48:13, ★★★¼)

**BY JUNE, MANY PEOPLE** were shocked that Chris Benoit was still World champion on RAW. He had won the belt in March, and three months is normally a long time for HHH to be without "his" title. Unfortunately, there never seemed to be any intention of putting Benoit forth as the leader of the show and the guy carrying the belt into a new generation, because he was mainly used as an undercard attraction or tag team partner for Edge, even while wearing what was arguably now the most prestigious title in wrestling.

Those tag matches with Edge had an interesting side effect, however. Edge had returned from yet another injury in 2004, re-debuting in a crappy match with Kane at Backlash in April and failing to set the world on fire. Essentially, after four years of pushing Edge as the "hot new babyface" attraction and then never delivering a main event push for him, the WWE had burned out the fanbase on the guy. Lacking anything better to do with him for the time being, Edge teamed with Benoit and won the tag titles from Evolution in April, holding onto them until June. The idea behind it seemed to be a fairly straightforward one: Edge needed a heel turn to freshen him up, so you team him with the guy who is supposed to be your #1 babyface, then have Edge turn on him and voila! Instant title match. Edge is "fresh" again, Benoit has a natural challenger for the summer months, birds are singing, flowers are blooming, etc. The problem was that they kept having Edge do all these subtle mannerisms to indicate tension with Benoit and thus tease a heel turn, but he never turned. In fact, they lost the tag team titles quite innocuously to La Resistance (this time the permanent combination of Sylvain Grenier and Rob Conway) and it seemed to be a perfect setup for the turn, but again nothing. And with a PPV coming up that month, Benoit still needed a challenger. Most assumed it would be HHH for the third show in a row, but instead they went with the *thrilling* notion of yet another #1 contender battle royale and had Kane be the lucky recipient instead. Apparently, forcing women to have sex with you is an effective way to advance up the company ladder within the WWE. Not that it shocks me or anything, but this *is* the company that says they don't do rape angles. Or murder angles, even though Undertaker was murdered by Kane at Survivor Series. At any rate, Kane lost to Chris Benoit relatively clean, as Benoit once again did the only thing he knew how to, and carried Kane to the match of his life. In between lousy feuds against rapists and teaming with Edge against the evil forces of Quebec (Benoit actually wrestled in the opening match of the PPV, challenging

La Resistance for the tag belts and losing, and also wrestled in the World title match against Kane later in the night, showing how shallow the roster was getting), Benoit even had time to wrestle a Match of the Year Candidate level match against Shawn Michaels on RAW, just because he was that kind of guy. Sadly, there was never any plan to go with Benoit past Summerslam, which he was told back in November before even winning the title. I guess all those **** matches would have dragged down the bottom line or something.

Speaking of Shawn, within the story line he wasn't giving up the HHH thing very easily. Keeping in mind that he got his first shot at the title in December and lost (through his own fault), then challenged HHH again at Royal Rumble and didn't win the title, then challenged HHH at Wrestlemania and didn't win the title, then challenged Benoit and HHH for Backlash and lost the match, *then* challenged Benoit in a singles match and didn't win the title . . . well, really he should have read the part in the Bible about "thou shalt quit being a whiny jerk and let someone else have a shot at it." Oh, it's in there, go ahead and look. At any rate, Shawn was beating the drum about "this thing with HHH isn't over by a longshot" pretty much nonstop, until even HHH got bored by it and wanted him to shut up about it already. And when HHH thinks your whining is tiresome, you're pretty whiny. So the result was HHH's favorite match, Hell in a Cell. The problem is that, of course, Shawn Michaels is one of the greatest workers in history, and HHH thinks he is.

So if someone like Scott Steiner, generally considered the worst of HHH's in-ring victims, is booked to go twenty minutes with him, you can only imagine what HHH would demand for someone good. Well, imagine no more, because the epic final match (well, sort of) between HHH and Shawn was booked to go an astounding forty-eight minutes, complete with an equally astounding amount of both guys laying around on the mat selling how tired they were. I kind of felt the same way, except I think I actually did fall asleep at about five different points during the match. Although the match was technically sound, it was a pretty passionless effort from two guys who were supposed to hate each other and had collectively engaged in three matches that were near the top for Match of the Year honors. Even more insulting was not only giving them more time than any other wrestlers on any other show in years, but then making sure that only Shawn and HHH were able to use a ladder and table for their match, gimmicks that are generally reserved for helping those who cannot help themselves. I had it at ***1/4 out of the intellectual knowledge that the match was "good," but I have no desire to ever watch it again to confirm that. The thing that really blows my mind is that they booked *another* match between them a few months later and expected people to care.

**RIGHT: Scott Steiner**

Speaking of divas and weird notions of what people care about, wrap your head around this one: the WWE cuts talent (every year it seems like) for cost-cutting reasons, but comes up with the idea of their own reality competition outside of Tough Enough . . . the Diva Search. Since apparently they didn't have enough dead weight in the women's already, they not only wanted more, but offered a prize of $250,000 for whoever won the contest to be the next diva. And man was there a lot of dead weight in the women's division as it is. As of mid-2004, the division on RAW consisted of champion Victoria, hot heel Trish Stratus, terrorized rape victim Lita, soon-to-be-fired badass black chick Jazz, solid puritan heel Molly Holly, and rapidly improving submission specialist Gail Kim. And that was the whole division, outside of occasional freakshow additions like Stacy Keibler or ring announcer Lilian Garcia. Even worse, by the beginning of 2005 they had fired Jazz and Gail Kim as a result of cost cut-

ting and Molly Holly had quit for reasons that she refuses to discuss to this day. Victoria basically only sticks around because she apparently needs the money and is willing to pose naked for *Playboy* should the situation present itself, but otherwise she isn't used in any story lines of note and basically just inhabits space on the roster as an occasional opponent for the women that they care about. Gail Kim was actually a rather unfortunate cut, because she was thrown right into the mix in 2003, winning the Women's title in her debut as a babyface, at which point backlash was harsh and immediate. Well, she was terrible, so they were right to boo her, but after dropping the title just as quickly back to Molly Holly, she actually went to the OVW and improved hugely in the ring, changing her style from "spunky babyface" to "calculating Asian bombshell," like something out of *Kill Bill*. It worked wonders, as she innovated all sorts of wacky submission moves that actually looked painful and had her positioned as a serious challenger to Victoria's title by June 2004. Of course, given that tremendous improvement and the fact that they needed to pay some chick a quarter of a million dollars, they fired her and decimated the division in the process, to the point where Lita and Trish were literally left as the only legitimate contenders to the Women's title. Gail resurfaced as a main event level manager with NWA-TNA, so she's doing okay now.

But back to the Diva Search.

The qualification process was quite strenuous to begin with, as apparently the key things needed were being a model, being a former model, being an aspiring model, being as dumb as a model, looking like a model, or having big hooters. Mainly the last one. Then in fine reality show fashion, we got the usual dramatic fan voting, somber elimination ceremonies, and immunity challenges that had all been done to death by shows with higher ratings before. Much like *American Idol*, one of the shows being ripped off, the top ten contestants' fates were controlled by a fan voting system, with a new contender being voted off each week. However, instead of situations where personality could actually shine through or actual wrestling matches to demonstrate that they could, you know, wrestle (which is such a ludicrous concept for a wrestling promotion that I don't know why I would even bring it up), we got week after week of "challenges." Sample challenge: In thirty seconds or less, "seduce" retired wrestler Kamala, who responds by patting his belly and groaning in Ugandan. It was as hilarious in practice as it sounds on paper, believe me. Amazingly, even through all the stupidity involved in the "challenges" assigned to the contenders, two of the women actually managed to show personality and the votes were rigged accordingly. Not that I would ever accuse such a fine organization with strict moral standards such as the WWE of rigging anything, because that would totally be out of character for them, but that's my speculation. Anyway, overly enthusiastic redhead Christy Hemme, who actually looked like she cared about being there, was matched up against Carmella DeCesare in the finals. This was interesting because Carmella was not only a bigger media darling than many of the wrestlers on the roster due to a tawdry relationship with quarterback Jeff Garcia and a resulting bar fight with another woman, but because she actually went out of her way to bury her opponents and even wrestling in general in all her interviews. She was the perfect heel for the women's division, in short. Sadly, Hemme won the vote, and Carmella was left to fade away into Hollywood. As an added sick joke on top of the whole thing, they hired essentially every loser and gave them fairly substantial roles on television. Hey, you might not *think* that Maria and Joy standing around talking about how HHH is hot is a major role, but it's more than someone like Val Venis tends to get on the average RAW. To date, the only one of the Diva Search rejects to survive cost-cutting bloodlettings and emerge with an actual character is Maria, who has a gimmick of being a backstage interviewer so stupid that she borders on being mentally challenged.

Which brings me back to Eugene. Hey, you think these segues write themselves? Anyway, with Eugene's character suddenly established as a capable wrestler despite his childlike antics outside the ring, he suddenly started to get popular. In fact, after weeks of abuse from Coach had deflated his self-esteem, they suddenly exploded the character into the stratosphere by having the Rock reappear for one of his semiannual visits and make the verbal save. It was actually a wonderful segment, as Rock played the cool guy standing up for the bullied slow kid to counteract the arrogant jock who was making fun of him to hide his own deficiencies. You can trace a lot of relationships in the WWE back to the schoolyard, which I think has to do with Vince getting beat up and shoved in a garbage can somewhere back in his nebulous past. Anyway, Rock's endorsement of Eugene was exactly what the character needed to move him from midcard novelty act into a truly hot babyface. Fans actually cared about him now and invested some emotions into his character. So of course, in their desperation to find a new babyface act to push to the top, they made the two classic errors that kill every babyface:

1. **They immediately overexposed him to the point where people shifted from liking him to being sick of seeing him. Case in point: One week after his massive move up the card, he was programmed into a main event match on RAW against Kane, another poster boy for overexposure, and the match bombed in the ratings.**

2. **They programmed him in a feud with HHH.**

Now, #1 can be survived. The Rock did it, Randy Orton did it twice, it's very much possible. With time and patience and a well-timed heel turn, you can shift the heat from "we're sick of you" boos to "we don't like you" boos, and then the character is a success again. Had they stopped at #1, Eugene could well be a star attraction today.

But that HHH program . . . well, just ask Booker T, Rob Van Dam, Scott Steiner, Kane, and a few others about where you're left. HHH is a heat vampire—he latches onto hot babyface acts, puts himself over them until fans boo him for beating their new favorites, and then when he's sucked all the fanbase's attention away from his opponents, he buries them with one final interview, declaring them to be not in his league, and leaves them for dead in the midcard. That's what he does. That's the Game. HHH in real life actually objected strenuously to being part of the feud, because he thought it was beneath him working so far down the card, but Vince was convinced otherwise and it went through. So to compensate, he just went out and buried Eugene extra hard, running an angle where Eugene was mesmerized by "favorite wrestler" HHH into being a whipping boy for Evolution, to the point where Eugene was even coming across as so naive and stupid that he was making real mentally challenged people look bad. Fans immediately picked up on this and started booing Eugene, instead of getting behind him to stand up to insincere jerk HHH. Why? Because no one wants to back a loser, and not only was Eugene acting like one by blindly hero-worshipping HHH and turning on his friends but also there was no chance of him actually emerging from the feud with anything resembling a win. Eugene's push was destroyed in one fell swoop, and after a brutally one-sided loss to HHH at Summerslam and a resulting injury angle to get him TV for a while, he reemerged later back where he was originally slotted to go: a fun novelty act for the midcard that could open house shows and work tag matches.

Keep in mind the lessons learned about shooting babyface acts up the card too fast and then programming them with HHH in mind, because we'll get back to that a bit later when we get to Randy Orton again.

## THE GREAT AMERICAN BASH (SMACKDOWN)

FROM: Norfolk, VA
DATE: June 27, 2004
ATTENDANCE: 6,500
BUYRATE: 250,000 buys
ADVERTISED MAIN EVENT: Eddie Guerrero v. JBL

### RESULTS:

U.S. champion John Cena d.
Rob Van Dam, Booker T, & Rene Dupree (15:52, ★★¼)

Luther Reigns d. Charlie Haas (7:11, ½★)

WWE Cruiserweight champion Rey Mysterio
d. Chavo Guerrero (19:39, ★★★¼)

Kenzo Suzuki d. Billy Gunn (8:06, -☆☆)

Sable d. Torrie Wilson (5:42, -☆☆)

Mordecai d. Bob Holly (6:31, ½★)

JBL d. Smackdown World champion Eddie Guerrero (21:06, ★★★¾)

Undertaker d. The Dudley Boyz (14:42, ¾★)

**IN JUNE, SOMEONE DECIDED** that it would be a great idea to run two PPVs instead of one—one featuring Smackdown at the end of June, and another one featuring RAW just two weeks later. The theory behind it was kinda sorta sound: instead of one month's worth of PPV revenue (325,000 buys in July 2003 multiplied by $35 a pop), you'll get two months' worth in the same month. And even if the experiment flops and you only draw, say, 175,000 buys (which would be an absolutely dismal number for a WWE PPV), then you're still ahead of the game by about a million dollars, and that ain't not bad.

However, where the theory breaks down a little bit is when you start to look at it from the perspective of the Big Picture. In this case, by putting on shows that are obviously designed for fans to pick one or the other, you train fans to skip certain shows and wait for the ones they really want to see. And that is a very dangerous habit to get the fanbase into, because history (and specifically the history of the WCW) has shown that once fans are trained to start skipping shows, they don't start not skipping them again.

But hey, if the Smackdown show had an unskippable main event with a compelling heel challenging Eddie Guerrero for the Smackdown World title, that wouldn't be a problem anyway. Sadly, that challenger was JBL.

Now, we all know that wrestling is a sleazy business. I think I've hammered that nail into the ground as far as it will go. However, never let it be said that they don't know how to scrape another layer off the bottom of the barrel and go a little bit deeper than rock bottom. For instance, the newly pushed Bradshaw version 18.1 was capitalizing on his reputation as a financial wizard by repackaging himself as a Repub-

lican econo-terrorist, and in real life he was starting a cushy job as a financial analyst with CNBC. Sure, not exactly the zenith of extended cable fame, but it was a good gig for him and gave him some real-world street cred with the rough-and-tumble bankers of Wall Street. Now, for the previous main event match against Eddie, he had merely resorted to pushing the elder Mama Guerrero down at a house show and didn't really exploit the full tasteless potential of his character the way that we all knew he could. Of course, that all changed on a tour of Germany, as JBL was looking for some extra heat during the match and decided that a fun and interesting way to get fans to boo him would be goose stepping up and down the ring apron while giving the Nazi salute. Wolfgang Stach of the German wrestling magazine *Power-Wrestling* chimed in with the following statement, trying to explain his actions:

> **Bradshaw, as one of the major heels in WWE, was trying to produce still more heat from the fans. So he was showing the goose step and the Nazi salute. I don't think that this was the most intelligent thing he could do and he was also criticized by us, but it was just part of the show (also in small independent shows in Germany this happens sometimes from foreign wrestlers). Bradshaw wrestled many years for Germany's CWA and he lived here during this time. I know him in person and I know that he loves Germany. And I also know that Bradshaw never thought that his behavior would cause so much problems and so much negative response by just a minority of fans. Most of the German fans took it as what it was—just a part of the show. Also: Doing the Nazi salute is USUALLY illegal—but NOT in every case. As long as it is part of a show, a movie, a theatre act, a musical (please think about "Cabaret"), a soap opera and other performances it is NOT illegal, just if the movie etc. is glori-**

**RIGHT: JBL and Rikishi**

> **fying the Nazi regime or is an incitement of the people. But Bradshaw's behavior was part of the show, part of his role as a major heel and because of that it was NOT illegal.**

So it was obviously an innocent gesture on his part, but some *crazy* people got offended by it and had a video camera with them at the time. Because that's what crazy people do. In fact, they were so crazy that they decided to send a copy of the video to CNBC and inform them of the wacky antics of the guy they had just signed to a major TV deal. To top it off, CNBC was also hit with the dreaded Internet petition. Now, personally I hate the things, as going to a Web site and clicking on a link to electronically "sign" your name on the cause of the day is about as taxing a chore as, say, clicking on a porn link that looks particularly interesting. In fact, I'm thinking about starting up an Internet petition to have them banned for good. Regardless, the

petition in this case was effective, as apparently the technologically ignorant executives of CNBC didn't understand what a joke they are and took the thousands of "signatures" asking for JBL to be fired to actually mean something significant. The statement from on high was short and sweet: "CNBC has terminated its relationship with John 'Bradshaw' Layfield following his conduct this past weekend in a wrestling match. We find his behavior to be offensive, inappropriate, and not befitting anyone associated with our network."

Bradshaw immediately replied with an interview in the *Washington Post:*

**They hung me out to dry. I was playing a character. It's the same as Vin Diesel playing a Nazi. I'm a bad guy. I'm supposed to incite the crowd. I've done it for decades. I really didn't think anything of it—I know how bad it is, I've lived there. I've been to Dachau, seen those places where they exterminated millions of Jews. I draw the line between me and my character. That's like saying Anthony Hopkins really enjoys cannibalism. The only thing they asked me not to play was a stock market cheat or fraud. Other than that, they said they totally understood, that it was like Arnold Schwarzenegger playing a cyborg. I thought I had it covered. I thought they understood the character is a bad guy and is going to do bad things.**

Now, as much as I dislike JBL as a character because he does ignorant and offensive things to draw heat, and as much as I dislike John Leyfield as a person because he's a locker room bully who intimidated his way up the card because he couldn't get over on his own, he got shafted there. Overzealous fans overreacted, like they do every time the WWE crosses another line and does something stupider than the last time they did the stupidest thing ever, and this time one of their guys paid the price for it. Still, the lesson here is an important one, as Vince had been underestimating the power of the electronic media for years and was hoping to fly under the radar of the mainstream press like he did with the deplorable Gulf War exploitation in 1991, and someone finally called him on it.

This unfortunately caused an immediate, Vince-like reaction to the actions of the fans on the Internet, as he lashed out at them in the worst way possible by making John Bradshaw Leyfield the Smackdown World champion at the dismal Great American Bash PPV. Some punishments are just too harsh. Great match, though. The title change was actually quite explainable in hindsight, as Eddie had done a gory bladejob at the previous PPV and the blood loss left him so disoriented and shaken afterward that those backstage described him as being a totally different person afterward. He clarified things during an interview with the *Sun* newspaper in the United Kingdom a few months later:

**It's a great responsibility being champion, as you're the one carrying the ball, and I found**

it very difficult. It was the first time I'd held the title and I don't think I was ready. I was ready to win the belt, but not for what lay ahead of me. I wasn't prepared mentally for what happens outside the ring—because I think that's where the real challenges lie. I was taking things like attendances and ratings very personally. I'm an extremist and that's one thing I'd like to change in my life. It's good to be hard on myself but not to the point where I beat myself up about things. And if I'm honest and look back at my mistakes then I was too hard on myself when I was carrying the title. I let things eat me up inside and I questioned myself when I shouldn't have. But it's a lesson learned and I won't make that mistake again.

At the time, however, this was a huge blow for his fanbase, as career midcarder JBL was clearly not the guy to be carrying the title either, and most expected his reign to be short lived. Boy, that one didn't work out the way we wanted, either.

Speaking of not working out the way anyone wanted, Undertaker was still hanging around at the top of the card, and it was

**RIGHT: Bubba Dudley and Jamal**

getting harder to watch the stuff he was involved in without feeling your IQ dropping a few points. For instance, Paul Heyman (back on the good side of Vince and thus on TV again after getting booted from the general manager position for pissing people off backstage) had a new role managing the Dudley Boyz in a last-ditch attempt to freshen them up, and boy did they hate Undertaker. So much so in fact that Heyman had Undertaker's formerly estranged manager Paul Bearer held in a vat of concrete while Undertaker wrestled the Dudley Boyz in the main event. If Undertaker didn't throw the match and let them win, Paul Bearer would "die." I'd like to remind any Smackdown writers who are reading this that *is* the twenty-first century and we're all aware that matches are fixed and people don't actually die in giant vats of concrete without the police investigating and making arrests. Ah, but see Undertaker won the match anyway, even though he was wrestling two-on-one against the tag team cham-

pions at the time, because that's what he does. And then just to show how badass he was, he buried Paul in concrete himself and finished him off.

I'd once again like to remind you that the WWE does not do murder angles. In this case, the WWE Web site clarified that Paul was rescued from the concrete mixture before dying and was only seriously injured and would live. So you see, they only do *attempted* murder, which is perfectly fine for the kids to watch. But then as Sideshow Bob once said, they don't give Nobel Prizes for attempted chemistry. This idiocy was supposed to lead to a summer program with the newly heel Undertaker challenging Eddie Guerrero for the title and putting him over, but Eddie's breakdown and subsequent title loss left that idea up in the air, and the next week they simply ignored the whole (attempted!) murder thing and just had him carry on like nothing happened. Not coincidentally, at that point I stopped watching Smackdown altogether and just did the PPVs.

But over on RAW, things were looking up for the summer and the big push was on to make stars out of those considered to be the future, and do it fast. Sadly, one of those attempts was just faking us out.

That attempt was that of Matt Hardy, who you will recall was stuck in a god-awful feud with Kane, as poor Matt was booked to look like a cuckolded husband, watching his woman, Lita, whore herself out to Kane in exchange for his continued well-being. Truly a story line for the whole family to enjoy together. Then, the next logical step in this chain of stupidity is that

Lita is pregnant, and we don't know whose baby it is. But really it could only be one person, because that's the option that makes the least sense and annoys the most people. Yes, the baby belonged to Kane, and of course they had to have a match to settle things. Everyone expected Matt to get squashed, but he only got squashed for a while before getting the fluke win. If that was the end of it, fine, but it wasn't, and that's where it really fell apart for poor Matt.

Everyone also expected Chris Benoit to finally drop his hard-earned title back to HHH in the main event of Vengeance, but surprisingly HHH put Benoit over for a third time to further his own feud with Eugene instead. And then in an Iron Man match on RAW, a fourth win for Benoit. In fact, outside of a couple of meaningless jobs to HHH once he lost the title, Chris Benoit remains one of the few people to decisively win a feud with HHH. Of course, we all know who ended up with the title in the end, but it was nice to have them take *some* steps, however small, toward letting someone else run with the ball on Monday nights.

But the guy who was really starting to run with the ball (in between harassing divas backstage) was Randy Orton, as his showdown with Edge, for the Intercontinental title that he had held since December, was clearly positioned as the featured match for the PPV. The match garnered instant and overwhelming praise from most reviewers, as it saw them exchange an exciting series of near falls to end the match after a slow start, and Edge finally seemed to get over the hump as a top guy by winning the belt from the super-hot Legend Killer. Of course, the teased heel turns for Edge were still lurking in the background, seemingly forgotten about, but at least he had a direction now. The wisdom of taking the #2 belt in the promotion off the guy they wanted as the top heel was questioned somewhat, but when he won (you guessed it) a #1 contender battle royale the next week to set himself as the challenger for Benoit at Summerslam, the second-biggest PPV of the year, the questions seemed to be answered.

They were, however, only beginning.

# 17 AUGUST 2004

## SUMMERSLAM 2004 (BOTH BRANDS)

FROM: Toronto, ON
DATE: August 15, 2004
ATTENDANCE: 17,460
BUYRATE: 400,000 buys
ADVERTISED MAIN EVENT: Chris Benoit v. Randy Orton

### RESULTS:

The Dudley Boyz d. Paul London, Rey Mysterio, & Billy Kidman (8:07, ★★)

Kane d. Matt Hardy (6:09, ★)

John Cena d. Booker T (6:25, ½★)

Intercontinental champion Edge d. Chris Jericho & Batista (8:25, ★¼)

Kurt Angle d. Eddie Guerrero (13:37, ★★★)

HHH d. Eugene (14:06, ★★½)

Smackdown World champion JBL d. Undertaker (DQ, 17:39, ★½)

Randy Orton d. RAW World champion Chris Benoit (20:09, ★★★½)

**BY AUGUST, THE GOAL** was clearly to make bigger steps with some of the guys who they had earmarked for the top of the card in the months following. Chiefly among these were Randy Orton and John Cena, although there was soon to be a surprise addition to those ranks.

John Cena, since turning babyface in the winter of 2004, had gone from an edgy and bile-spewing white rapper into a crowd-pandering clown who depended increasingly on gay jokes and making fun of Michael Cole to support his act. That's not to say the act wasn't working, because the crowds were definitely still reacting to him strongly, but to my way of thinking he was no longer the kind of underground cool that transcends the business and makes a bigger star out of them. He was now part of the WWE system instead of getting over by working outside it, which was doubly ironic because the main issue being built up for him was against Kurt Angle, in yet another dopey "authority figure against loose cannon rebel without a cause who plays by his own rules" story line.

Kurt Angle had been out, yet again with serious neck problems, for much of 2004, and to find a way to keep him on TV without aggravating things further he was made into the figurehead of Smackdown, replacing Paul Heyman as general manager. However, the role was an immediate problem for him, as it required a certain personality type, which Angle didn't have. First, he wasn't particularly authoritative after years of playing a happy-go-lucky dork on WWE TV, and it just didn't come across believably for someone portrayed as a clown for so long to be suddenly acting all stuffy and conservative. Second, the role of overcompensating egomaniac requires someone who can talk like a big man and yet someone that the fans know deep down can't back up his words with action. Kurt

**BELOW: John Cena**

Angle is not only a gold medal–winning Olympian, but a multitime World champion and one of the most dangerous submission wrestlers in the history of the sport, within the context of the story line. Generally speaking, if a guy like Kurt Angle makes a threat, he backs it up, and that's the kiss of death with this kind of character. Third, they recruited some developmental guys for him as backup, bringing in recent Smackdown draftee Mark Jindrak (who was coming off a failed gimmick as the 2004 version of "The Narcissist" Lex Luger) and Luther Reigns (who was best known as being a WCW jobber named Horschu), which again doomed him for using guys who were obviously huge jobbers and would never amount to anything. I mean, if Mark Jindrak makes threats toward me, it's not exactly going to make me quake in my boots. Ditto Luther Reigns, no matter how tough Michael Cole tries to make him sound (and you know if Michael Cole endorses someone as a badass, he must be). Fourth, people like to watch Angle in the ring and don't generally like to boo him. Well, let me rephrase that. They enjoy booing him because it's an effective and fun heel character to boo, but they do it out of respect for him, rather than because they think he's a sleazeball like Eric Bischoff on RAW or Paul Heyman before him.

The silliness of Angle's run as GM of Smackdown was summed up nicely by one of the first angles he was involved with, in April, as he tried to channel the inner monster of Big Show and the result was getting thrown off of a twenty-foot balcony by the enraged

Show. Amazingly, despite landing on his head and apparently shattering his spine, he returned to the show a couple of weeks later, with a cast on his leg. Now *that*'s a real man! To be fair, HHH set the standard for surviving life-threatening injuries in 2000 when he was dropped from 100 feet in the air in a car and showed up the next night with a Band-Aid on his cheek, but then HHH does book himself to be exceptionally tough.

**ABOVE: Kurt Angle and Big Show**

Besides, I can't in good conscience call myself a fan of the show *24* and still seriously complain about any character on TV returning too soon from death, so I can easily cut the writers a break on the whole balcony-diving thing and move on with my life. Anyway, back to my original point with the Cena-Angle "feud," as Cena was not only embroiled in rehashed ideas from the '90s to get him over, but was actually degenerating in the ring. Whereas early matches with him during his debut period in 2002, with guys like Kurt Angle oddly enough, had shown some flashes of in-ring brilliance akin to a young Sting, later matches with Big Show and Rene Dupree showed flashes of in-ring mediocrity akin to the later Sting. It was clear that Cena was a guy who could keep up with a better wrestler if he needed to, but was unable to carry someone worse than him to anything watchable. Part of the fault was, in my opin-

ion, simple laziness on his part, as he essentially did the bare minimum to pop the crowd. He would work matches as a babyface where he'd take punishment for a few minutes, then come back with his standard offensive flurry (flying shoulder tackles, Five-Knuckle Shuffle fistdrop, and F-U) to finish the match. The formula varied very little from match to match and the matches got progressively worse through the year. This was in stark contrast to people like Rock and Steve Austin, both of whom Cena was aping for his act, who reinvented the art of the sport on their way up to the top and still had ★★★★½ matches with each other on their way down again. Really, the last thing that Cena needed to further his development was a feud with someone more unmotivated in the ring than him, which is why it was such a problem when Booker T was made into his next program, leading into Summerslam.

Booker was a really sad case, actually, because this was obviously a guy who had seen the cracks in the glass ceiling in 2003 during his feud with HHH, and then had them sealed shut again just when he thought he was through to the other side. The loss to HHH in the RAW World title match at Wrestlemania XIX was a crippling blow to his career, and he never recovered from it, moving from face to heel in aimless fashion and never seeming to give a crap in the ring any longer following that period. By the time his feud with Cena rolled around, he was a heel again, coming off a really bad idea. That idea was the brainchild of the Smackdown writer Dan Madigan, who was coming to the show with aspirations of being a TV and movie screen writer. Sadly, the only one of his ideas to make it to the screen was one for Booker T, who was searching for help in his feud with Undertaker after Wrestlemania XX. Booker met with a voodoo priestess and searched for a bag of dirt to give him mystical powers to fight the undead powers of Undertaker, but then someone thankfully came to their senses and dropped the whole thing. On the bright side, it's still better than feuding with Edge over shampoo commercials in 2002. Madigan, for his part, moved onto writing movies for the WWE instead, although the only one in production as of 2006 stars Kane as a serial killer and has to date gone through three name changes, from *Eye Scream Man* to *Goodnight* to *See No Evil*. Most people doubt it will ever see the light of day.

The idea with the Booker-Cena feud was to hold a best-of-five series of matches that would take place over the course of two PPV shows and several episodes of Smackdown and thus do for Cena's career in 2004 what the same concept did for Booker T's career in 1998 when he wrestled a best-of-seven series against Chris Benoit. However, while that series was amazing in execution and catapulted Booker T into the ranks of serious uppercard wrestlers, John Cena is not Chris Benoit and he was already above Booker on the pecking order by that point anyway. The match at Summerslam, first in the series, was a huge disappointment for those expecting a repeat of the epic feel of the original series, but that's often the case with sequels anyway.

One case where the sequel exceeded the original, however, was Randy Orton. Although he was a third-generation wrestler, both his father and grandfather were midcarders at best and had only tasted the occasional run at the top. That was definitely not the case with Randy, who was riding high and booked in the main event of Summerslam against Chris Benoit on the strength of his Legend Killer persona. Orton had spent months building up a cocky heel character, although one that was definitely second-banana to HHH in Evolution. However, because he was constantly booked to win matches and emerge victorious from situations where it appeared that he was beaten, fans started cheering him. This was not because they liked the person or felt the character was a good guy to represent their interests. It was a much more basic reaction by the fanbase: people cheer for winners and won't get behind losers. Since all the babyfaces on the

RAW side had been emasculated by HHH, the crowds were left to be entertained by Orton, who wouldn't let them down in the ring because he rarely ever lost matches. Thus, it became the cool thing to cheer for Orton, and that's what undid his success in the summer of 2004.

Vince McMahon is a very "what have you done for me in the last five minutes" kind of guy, as noted previously here, and he comes up with stuff based on what's hot *now*, very rarely going for the slow build these days. So when Orton started getting cheered by a fanbase that wanted desperately to get behind anyone, that was the sign to Vince that they had a new top babyface. This was completely opposite to the prevailing viewpoint of everyone else watching and looking ahead to Wrestlemania, who had Orton pegged as the heel who would add HHH to his "Legend Killer" list and thus turn him babyface for their big showdown. Orton in fact won the RAW World title from Chris Benoit in the main event of Summerslam to start down that road, wrestling probably the best technical match of his career to do so and winning with the RKO clean as a sheet, and the road to Wrestlemania seemed to be pretty clear from there. Orton wins the title, thus making HHH jealous, and starts rubbing the win in his face like a jerk until fans actually feel sympathy for HHH, at which point Orton kicks him out of Evolution and takes the group in his own direction. HHH vows revenge—instant main event feud. However, Vince now had it in his head that Orton was to be the big babyface for the winter months, so in-

stead of anything resembling that kind of buildup, Orton defeated Benoit again in a rematch the next night on RAW, needing Evolution's help to do so this time, and HHH turned on him afterward and kicked him out of the group, thus turning him face.

Problems with that were immediately apparent, however. First, Randy Orton didn't actually turn face, he was turned on by the heels, and that's far from the same thing. There was no organic reason for fans to cheer Orton, because the turn was dictated to them instead of them dictating who they wanted as the top babyface. Second, Orton's personality as a heel was that of a cocky dickhead who did things to further his own selfish agenda, not someone who the fans could respect as an athlete because he was better than everyone. Although they cheered his constant wins, he won by cheating and was generally outclassed leading to the big RKO finish. Third, his methods of revenge on HHH were the same clichéd stuff that every failed babyface has been doing for thirty years, from hitting him with the belt, to using his own weapons against him, to actually jumping out of a giant birthday cake one week and sneak-attacking him. That they would book the guy they wanted to main event Wrestlemania this way was amazing to me, but even more amazingly they actually paid attention to these lessons when they failed and did exactly the opposite in each case with Dave Batista. This marked one of the few instances where they did see what was wrong with a previous attempt and made an effort to correct it. However, it wasn't enough to save Orton's push, which was floundering out of the gate and looked doomed when they announced that he would defend the title against HHH the next month at Unforgiven.

Speaking of doomed people, with Lita "pregnant" and carrying Kane's baby, they made poor Matt Hardy look like even more of a wuss by having him still be supportive and wanting to marry his slutty girlfriend. So in the most unique match stipulation I had seen in a while, we got Kane v. Matt Hardy at Summerslam, with the winner getting to marry Lita. Now, if you stop to think about the mind-boggling legal ramifications of something like that, you'll go nuts, so I'd advise not doing so. To no one's shock, Kane won, thus allowing him to live out his dream of domestic bliss and marry the sweetheart that he had so brutally raped just a few weeks previous. Now, I personally got married in February 2005, and I had never actually been to a real wedding before that, so all my knowledge of the subject came from watching wrestling through the years and seeing a succession of wrestling weddings.

Generally speaking, wrestling weddings are the sign of true desperation among the writers of a show, much like a baby on a sitcom. And hey, Lita was pregnant, too, so we hit on all the bases with this one! At any rate, there has been a long tradition of crazy matrimony in wrestling, and with that in mind, you can imagine how strange my own ceremony was for me. First, it wasn't held in a converted wrestling ring, which threw me off right away. The official who mar-

ried us didn't turn out to be someone else under a mask. And in fact, he actually had the power to marry people and wasn't just an actor playing one. There were neither midgets nor hillbillies in either of the wedding parties. When the time came for someone to object, the bride's former boyfriend did not run out and try to hit me with a steel chair, nor did my archenemy appear on a giant video screen and reveal that he had already married the bride in Las Vegas while she was drugged. In fact, no one in the crowd even turned around and looked to the entranceway for a run-in when asked about objections. No one directly involved with the wedding was gay (that I'm aware of ). At no point did myself or anyone on my side of the wedding party throw up a giant wall of fire by the entranceway to prevent someone from escaping. And finally, the wedding was actually allowed to finish without anyone beating up the official. All in all, it was much different than I was expecting.

The wedding of Kane and Lita, however, adhered a little more closely to the rules of weddings that I'm familiar with, as the bride was knocked up with the seed of evil in her belly, and when the fake priest asked if anyone objected, Matt Hardy ran down and tried to beat up Kane, getting chokeslammed through a table for his troubles and thus getting written out of the WWE universe, seemingly for good. However, where the story line went next, even I didn't believe at first.

★ ★ ★ **UNFORGIVEN (RAW)** ★ ★ ★ ★

FROM: Portland, OR
DATE: September 12, 2004
ATTENDANCE: 8,313
BUYRATE: 250,000 buys
ADVERTISED MAIN EVENT: Randy Orton v. HHH

**RESULTS:**

Chris Benoit & William Regal d. Ric Flair & Batista (15:06, ★★)

WWE Women's champion Trish Stratus d. Victoria (8:20, ★¼)

Tyson Tomko d. Steven Richards (6:24, -☆☆)

Chris Jericho d. Christian to win the vacant
Intercontinental title (22:28, ★★¾)

Shawn Michaels d. Kane (18:09, ★★★)

RAW World tag team champions La Resistance
d. Tajiri & Rhyno (9:40, ¾★)

HHH d. RAW World champion Randy Orton (24:35, ★★★¼)

**SOMETIMES A NEW CHARACTER** is introduced and gets over in such a weird, ass-backward way that you don't even know where to begin to explain it, and that's the case with Gene Snitsky.

Snitsky was supposed to be the means to an end for the writing team of RAW, and it was quite an ingenious end-run around any kind of responsibility at that. The idea is that Lita is "pregnant," but the real person is of course not with child, so you have to get rid of the story line baby somehow. So in the fine tradition of tasteful wrestling angles that preceded it, they decided to go with the old miscarriage option, which worked fine for Terri Runnels years before. However, sensitive to the needs of sure-to-be-outraged parents groups as they were, they had to make sure that it was as a result of someone not on the roster. So this led to happy new hubby Kane squashing a guy on RAW who I just referred to as "some jobber" because I never thought we'd see him again. During the course of the match, Lita got involved, trying to screw over her husband, and the jobber fell on top of Kane, who fell on top of her, causing her to miscarry and thus lose the baby. Ah, irony. Like rain on a summer day or the free ride when you've already paid. That jobber was OVW developmental wrestler "Mean" Gene Mondo, who wrestled under his less imposing real name of Gene Snitsky for that match. Things got much sillier the next week, however, as a tearful Kane saw his progeny lost to the machinations of the story line and Lita suddenly loved the man who raped and tormented her for months, which led to a wedding against her will. It only got better from there, as they actually gave raw rookie Gene Snitsky promo time for doing such a good job killing off the baby, and he declared to the world: "It's not my fault!"

This scared the hell out of me. Not because of the delivery or the inherent imposing nature of someone like Snitsky who is over six feet tall and has skin covered with acne from steroids. No, because of something much more hideous: He was now a really big wrestler with a *catchphrase*. And a character—he's Gene Snitsky, the baby-killer! I dubbed his pump-handle slam finisher the "Coat Hanger" immediately after his debut, but sadly it never caught on with the announce team. Regardless, a big wrestler with a character and a catchphrase is the holy trinity that guarantees someone a push, and that's exactly what happened, as suddenly Gene Snitsky was all over the program, leading up to a feud with newly turned baby-face Kane over the dead baby from a wife he forced in marriage. Even scarier, Snitsky was an attentive student backstage who listened to everything told to him, so he was not only getting pushed but he was also a favorite of the agents and probably wouldn't do anything

stupid and get himself fired. The world didn't need another version of Sid Vicious, but we were sure gonna get one whether we liked it or not, because the WWE had just backed ass-backward into the biggest monster heel they had created in years.

For his part, Kane was involved in one of the bigger missteps of the year from the people who are supposed to be in charge of continuity. While feuding with Matt Hardy earlier in the year, Kane had gotten temporarily side-drained with Shawn Michaels (or maybe it was the other way around, depending on who you like better), putting him out of action with a "crushed larynx" in a TV angle designed to get Shawn off TV for a few months so he could heal injuries and help his wife with having a baby. This stuff was right out of the '80s, which is fine, but in cases like that buildup and payoff are everything. An injury to Shawn that prevents him from alternately talking about himself and how great he is, or how much he loves Jesus, should have been a crippling blow to his character. Instead, after a week of followup for the fake injury, it was forgotten about entirely until it was time for him to return for revenge against Kane at the Unforgiven PPV. However, this proved to be a problem, hype-wise, because no one remembered that he was injured by Kane in the first place! The killing blow for the whole stupid angle came the week before the show, as Shawn had yet to make his dramatic return to the world of the speaking, but was shown at the Republican National Convention doing coverage for the WWE as though nothing was wrong.

(Sidenote: The fact that the WWE was covering the convention as though they were journalists or their fanbase gave two drizzling shits about politics, speaks volumes about the screwed up state of their priorities at that point. In fact, I think if Vince McMahon could have gotten away with coming on TV and endorsing George W. Bush on his shows each week, he would have taken a run at it.)

Anyway, Kane, the rehabilitated monster who needed new victims to wipe out every year so he could rise to the top of the card again, lost cleanly to Shawn and didn't look like much of an unstoppable demon spawn that night. Maybe having his fake offspring killed by Gene Snitsky had him down, I dunno.

The other monster heel on RAW, albeit one who has never killed any babies that I'm aware of, was HHH, and we all succumbed to the inevitable at the Unforgiven PPV in September, as he regained the RAW World title from Randy Orton. The match foreshadowed bad things for the upcoming Wrestlemania rematch that we were all supposed to be chomping at the bit to see, because as main events go it was pretty disappointing and featured the same predictable run-in finish from the same people and HHH winning with the pedigree again. In fact, the HHH show was getting so out of control

at that point that it actually drove Pat Patterson, longtime Vince crony and match finish–planning god, out of the WWE due to conflict with HHH and feeling like his position was being usurped. Of course, this was completely true and seemed like the first in a long series of bad signs for the promotion at that point.

The loss to HHH was pretty much the kiss of death to Orton's big babyface push only a month after his initial turn, because he was not only a babyface who fans didn't like but also one who could no longer back up his big talk now. He was, in other words, a hastily updated version of Ronnie Garvin, the biggest lame duck champion in history. That's a bad position to be in, because once the fans stop believing in you, you're done. However, in quite the opposite manner, people were starting to believe in Dave Batista.

Batista had been initially called up from the

**RIGHT: D-Von Dudley**

OVW in 2002 in a loser gimmick on Smackdown, playing "Deacon Batista," the evil priest who assisted evil Reverend D-Von Dudley in his quest to take over the WWE through evangelical means. After ditching that act when D-Von's singles push went down the toilet, Batista was moved to RAW and pushed as a more traditional muscleheaded power wrestler. Feuds with Kane and other midcard wrestlers failed because he wasn't ready in the ring for anything bigger than opening shows at that point, but because of his size and scary tattoos, as well as a friendship with HHH, he was consistently booked on TV and used. He was thus a natural choice to join HHH's Evolution group when it became a permanent foursome in 2003, and the result was a role as the power guy, who was sent against HHH's enemies (like Shawn Michaels) to soften them up for later matches with HHH. Essentially, his "thing" was standing in the background during HHH interviews and looking imposing while wearing stylish suits. By mid-2004, his "thing" was becoming one-half of the tag team champions with Ric Flair and doing quick bursts of power wrestling while mainly standing on the apron. After filling that role at Wrestlemania XX in the super-entertaining Rock and Foley v. Evolution tag match, his list of opponents was mixed up a bit more, generally resulting in combinations of himself, Flair, Orton, and HHH against combinations of Chris Benoit, Edge, Chris Jericho, and Shelton Benjamin night after night. And then something interesting started to happen, as night after night of wrestling with high-quality oppo-

nents started to rub off on him and suddenly he was no longer the weak link in the matches, he had a well-defined role to play in them and filled it well. He started picking up timing mannerisms that lent his moves a better snap, like the way he would execute the spinebuster and then pop right up to his feet again. Essentially, he would do every move as if he really believed he was doing that move to his opponent, and would sell it himself with facial expressions and a real air of intensity about him. This was a radical change from his demeanor in 2003, when he was seemingly nervous about wrestling on the big stage and would botch simple moves in important situations.

By August 2004, he was getting moved into a peripheral role in a feud between Edge and Chris Jericho over the Intercontinental title that was going nowhere, and it proved to add another dimension to his cool factor. Although he didn't win the title at Summerslam in a three-way match with Edge and Jericho, he had a singles match with Jericho on an episode of RAW leading up to it and got a better boost from it. While coming out of the corner, he hit Jericho with a hard clothesline that looked visually impressive and more importantly was sold by Jericho as though he was touched by the cold clammy hand of death itself. That's an important thing, because it really established Batista as the kind of dangerous badass that he needed to be to take another step up the ladder. From then on, the clothesline, simple a move as it is, was considered a potential finish to his matches, especially where Jericho was involved. Any time you can take a simple transition move and turn it into a potential end to the match, you've accomplished something. With the dangerous cool factor added to his in-ring persona, Batista found himself the #2 man in Evolution behind HHH, what with Orton being bounced from the group and all. In stark contrast to Orton's brash and mouthy promos, Batista's approach was to stand behind HHH with women on his arm and look cool. Since talking wasn't his strong point anyway, having HHH do all the talking (which was certainly not something you had to ask him twice to do) allowed fans to see the "strong silent type" in him. And when HHH continued beating his own drum in promo after promo, Batista started giving sly looks to the audience to indicate that maybe he wasn't quite the toady that Ric Flair was. This was a subtle but interesting twist in the character, one that wouldn't even get paid off until much further down the road but showed the kind of foresight that was missing in the Randy Orton face turn just a month earlier.

However, foresight works both ways, sometimes not for the best. Take for example what happens when you truly have nothing interesting to do with someone. The result was poor Stevie Richards running around in drag for most of the summer, trying to win back estranged life partner Victoria with some sort of bizarre plan apparently involving becoming a transvestite. The angle was alternatively dropped and picked up again depending on how much attention

**ABOVE: Stevie Richards and Spike Dudley**

the announcers were paying on any given week, and really I only give mention to it because it led to what was far and away the worst match of the year. After weeks of Richards running out with a bad wig and the fans literally screaming "Stevie!" while Jim Ross was forced to play dumb to sell the ridiculous angle, they finally decided to go somewhere with it. Victoria lost to Trish Stratus at the Unforgiven PPV in a forgettable match, and Stevie tried to save her from Trish's monkey boy Tyson Tomko. Now, considering that Tomko is gigantic and covered in imposing tattoos, you wouldn't think that a skinny guy in a dress would be a suitable challenge for him, but apparently they thought he was and made us sit through the match. And after three months of buildup, Tomko and Richards went out and absolutely redefined "stinking the joint up" in a hellishly bad six-minute match that featured essentially nothing but choking from Tomko and Richards trying to navigate around the ring in a bra and panties. And the result of all the build was Richards losing like a jobber and thankfully disappearing back to Sunday Night Heat again with no point ever demonstrated. I mean, I can live with bad wrestling, as long as it *goes* somewhere.

And as if that wasn't bad enough, their worst idea was yet to come in October . . .

# 19 OCTOBER 2004

**OCTOBER WAS YET ANOTHER MONTH** of two PPVs in the same month, hooray. And not just any two PPVs, two unrelentingly awful and depressing PPVs. On the bright side, both of them managed to top each other by scoring consecutively the two worst buyrates in the history of the promotion, so at least there was the historical aspect to them.

No Mercy at the beginning of the month (unofficial subtitle: "Oh My God, JBL Is Still Champion?") was indeed mercilessly crappy, thus living up to the name bestowed on it. However, there were attempts, misguided as they were, to at least try out new acts in the midcard, which was kind of a step forward for the promotion compared to the backward-thinking philosophy that normally defined them. Probably the biggest potential star out of the bunch of experiments was Paul London, although I'm sure that he's not viewed that way by those who attempted to push him, oddly enough.

Growing up with Latino roots while living in Austin, Texas, London was a product of the failed but shockingly influential wrestling school founded by Shawn Michaels, which produced such talent as London, Brian "Spanky" Kendrick, and Brian "American Dragon" Danielson. Building up a buzz on the indy circuit with a notable run in Ring of Honor and then a short stint in TNA, London was big enough to be a natural for the WWE developmental system, but not big enough that anyone thought he'd amount to anything once he got there. That description unfortunately applies to a lot of guys stuck in the system these days, but London's matinée idol good looks at least got

him some shots on the weekend shows as enhancement talent thanks to his flashy style and charismatic presence. From there he was put on Smackdown and given a surprising amount of protection for someone not born and bred in the WWE system, as his first big shot on TV came as the mysterious "El Gran Luchador," champion of Mexico and victim of JBL's early run as a main eventer in April. Well, everyone's gotta start somewhere. Luckily for him, his performance in that limited role earned him a step up the ladder, and he formed a tag team with fellow cruiserweight Billy Kidman, doing the standard pretty boy tag team deal for the screaming girls. Apparently, that

worked out well enough for another shot, so they were booked to upset the Dudley Boyz and win the Smackdown tag team titles in July 2004. Sadly, they never really got a chance to go anywhere as a team, as the writers stumbled across a more interesting direction for them as singles, entirely by accident. That seems to happen a lot.

The deal was that during a match in August on TV against Chavo Guerrero and Jamie Noble, Billy Kidman went for his trademark Shooting Star Press finisher (an inverted backflip off the top rope) and accidentally knocked Chavo into the middle of next week with his knees. It was entirely an accident (although one that has happened more than once with Kidman's notably sloppy version of the move), but with Chavo out of action as a result, they decided to turn it into an angle, and an interesting one at that. From that point on, Kidman was scared to do the move and chickened out whenever he was in position to do it. Eventually, he took out his frustrations on London, costing them the tag titles to the unlikely pairing of Kenzo Suzuki and Rene Dupree, and a feud

was born. I would have preferred for them to stretch out the team a bit further, but at least they were handed a real-life story line that could be used to get both guys over, so great. They ended up having a show-stealing match at No Mercy to blow off the feud, with Kidman going decisively heel by not only getting over his fear of the Shooting Star Press, but using it to beat London and then further injure him. This was an interesting dynamic for a wrestling character, as they had not only established the move as a finisher, but a finisher that was legitimately injuring people "in real life," so that the fans *knew* that when he went for it, he meant business. In fact, Kidman started drawing extraordinary heat with this new act, especially in proportion to his relatively lowly position on the card, since the creative team ignored the match in the fallout of the PPV and the whole thing was dropped soon after anyway. London, however, looked like enough of a star coming out of the feud that after taking an insane bump in the Royal Rumble match in early 2005, he was rewarded with the Cruiserweight title later in

the year. Sadly, Kidman's vicious streak didn't pay off with any increased exposure or push and he was fired midway through 2005.

Um, maybe that one was a bad example.

On a more positive note, after five crappy matches in the best-of-five series against Booker T, John Cena emerged with the U.S. title for the second time at No Mercy and immediately dropped it to newcomer Carlito Caribbean Cool at the next Smackdown taping. Carlito is the son of semilegendary Carlos Colon, the kind of guy who owned the WWC promotion in Puerto Rico and booked himself to win the "Universal title" (yes, that was really the name of the belt) an astounding twenty-five times before retiring in 2000 and then passing on the legacy to his son, who was booked to win it ten times himself. Gosh, I bet the fans were really scratching their heads as to who the real power behind *that* promotion was. Carlito was introduced over the course of the summer with a series of vignettes "paying homage to" (as Jim Cornette would call it) the character vignettes originally done for Scott Hall in 1992 when he debuted as Razor Ramon.

Sidenote: Plagiarism in wrestling, as with any entertainment media, is easily dismissed by remembering the two basic rules covering the subject:

1. **The statute of limitations for stealing any good idea is seven years.**
2. **As long as everyone knows you're stealing the idea, you're not actually stealing it, you're paying homage to it. When an idea is obscure enough that no one else got a crack at it first (i.e., Eric Bischoff converting the Ishigun story line from Japan into the New World Order),** *then* **people get pissy about it.**

Anyway, Carlito "borrowed" a cheesy accent from Scarface and grew out his afro, and actually had a very neat character building, as a jerk who spits in the face of people who aren't cool. Literally. And the WWE creative team liked it so much that when Cena was scheduled to go shoot a movie in the fall of 2004, Carlito got to beat him for the U.S. title and then "put him out of action" by allegedly stabbing him in a bar.

Now, I don't mean to get off on a rant here, but is this what we've been reduced to for writing a guy out of the story line? As if the business didn't insult the intelligence of the paying customer on a minute-by-minute basis as it is (sometimes working extra stuff into the commercial breaks as well), we're supposed to buy that it's actually a better idea to say that someone attempted *murder* on the guy? Like saying that "he's off shooting a movie" isn't a good enough plan? Whatever happened to the good old days of someone jumping someone else in the aisle and rubbing his face into the concrete floor, or throwing a fireball at him and blinding him? Furthermore, it kind of makes Cena look like a punk who can't back up his street credibility when he gets shanked while hanging out and chilling with his homies. Wrestling itself is built on the backs of guys who would tell stories that started "I was on the way to the ring and some guy slashed my throat from ear-to-ear and poured lemon juice in the wound, but I finished the match anyway" and then get more graphic from there. It's not only disheartening that they couldn't even book an on-screen angle to get rid of Cena, but would have him taken out of action in a way that would make most old-timers laugh at him for being such a pussy.

Carlito, ironically, suffered an injury himself while Cena was off in his cushy movie trailer, and the U.S. title ended up back on Cena again within a few weeks. I don't get the thought process myself sometimes, believe me. I'd give a review of *The Marine*, the movie made by Cena about a marine who returns home from the war to find his family kidnapped, but it was apparently such a disaster that it was immediately shelved. Linda McMahon's evasive strategy when confronted by angry investors who sunk their money into the project seems to indicate that there's little chance of it ever appearing on movie screens or any other screen for that matter. But at least they settled on a title for it and didn't change it three times. I'll give them that.

Next up on the parade o' new faces is Simon Dean, played by the former Nova, Mike Bucci. Another guy stuck in developmental hell in the OVW with little chance for escaping via a character created by himself, Bucci came up with the concept of an evil fitness guru who called people fat. This was truly enough of an earth-shaking concept for a heel (a heel who calls people fat? Call the press!) that he was actually brought up to RAW with this loser gimmick and

**ABOVE: John Cena**

given the name Simon Dean, which was an inside joke for those who knew that road agent Dean Malenko's real name is Dean Simon and was also because they're lazy and name all their characters after people employed by the WWE. Despite weeks of buildup and prominent placement on the show, his debut was a massive flop and he failed to get over with the gimmick, then was humiliated further by being turned into a glorified jobber within two weeks of his start on RAW, getting decimated by midcarder after midcarder until finally being traded to Smackdown in 2005 and essentially left for dead there. He's not a particularly good wrestler anyway, but it's a bit of a downer when someone actually takes the time to fashion his own cheesy gimmick and works his way past the bureaucracy, only to discover that he probably shouldn't have bothered in the first place.

Another guy who rarely bothers to show up in

spirit these days is Undertaker, who increasingly leaves me wondering why he doesn't just find something else to do with his life at this point. Here's the formula for those who haven't had the misfortune of tracking his seemingly endless career with the WWE:

1.  Undertaker gets a big win at Wrestlemania to build him up to challenge whoever the next big World champion is.

2.  Undertaker gets involved in a meaningless feud during the spring to ensure that he doesn't lose heat leading up to his title challenge.

3.  Undertaker wrestles the hot new thing in the main event scene at a pair of the fall PPVs, being heavily protected each time and not doing a job unless the hand of God himself strikes him down in the middle of the ring.

4.  Undertaker is screwed over by someone in the winter months, establishing a feud that will lead to Wrestlemania, where he never loses.

5.  Go back to step one.

I mean, seriously, it's every year that this happens. You can set your watch to it these days. In 2002 it was a pair of matches with Brock Lesnar, in 2003 it was another series with Brock, in 2004 it was JBL, and even in 2005 he looked to be following the same pattern again against Randy Orton. And between 2003 and 2005 he didn't lose very much at all. The justification

is generally, "Well, we don't want him to lose matches because we want to keep him strong for title matches," but the matches don't draw and all you're doing is hurting the guys who have to keep losing to him. Besides, no other main event guys are protected with that kind of argument. Hell, look at Kurt Angle, who will work comedy angles with local jobbers if it means getting a laugh and entertaining people. Even more irritating was the treatment by the announce team, constantly telling us how honored we're supposed to be watching him on TV. Apparently, watching an aging gimmick wrestler doing a triangle choke with a foot of space between his arm and the neck of the victim is "classic Undertaker." Not to say that he doesn't have his moments these days—he was nice enough to put over hot newcomer Vince McMahon in his own Buried Alive specialty match in November 2003 and also let John Cena pin him after wiping the mat with him for twenty minutes and taking a few shots to the head with a chain to put him down. But outside of the occasional anomaly like that, it's been much of the same for the past few years now, as he occasionally shows up and loses the big title match between moving onto the next big feud, like Heidenreich or Voodoo Priest Booker T or estranged family members. Occasionally, he freshens himself up by changing up the gimmick. In 2000, he switched from undead mortician to grumpy biker. In 2003, he added "shoot fighter" to that list. When asked to change back to the "old school" Undertaker for Wrestlemania XX, he added a cowboy hat and leather duster to the ensemble. I don't know how that's supposed to work, either, man. The general direction for most of 2005 was supposed to be leading toward Kurt Angle v. Undertaker for Wrestlemania XXI, with Undertaker deciding not to do any jobs in the *year* leading up to the show, to keep the feud strong you understand, while Angle did several jobs. By the winter, that idea was scrapped, and Undertaker still wasn't doing jobs. He was getting better by October, however, with this PPV—he lost yet another title match, this one to JBL (who was going on an astounding three months as champion by that point) in a "hearse match," where the loser gets stuffed in a hearse. In the spirit of making sure that JBL got put over strong, he needed chloroform to knock him unconscious, plus Heidenreich to stuff him into the hearse, and then Heidenreich made sure to drive a truck into the hearse and kill Undertaker. Again. That didn't even put him out for a month, as he was back for Survivor Series to seek revenge on the guy who killed him for, like, the seventh time. But *this* time, it's *really* personal!

But even Undertaker dying multiple times to further a feud with a guy whose big highspot is reading poetry before the match couldn't compare with the dumbest idea that the WWE has ever had, bar none. And I don't throw that around lightly, because this is the company that produced the XFL and released more than one album of wrestlers singing popular music. Indeed, I can only be referring to the giant turd-burger floating in the toilet tank of life that was Taboo Tuesday.

An interesting idea on paper (much like communism and Debbie Gibson's attempts to be a serious musician), Taboo Tuesday was an oddball PPV scheduled on a Tuesday (hence the name), stemming from Vince McMahon's sudden desire to do an interactive PPV. The idea was a continuing part of his appropriation of (or "homage to") reality TV in general, which had already produced Tough Enough and the Diva Search. In this case, the idea was that fans would vote for HHH's challenger in the World title match main event and then vote for undercard matches that they wanted to see. We fans had the power! Yeah!

Slight problem. The list of challengers for HHH went Randy Orton, Chris Benoit, Edge, and Shawn Michaels. Randy Orton had just lost the title to HHH and was freefalling like a skydiver with an anvil for a parachute, and if they threw him out there with someone like Michaels, who the fans genuinely cared about, voting results might not reinforce what those in charge wanted to hear. That's never a good option, so out goes Orton and the vote is left divided between Benoit, Michaels, and Edge. None of these guys was any threat to win the title at that point—Benoit's push was done and he was well on his way back to the midcard, Edge was in a transitional mode between heel and face and wasn't accepted by the fans in that position anyway, and Michaels was in need of knee surgery and needed time off. So that left the undercard.

Slight problem. Fan sentiment seemed to lean toward wanting something like Edge v. Jericho for the Intercontinental title, but the promotion wanted potential classic matchups like the long-awaited Gene Snitsky v. Kane showdown or Eugene v. Eric Bischoff, matches that were unlikely to be picked as favorites by those watching the show. So Vince did what he always does: he told the fans one thing to start and then changed his mind later as the situation warranted and did what he wanted anyway. In this case, what he wanted was Snitsky v. Kane, a bunch of chicks in a battle royale, a match featuring Diva Search champion Christy Hemme to put her over, Eric Bischoff getting humiliated for the millionth time, and Randy Orton getting a big win in the main event to continue the facade of fans caring about him as a face. So that's what we got, but to throw a bone to those foolishly expecting actual interactivity as promised, fans got to pick match stipulations. Oooo. They also got to pick the challenger to Chris Jericho's Intercontinental title, although the guy built up as the natural challenger for the past few months (Edge, who never lost the title) was unavailable to actually be voted in as challenger. Instead, fans got to pick from a veritable smorgasbord of jobbers and Sunday Night Heat regulars, with Shelton Benjamin and Batista thrown in there to actually give people someone to vote for. And just because I might as well finish going all the way with breaking this nonsense down, here's a

**ABOVE: Christian chinlocks Shelton Benjamin**

match-by-match listing of what we had to choose from and what we got:

- **Shelton Benjamin d. Intercontinental champion Chris Jericho (10:56, ★★½). Benjamin was "endorsed" by Vince McMahon on the last RAW before the show, thus clearly positioning him to be the guy that the fans wanted to see in there. It should be noted that Batista also got a fair amount of votes himself, although as a heel he wasn't likely to win the popular vote. Benjamin still had enough momentum coming off his spring wins over HHH on RAW to be a player in the midcard and won the title from Jericho here, clean with the exploder suplex (or "t-bone," as Jim Ross refers to it). The match was rather lackluster be-**

cause Jericho obviously didn't know who he was facing beforehand (despite the WWE's best efforts to influence the vote beforehand) and Shelton didn't know he was winning the title until the ref told him so at the start of the match. Still, given the limitations, they improvised a pretty decent match, and it kicked off an astonishing (by modern standards) eight-month title reign for Shelton. Of course, you could argue he mainly held the title that long because they had nothing better for him to do, but I'm very much a glass-half-full kind of guy, as you can probably figure out.

- WWE Women's champion Trish Stratus won a battle royale (5:37, no rating). The voting gimmick here is that fans got to pick what the women wore to the ring. You could vote for schoolgirl uniforms, nurse uniforms, or French maid uniforms. Lucky us. Basically, each would be the same slutty outfit with minor variations anyway, but if you care, schoolgirl outfits won. Trish Stratus, untouchable as Women's champion for most of 2004, was not only the hottest thing in a miniskirt and pigtails, but destroyed everyone to win the match as well.

- Gene Snitsky d. Kane (14:20, ¾✶). For the inevitable blowoff to their feud, fans could vote for which weapon was used in the match: a chain, a chair, or a pipe. Truly a revolutionary concept, this show. The chain won, and the chair got involved anyway. The funniest part of the match (not counting Kane and Snitsky trying to have a serious blowoff match) was Jim Ross getting indignant with a straight face, because the chair had not been voted into the match. I can't make this stuff up. This actually did a great job in making Snitsky look like a killer, as he destroyed Kane and pinned him, but would mark the high point for his career in the promotion to date.

- Eugene d. Eric Bischoff (2:09, DUD). The most ridiculous of the stipulation matches (and that's saying something) was this one, as you could vote for what would happen to the loser: forced to wear a dress, forced to shave his head, or tarred and feathered. Eugene was jobbed into oblivion leading up to this show and had zero momentum going in, and of course easily beat his "Uncle Eric" and got to shave his head. Picking lame stipulations for a match no one wants to see is hardly "interactive" by my way of thinking.

- Chris Benoit and Edge d. RAW World tag team champions La Resistance (16:14, ✶½). Another case of them changing their mind on the fly was this match, as the show was originally hyped as "You won't know who HHH's challenger will be until he's introduced by the ring announcer," but then with a week left until the show, they changed their mind and decided to have the two contenders who lost the vote team up and challenge for the tag titles instead, which was truly the definition of filling time on the show. It also gave away who won the vote, so they just scrapped that idea and announced the winner before the show started so they could get some extra buys out of it. Since Edge was turning heel at this point, he abandoned Benoit, who then won the belts by himself in a bad match. La Resistance regained them shortly after, leaving many to wonder what the hell the point was. Edge's bitterness at not winning the popular vote on the night ended up being the catalyst for his long (loooooooong) awaited heel turn, although his longer-awaited World title run wouldn't come until January 2006.

- Christy Hemme d. Carmella (1:49, - ☆☆). This would be Carmella's swan song in wrestling after losing the grueling (for the fans) Diva Search competition, and us lucky fans got to vote whether this was a lingerie pillow fight or two other lame stipulations, although it ended up being a quickie two-minute match that was brutally bad and helped no one.

- RAW World champion HHH d. Shawn Michaels (14:04, ✦✦✦). This was of course the main event voted by the fans, as Shawn won with about 40 percent of the popular vote and got to be the one to lose to HHH before the smallest PPV audience in WWE history. Sadly, Michaels had blown out his knee at a house show and needed surgery right away, so the match was abbreviated (by their standards, fifteen minutes is a quickie) and was mainly HHH working on the knee and pinning him with a Pedigree. It was a good match and something different compared to the cut-and-paste copies they had been doing all year, but *enough* with Shawn Michaels v. HHH already, ya know?

- Randy Orton d. Ric Flair (10:35, ✦✦✦¼). This was set up by Flair faking yet another face turn, as he seems to do every year when the writers run out of ideas, thus wasting the perfectly good angle whereby Flair actually does turn on HHH and helps to get the failing Randy Orton over by acting as a mentor for him. But since the fans really like Flair and want to cheer him and that would have immensely boosted the fortunes of Orton, you can see why they didn't go for it. Fans got to vote here between a cage match, submission match, or a First Blood match. The shows leading up to this were heavily pushing the cage match, so that's what won. Plus people like cage matches. Orton went over big and they did the big respect thing afterward and everyone thought it would lead somewhere. Of course, it didn't, but you can probably name that tune in one note by now.

Despite all the "innovation" of Taboo Tuesday, the show was a total bomb, scoring a 0.31 buyrate, or 160,000 buys. This was the lowest number since the real PPV numbers started to be reported for reasons related to the public trading of the company's stock, and possibly the lowest number in the history of WWE PPV. It was almost certainly the lowest number since the previous low point of the promotion, in 1995. And there was nothing looking to be on the horizon that would save them from themselves.

Even worse for the WWE, competition was about to begin, although on a small scale, as the NWA-TNA switched to monthly PPV shows in November.

# 20 NOVEMBER 2004

## ★ ★ TNA VICTORY ROAD 2004 ★ ★ ★

**FROM:** Orlando, FL
**DATE:** November 7, 2004
**ATTENDANCE:** 700
**BUYRATE:** Unknown, estimated to be 30,000
**ADVERTISED MAIN EVENT:** Jeff Jarrett v. Jeff Hardy

### RESULTS:

Hector Garza won a twenty-man "Gauntlet" match (24:41, ★★★¼)

Erik Watts, "Empire Saint" Pat Kenney, Johnny B. Badd, & Ron Killings
d. Kid Kash, Lance "Dallas" Hoyt, Andy Douglas, &
Chase Stevens (4:37, ½★)

Mascaritas Sagrada d. Piratita Morgan (2:56, no rating)

BG James & Konnan d. NWA World tag team champions
Booby Roode & Eric Young (6:54, ★)

Trinity d. Jacqueline (1:51, ½★)

Monty Brown d. Raven and Abyss (9:25, ★½)

NWA X champion Petey Williams d. AJ Styles (9:47, ★★★)

America's Most Wanted (Chris Harris & James Storm)
d. Triple X (Christopher Daniels & Elix Skipper) (11:31, ★★)

NWA World champion Jeff Jarrett
d. Jeff Hardy in a ladder match (18:33, ★★)

**BY NOVEMBER,** it was starting to get pretty expensive to be a wrestling fan where PPV was available, as up-start challengers to the wrestling throne the NWA-TNA began running their own monthly three-hour PPVs to compete directly with the WWE ones. Now, this didn't exactly have anyone in Connecticut shaking in their boots, since best industry estimates place the TNA's PPV presence at about 30,000 to 50,000 people per show, but even a little competition is better than none, I guess.

## SURVIVOR SERIES (BOTH BRANDS)

FROM: Cleveland, OH
DATE: November 14, 2004
ATTENDANCE: 7,500
BUYRATE: 390,000
ADVERTISED MAIN EVENT: Randy Orton's team v. HHH's team

### RESULTS:

WWE Cruiserweight champion Spike Dudley
d. Chavo Guerrero, Billy Kidman and Rey Mysterio (9:04, ★★★½)

Intercontinental champion Shelton Benjamin
d. Christian (13:22, ★★★¼)

Big Show, Eddie Guerrero, John Cena, & Rob Van Dam
d. Carlito, Kurt Angle, Mark Jindrak, & Luther Reigns (12:24, ★★)

Undertaker d. Heidenreich (15:53, ★)

WWE Women's champion Trish Stratus d. Lita (DQ, 1:19, DUD)

Smackdown World champion JBL d. Booker T (14:44, ★★)

Chris Jericho, Chris Benoit, Randy Orton, & Maven
d. Gene Snitsky, HHH, Batista, & Edge (24:31, ★★★¼)

# A BRIEF HISTORY OF THE TNA

Really, the roots of America's current #2 promotion began back in 2000, as the WCW was on the ropes and longtime Memphis promoter Jerry Jarrett was making overtures about buying it from Time Warner. Jarrett had been running shows in Memphis so long that you'd have to resort to some sort of corny Jerry Lawler–type line about his Social Security number being "2" to properly convey how long he'd been in the business. But it was a long time, and Jarrett was certainly a well-respected promoter among promoters. In fact, had Vince McMahon gone to jail in the infamous steroid trials of the '90s, as was feared by many people close to him, Jarrett was the guy designated to take over the WWF and run it while he was "away." So when Jarrett started talking about buying the WCW, people knew he was serious. Too bad Time Warner was even more serious about getting rid of it at any price, because both Jarrett and Eric Bischoff were cut out of a potential deal when it was sold to Vince McMahon instead and essentially put out to pasture.

Speaking of put out to pasture, Jerry's son, Jeff Jarrett, had been a longtime midcarder in the WWF and

LEFT: Abyss

the final episode, the simultaneously airing episode of RAW featured Vince cruelly firing many of the WCW's top talent on-air to vent past grievances. Lex Luger in particular was harshly dismissed by Vince and never recovered from it, and probably the second-meanest firing went to Jeff Jarrett. To finally pay back a longtime grudge for Jarrett holding the WWF up for a PPV payday when they forgot to renew his contract in 1999, Vince declared that "Good ol' Double J was G-double-O-N-double-E." This spelled "GOONEE," which I don't think was the intention. Spelling issues aside, Jarrett was most definitely fired and not welcome in the new WCW-less world order.

So with no chance left to buy the #2 promotion and a son who wanted something to feed his ego, Jerry and Jeff teamed up to form their own run at the WWE. Going for an alternative feel and playing off fan feelings that the WWE was getting old and slow by 2002, they

even had ascended to being a WCW World champion in 2000 during the dying days of the promotion. Although the whole title reign was something of a joke; kind of like on the TV show *Night Court*, where they needed a new judge and all the other candidates were out golfing on Sunday so they just started calling down the line until getting to Harry Stone. Same thing with Jarrett, as Bret Hart was retiring, Goldberg was injured, Chris Benoit was jumping ship, and Sid Vicious was out playing softball. In fact, by that point even Jarrett himself didn't want the belt, because he didn't want to be known as the lowest-drawing champion in history. Luckily for him, David Arquette earned that dubious honor in May 2000, so Jeff could rest easy. Anyway, when the sale of the WCW went through in March 2001 and Nitro was turned into the Vince McMahon Show for

RIGHT: Abyss

called their new promotion Total Nonstop Action (TNA). Backed by the former WCW announcer Mike Tenay and the wrestling Web site owner Bob Ryder, they came up with a fairly unique concept that was toyed with in the early '90s by Vince McMahon before being discarded: weekly PPV shows. Born out of necessity because they couldn't get a TV deal, the Jarretts came up with the idea of staging their own weekly two-hour TV show and airing it on PPV, for $10 per show. They would need a truly miraculous number of buys to break even, but the hope was that they could build a following and then turn it into a TV deal. To maximize the available talent, they partnered with the bastard cousin of the former WCW: the National Wrestling Alliance (NWA). Formerly the biggest coalition of wrestling promoters on the planet until being discarded like a chewed-up piece of gum by the WCW in 1993, the NWA had become something of a running joke in wrestling since that point; getting symbolically curb-stomped by the ECW in 1994 and then turned into a play thing for Vince Russo to mock Jim Cornette with in 1998. Left with not much choice, the remaining NWA members rolled over and played dead for the incoming TNA, merging with them to produce the NWA-TNA and giving total booking control of the champions to the Jarretts. Dan Severn, who had been the NWA World champion in what felt like forever, was callously stripped of the title on a technicality so that the Jarretts could crown their own champion at the first show, and ditto for tag champions the Shane Twins, although at least they were offered a job with the TNA.

With champions secured and the NWA behind them, the TNA got down to the business of flushing their integrity down the crapper as soon as possible, handing over creative reins to the estranged WCW bookers Vince Russo and Ed Ferrera. They denied Russo's involvement from day one because otherwise he would be in breach of his iron-clad WCW contract, but then Russo made a brilliant end run around it by getting a job with the WWE (thus necessitating Vince McMahon buying out the contract himself) and pitching the stupidest ideas possible until he was fired a week after starting with the company. Thus, he was free of the contract and ready to start sinking the TNA. The first show demonstrated the kind of direction it appeared they'd be going with, as former shopping channel maven Don West was hired as one of the color commentators and the former NWA tag champions the Shane Twins were repackaged as a couple of guys who dressed like giant penises. Plus, there were midgets masturbating in garbage cans, Japanese guys dressed like Elvis, more half-naked and swearing women than you could shake a stick at . . . you name it.

Despite the car-wreck nature of the early shows, there were definitely bright spots as they learned to adjust the style to meet fan expectations. The standard Cruiserweight or midcard belt ideas were merged into a catch-all division, called the X division. Rather than being defined by weight class, wrestlers would be defined by the style of match, as X division champions were expected to be the most exciting to watch in the ring and would wrestle fast-paced and risky matches.

This theory actually helped to keep the smaller wrestlers from getting squashed by the bigger ones, and soon it was producing new stars like AJ Styles, who had previously been part of a preliminary tag team in the WCW and nothing more. Styles started becoming more of a focus of the shows because of what he could do in the ring, and by 2003 he had actually broken through the confines of weight class to become a multiple-time NWA World champion himself.

The first NWA World champion in the TNA era was Ken Shamrock, who they intended to build up for a feud with Jeff Jarrett, but soon they stumbled onto another new star. Ron Killings debuted in the TNA as K-Krush, his longtime indy gimmick (altered slightly into "K-Kwik" for a brief run in the WWF in 1999) and got a minor heel push right from the start of the promotion. However, it wasn't until he started doing a more "angry black man" style of interview, claiming that the southern racists running the promotion were holding him down, that his more serious push began. With a name change to Ron "The Truth" Killings and a new interview style, he was soon pushed all the way to being a NWA World champion, winning the belt from Ken Shamrock. Unfortunately, this also showed how desperate they were to find a breakthrough star to begin with, because

**RIGHT: Abyss**

Killings may have been a hot act as a midcard heel, but he flopped as champion and was unable to hang with other main eventers in the ring. The inevitable consequence was Jeff Jarrett winning his first NWA World title in November 2002 and hanging onto it like a boa constrictor pretty much all the way into 2005.

The other major stars created by the early days of the promotion were a tag team known as America's Most Wanted, who quickly became one of my favorite teams. Comprised of James "Tennessee Cowboy" Storm and Chris "Wildcat" Harris, they were discovered by Jerry Jarrett after years on the indy circuit when they were wrestling each other, and he decided to pair them up as a team in the new TNA. They quickly gained in popularity, running through the tag ranks and winning the NWA World tag titles multiple times, essentially dominating the division with their crowd-pleasing looks and '80s-throwback double-team moves. Years of teased splits and losing and regaining

the belts have yet to truly diminish their star power in the promotion, as they've remained the top babyface team since the inception of the promotion with no signs of slowing down. I was frankly shocked that the WWE didn't throw money at them in 2003 and sign them away, as they hit their career peak with a legendary cage match against Christopher Daniels and Elix Skipper shortly after the one-year anniversary of the promotion.

With their mixture of old and new stars, the TNA actually managed to survive for longer than most gave them a chance at. However, by their first year as a promotion, money levels still weren't going anywhere positive, aside from a brief blip caused by a brilliantly hyped and booked showdown between Jeff Jarrett and Raven for the NWA World title. Most wrote the promotion off and started waiting for the death knell, but the Jarretts surprised everyone by bringing in the financial backing of the Panda Energy Group to keep them afloat. With seemingly limitless monetary resources now behind the shows, they could afford to be patient and wait for the audience to build. However, by 2004 the weekly shows were hemorrhaging money and a new strategy was quickly needed.

Part one came when the TNA scored a fairly important guest slot on Fox Sports Network's *Best Damn Sports Show Period*, running taped matches as a feature in hopes of impressing the network enough to give them a weekly timeslot. The ratings for the TNA-themed shows were okay at best, but they got a timeslot regardless, mainly due to them paying for the space.

Part two came when they dropped the weekly PPV format and went on hiatus, prepping for a return in November 2004 with a monthly, three-hour PPV format. The show was not exactly a critical success, and it was oversaturated with castoffs from the WCW and the WWE, but it was different enough from the competing product that most thought that giving them a chance would be wise. It also featured another innovation, as they had introduced a six-sided ring as part of their new show on Fox Sports, the TNA Impact. This truly made it a visually striking set and allowed for more freedom for the guys working the matches to improvise things.

The problems with the promotion remained, however, and their change of venue (from Nashville's fairgrounds to Orlando's Universal Studios) caused new issues. Chiefly among them was the smaller size of the crowd, and the fact that Universal wouldn't let them charge admission. Since they weren't running house shows and had no merchandising plan to speak of, this left their only source of income as the PPV buys. The promotion seemed in further trouble when they lost their TV deal in the summer of 2005 (but a move to Spike TV has left the company as a solid #2 promotion and in some ways a threat to the WWE). As for what I'd consider smart moves toward making the company financially feasible, I would have them actually learn how to run a wrestling company and thus do house shows, but that's probably crazy talk to the people running the TNA. I can certainly understand their viewpoint: they'd sunk millions of dollars into the promotion at that point and minor considerations like drawing money on the road or selling tickets to the PPVs are just a drop in the bucket, but you have to start somewhere in terms of building up an audience for the promotion Running the company like it's 1998 WCW, with a seventeen-person booking committee and big video packages to hype their nonexistent story lines, is just glossing over the fact that this company has yet to make a cent outside of their diminishing PPV revenues. They needed to fire most, if not all, of the nonwrestling people (i.e., the multiple bookers, women, managers, "enhancement talent," ring girls, whatever), strip down the roster to a manageable size, and actually act like a company that's a small wrestling promotion instead of trying to behave like the WWE's little brother. Either that or tour. But as noted, that's crazy talk.

The WWE's response to the TNA's throwing down of the PPV gauntlet was the Survivor Series, another show in a series of them where Randy Orton was booked to get the big win in the main event and look like a million bucks, and no one cared. By this point he had pinned HHH more than once in tag matches and was seemingly a permanent fixture as the #1 contender to the title, but just couldn't get over the hump and make people be-

**RIGHT: Eddie Guerrero's team and Kurt Angle's team**

lieve in him as the top guy. However, the elimination tag match (with Orton's team of Chris Jericho, Chris Benoit, and Maven defeating HHH, Batista, Edge, and Gene Snitsky) did carry one fairly interesting stipulation to it: The winning team would get control of RAW for an entire month, with each person getting to be the general manager for one week apiece. And wouldn't you know it, each guy focused the show on booking himself against HHH for the World title, with HHH being smarter than Maven, then Chris Benoit, then Chris Jericho, and retaining the title in all three cases. Once they got to Randy Orton, however, they finally found someone who could outsmart him (the ultimate compliment from HHH), as he first put HHH in a battle royale for the title, then was overruled by Vince McMahon and it ended up with a triple-threat match pitting HHH against Chris Benoit and Edge instead. That finally was enough to get the title off his HHHoliness, as it was vacated following a

controversial simultaneous pin/submission situation. Of course, we all knew where it would end up again, but it did have two interesting results:

1.  **It set up the extra RAW PPV in January with an Elimination Chamber match for the title that they could actually have time to hype properly this time around.**
2.  **It gave Batista more time to flex his acting muscles and subtly compete with HHH for the title.**

November also saw the introduction of one of the more controversial figures to emerge from the classy mind of Vince McMahon: Muhammad Hassan. Even the name pretty much gives away where the character was going from day one, doesn't it? Yes, with America having successfully invaded a sovereign nation over fictitious "weapons of mass destruction" and Vince being on the Bush bandwagon, you knew it would only be a matter of time before we had a positive role model for our Iraqi brethren on WWE TV. In this case, one played by Mark Copani, an Italian guy. But he wore a towel on his head, so he's *evil*. This was actually a pretty screwed up character, because all his interviews stressed how he was an American of Iraqi heritage, not an Iraqi native. His point was that people were booing him because of their own racism, not because of anything he had done or would do, and he kinda had a point with that. However, to really stress what a wonderful person that Hassan was, he used Iron Sheik's

clichéd camel clutch as a finisher, and often preceded the move by making a gesture that suggested he was cutting the victim's head off. Hassan was a major flop, both in the ring and as a potential draw, and by 2005 they were resorting to staged "terrorist attacks" on Smackdown to get him any heat at all. Despite the improvement of his talking skills, he was unable to put together a watchable match, even with great technicians like Chris Benoit and Shawn Michaels, and if you can't have a great match with either of those guys, you're worthless. He was fired, of course.

Speaking of worthless, November was also when the hammer fell on the dead weight clogging up the midcard, as it was time for the WWE's semiannual cutting of talent! Besides the previously mentioned firings of Gail Kim, Rodney Mack, and Jazz, also getting the ax were Billy Gunn, Test, A-Train, Chuck Palumbo, and Johnny Stamboli. While I shed no tears for Gunn, I have to shoulder some of the blame for Test, because there seems to be a curse whereby anyone on the cover of one of my books has his career go into a down cycle. Goldberg was on the cover of *The Buzz on Pro Wrestling* and he was put on the shelf for two years as a result of the WCW's demise soon after; Steve Austin was on the cover of *Tonight . . . in This Very Ring* and was retired by the time the book came out in 2003; and Test adorned the cover of *Wrestling's One Ring Circus* and was fired when *that* one came out.

I'm going to start putting HHH on all my covers and hope for the best.

# DECEMBER 2004

## ★ ★ ★ ARMAGEDDON (SMACKDOWN) ★ ★ ★

FROM: Atlanta, GA
DATE: December 12, 2004
ATTENDANCE: 4,500
BUYRATE: 250,000 buys
Advertised Main Event: JBL v. Booker T v. Undertaker v. Eddie Guerrero

### RESULTS:

Smackdown tag team champions Rob Van Dam & Rey Mysterio
d. Kenzo Suzuki & Rene Dupree (16:55, ★★★)

Kurt Angle d. "Santa Claus" (0:28, DUD)

Daniel Puder d. Mike Mizanin in a boxing match (no rating)

the Basham Brothers d. Charlie Haas & Bob Holly (6:51, ½★)

U.S. champion John Cena d. Jesus (7:55, ½★)

Dawn Marie d. Jackie (1:43, DUD)

Big Show d. Kurt Angle, Mark Jindrak, & Luther Reigns (9:56, ¾★)

Funaki d. WWE Cruiserweight champion Spike Dudley (9:29, ★¼)

Smackdown World champion JBL d. Eddie Guerrero,
Booker T, & Undertaker (25:36, ★★¾)

**LET'S FACE IT,** there was nothing going on in December of note, especially on Smackdown, so let's talk about the fates of people who have managed to escape wrestling instead.

### "I want to retire in two years and become a motivational speaker"

More than anything, that phrase seems to be the mantra of every top-level star in wrestling over the past, oh, ten years or so. Booker T said it near the end of 2002, almost word for word, and yet he's still around. DDP has said it more than once, and to be fair he got closer to achieving it than most, as he retired (once) and previously had a motivational speaker gimmick. For whatever reason, the only guy actually able to fulfill this long-standing dream of wrestlers everywhere was Jim "Ultimate Warrior" Hellwig, who passed a point long ago beyond which he was too crazy for even wrestling to accept him back. And this is the sport that keeps welcoming Roddy Piper back, so that shows how many bananas short of a bunch you need to be to cross *that* line.

To further put the fortunes of Mr. Warrior into their proper perspective, consider a talk he gave to an unsuspecting group of conservative college students in 2005. When liberally biased students showed up at the rally and began questioning Warrior's apparent hatred of homosexuals, he responded with, and I'm quoting here because god knows I can't make something like this up, "Queering don't make the world work." While the poor kids at the talk flipped out and accused him of hate-mongering while nearly rushing the stage themselves in the process, my main objection to this statement is that "queering" isn't a verb, as far as I'm aware. To be fair, he's a funny guy at times, and if there's one thing a wrestler knows instinctively after years in the business, it's how to incite a crowd. I think his main problem there, however, was that he was lacking that part of the brain that tells the mouth when to stop talking, as evidenced by his further verbal attacks on an Arab student, who he basically mocked for "wearing a towel on his head." That's the point when he probably should have cut his losses and shut the hell up. But the fact that he didn't shows what kind of dis-

ABOVE: Roddy Piper

connect from reality we're dealing with here. And to show another one, allow me to quote his response to the liberal students, from his very illuminating Web site:

I expected the behavior of the liberals. They were, this time, unusually animated but I thought that was great. It didn't become the fisticuffs I have often hoped for, but maybe next time. Hey, forgive me—I'm a romantic at heart and enjoy nothing like a good fight to bring out the love. Then again, there's nothing quite like the look in the eye of a radical liberal when he knows his bullshit isn't stirring up any fear in the person he's directing it toward. When you witness that realization happening, it's like seeing Velveeta melt. Maybe it's just that they know that if they throw something at me— whether pies or punches—there'll be no running except in the direction to catch and pummel their ass myself. Be forewarned liberals—I don't know how to pull any punch, physically or intellectually. Of course, in the interest of full disclosure, I say this part facetiously, part seriously—but it's up to you, squirrel nuts, to figure out to which side the scale leans more.[1]

There's another few pages of this stuff, but I have only one thing to add as a comment. "It's like seeing Velveeta melt" is perhaps one of the weirdest metaphors I've seen in a serious commentary, well, ever. That is how crazy you have to be to get thrown out of wrestling.

Running a distant second to Warrior's unique brand of dementia is Randy "Macho Man" Savage, a guy who I used to like. Randy's been less happy while out of the spotlight cast by the WWE than even Warrior has been, and he's been doing his best to be almost as psychotic. His asking price per appearance was rumored to be in the millions as of 2000, astronomical for a headliner today, let alone a senior citizen with rage issues like Savage. He scored a major victory for his public image in 2002 when he appeared in the blockbuster *Spider-Man* movie, playing basically himself, but followed up *that* stroke of luck by cutting a rap album about Hulk Hogan.

Apparently, this unexpected (and unwanted) foray into gangsta rap for the insane was spurred on by Hogan failing to accept Savage's challenge for a fixed fight. For charity, of course. Now—and this is the really crazy part, so stay with me here—most people were under the impression that if Hogan actually accepted Savage's ridiculous grandstand challenge, which

was just a ploy to get Savage back into the spotlight again, then Savage would attempt to fight him for real, to show how tough he was. When Hogan decided that this would be sinking to new lows of pathetic attempts at media coverage, even by his own standards, Savage began "calling him out" on any radio show dumb enough to book him and insisting that Hogan was a coward for not accepting his challenge to a fight that wasn't supposed to be real anyway, and then found an entirely new level of crazy by challenging Hogan to a "real" fight. So the idea was going to be that Savage would make everyone think it was a real fight, tell Hogan it was actually a fake fight, and then fight him for real anyway. I've seen episodes of *Batman* with smarter villains than this guy.

Hogan's continual declining of the challenge allowed the rage and hatred to build inside Savage, until he could only fully express it by hiring a team of song writers and producers to help him flow on his own CD. I wish I could include audio samples from the song, but since this is the printed media, here's some lyrics to hold you over:

> *Come on that phony fight the Rock spanked*
> *    you fast*
> *But when I challenged Hogan to a real fight*
> *    he passed.*
> *I called him out but the punk was scared*
> *    to go*
> *It was a charity event but the Hulk didn't*
> *    show.*

1. www.ultimatewarrior.com/08.04.2005UConnRetort.htm.

*Hollywood Hulkster you're at the end of your*
*rope*
*And I'm a kick ya in the butt and wash your*
*mouth out with soap.*[2]

This is how crazy you have to be to get thrown out of wrestling.

Now, I know that the feuds between hardcore rappers can be pretty rough, and people get, like, shot and stuff, but I don't think anyone has ever threatened to wash someone's mouth out with soap before. I mean, sure, 50 Cent has a bullet lodged in his tongue, and rappers have been shot to death over beefs with songs before, but how can we as a society stand by and allow someone to make threats about putting soap in someone else's mouth? Although Savage did have to listen to his own CD, so really he's been punished enough.

To be fair to Savage, although god knows I don't know why I would be at this point, the death of ex-wife Elizabeth Hewlett hit him pretty hard, and it was from that point on that his connection with sanity, however fleeting, seemed to snap for good. Cutting a rap album was one of the signs that this had happened. I should also point out that both Savage and Hogan are in the twilight of their careers as active wrestlers, to say the least, and both are falling apart physically. Savage's knees in particular are shot many times over, and Hogan endured a well-publicized hip replacement surgery. Savage is probably the least crippled of the two, so it would hardly have been a fair fight to begin with.

2. Lyrics taken from www.machoman.com, Savage's official Web site.

Say what you will about Hulk, but he knows how to pick his fights. As of this writing, Savage's collection of hard-hitting rap had yet to crack the Billboard Hot 100, but then that Sheriff song that went to #1 in 1989 sat on the shelf for about ten years too, so maybe there's hope for Savage yet. However, the record label sent me the CD for free and I still felt ripped off by it, so I'm not holding my breath. I think Savage should have shifted his focus and beefed with G-Unit instead—sure, he'd be taking his life into his own hands, but at least the payoff would be guaranteed to be more interesting.

Speaking of Hogan, his brilliant plan du jour in 2004 was to avoid trying his own comeback and attempt to live vicariously through his creepy lookalike daughter, as all great dads do. His ambitions for Brooke involved turning her into the next Britney Spears, although then someone would have to be the next Kevin Federline and I wouldn't want to wish that fate on anyone. Anyway, the bulk of 2004 saw Hogan shamelessly pimping his daughter at award shows, booking her to sing the national anthem at Tampa Bay Lightning home games, and even the inevitable reality TV show deal followed. However, to associate anything from Hogan's life with "reality" is a strange proposition indeed. He's certainly no more deluded about his own celebrity than, say, Nick Lachey, Ruben Studdard, or anyone who was ever on *The Real World* and thinks it means anything in the real world.

And much like Hogan's life is truly the surreal life,

that brings me to *The Surreal Life*, featuring another deluded wrestling "celebrity" has-been: Joanie "Chyna" Laurer. A TV show on VH1 about faltering celebrities who live together in a house, Real World-style, being on it marks the true point of a career where self-parody has set in. What makes it funnier is that those on the show rarely know or admit that this is true. Such is the case with Joanie, who retired from wrestling five years ago and yet still won't go away. As if reading her book wasn't enough of a trip to the twilight zone, the show allowed us, the common sane people, to truly get a glimpse into the mind of someone on the verge of a total breakdown any day now. Not that I normally take pleasure in the personal suffering of those who consider themselves better than me because of a short run in the business, but watching Peter Brady verbally bitchslap her boyfriend, Sean "X-Pac" Waltman, was indeed sweet payback for the years of having to watch Chyna and X-Pac sleepwalk through crappy matches.

Sadly, they put more effort into their XXX sex tape, which was titled *One Night in Chyna* and apparently looked like something made by a pair of drunken transvestites borrowing a video camera and using it for the first time. In the interest of full disclosure and to keep my reputation safe, I should note that I didn't actually watch it and I'm basing my judgment on the plethora of scathing reviews that the piece got. I mean, even I have my limits. Most reputable reviews of the "film" focus on Chyna looking coked up and drunk while trying to appear "seductive" and yet dressed like something off of LA's drag scene. To say nothing of the

actual sex involved, which was capped off by Joanie revealing sex organs that are best left to the imagination and best described as "unspecific."

Joanie of course still thinks of herself as both a big star and as being in full control of her mental faculties, which might explain her bizarre appearance on the Howard Stern show early in 2005. Highlights included her going topless despite no one asking and her breasts looking like a pair of socks with bars of soap stuffed in them. It was followed by attempts to sing, and the whole wonderful experience was capped off by Sean Waltman calling in to accuse her of breaking his heart. Or maybe it was to accuse her of beating him. It's hard to keep track with those two.

Sean himself is a noted headcase, although in a rare show of out-of-company generosity from Vince McMahon, the WWE bankrolled his trip to rehab in 2005. Perhaps due to his friendship with HHH, but perhaps to prevent him from writing any more bizarre and rambling love-hate letters to Joanie and posting them on his Web site. Sean found a temporary home in the wannabe WWE competitor TNA, along with fellow supposed retiree DDP, although the rapidly changing fortunes of that company meant that neither had stable employment for long.

Of course, not all exits from our so-called sport were as fun to discuss as the above. Chris Candido was on exactly the same sort of career path as Waltman, but the difference is that rehab appeared to work for him. He also emerged in the TNA as part of a comeback attempt, but ironically broke his leg soon after returning and refused drugs for the pain as a part of his new lifestyle. Sadly, he died during routine surgery to put a steel pin in his ankle mere days after the initial injury. Candido had essentially been out of the business since an ill-fated stint in the WCW during their dying days, doing indy shots here and there. The fate of his common-law wife, Tammy Sytch, is almost as sad.

Long considered one of the sexiest women in wrestling, Tammy split with the then-WWF in 1998 and spent time working for the upstart ECW to spend more time with Candido. However, soon the true reasons for her departure became known, as she exposed her own chronic drug use and abuse on ECW TV, as a ratings ploy. It didn't help the ratings. Tammy became something of a recluse, gaining weight and suffering through a humiliating arrest as a result of a complaint filed by her own mother, and by the time she arrived in the WCW to further support Candido in 2000, she was a shell of her former self. Still only twenty-four, she had ballooned in weight (by wrestling standards) and no longer projected the image that the major companies demanded of the women who occupied their shows. Tammy became an outcast from the business and hit rock bottom in 2001, when she co-founded the Wrestling Vixxxens Web site with the legendary skank Missy Hyatt. The idea was that it would be a Web site where Tammy, Missy, and any other disgruntled women would pose naked. Problems arose, however. First of all, the curiosity of horny fanboys, who had all but forgotten the fading Sytch by 2001, was not enough to sustain the business end of the site, ap-

parently. Also, Tammy was clearly not enjoying the experience, putting out unemotional photos that merely showed her body, and didn't give any sense of excitement like her WWF shots had done. I supposed part of this could be blamed on using such a shitty photographer, too. Third, Missy was already overexposed, and exposing flesh didn't help. Plus a series of grotesquely large breast implants left her looking like something out of *Baywatch* meets *Cocoon*. Finally, no other women (of note) joined the site to show defiance, choosing gainful employment instead. And they could only do so many shots of Tammy and Missy, together or alone, before the people lost interest. Plus, Tammy appeared unwilling to do anything truly sexual with Missy or anyone else. By the end, Tammy was doing a series of uninspired body shots, looking about as excited as a person stuck in a dentist's chair, while her weight grew past the point where she wanted to show it off any longer. Rumors also swirled about Candido interrupting photo shoots to prevent her from carrying on.

Tammy did, however, make something of a clean break from the business in 2002, printing the following angry rant on a messageboard dedicated to her (spelling and capital letters are hers):

I AM RETIRING THIS YEAR. IT'S ALMOST 14 YEARS IN THIS BIZ, IT'S NOT FUN OR WORTH THE AGGRIVATION ANYMORE. I HAVE A FEW MORE SHOWS AND TWO OVERSEAS TOURS BOOKED, AND THEN I AM BECOMING A FLIGHT ATTENDANT. MY LEG

HASN'T FULLY RECOVERED FROM A YEAR AGO DECEMBER 5TH—I TORE MY RIGHT QUADRICEP MUSCLE IN TEXAS IN A MATCH, AND I HAVEN'T BEEN ABLE TO TRAIN COR-RECTLY FOR A YEAR NOW. SO, YOU CAN SAY WHAT YOU WANT ABOUT MY CURRENT PHYSICAL CONDITION, BUT I AM INJURED AND I REALLY DON'T GIVE A SHIT ABOUT OPINIONS. IF YOU DON'T APPRECIATE MY WORK AND WHAT I'VE DONE FOR THIS BIZ, THEN, GET UP AND GO TO THE BATHROOM DURING MY MATCHES. I REALLY WON'T MISS THIS STUFF BECAUSE IT BASICALLY IS A CRUEL AND DEMEANING BUSINESS. IT DID A LOT FOR ME AND CC, BUT I DON'T HAVE THE PASSION FOR IT ANY MORE. SO, MAYBE I CAN SERVE YOU ALL A DRINK AND PRET-ZELS ON CONTINENTAL AIRLINES!! TA TA FOR NOW—TAM[3]

Well, needless to say, that didn't happen either, and as of the last time anyone cared enough to ask, her goal was to open up a tanning salon. Expect to see her go crawling back to wrestling any day now.

I think my point, which may have been lost in there somewhere, is that once you get sucked into the bizarre and incestuous world of wrestling, it gets in-creasingly difficult to escape and lead a normal life. Some, like Warrior and Savage, were never normal to begin with and thus apparently aren't equipped to deal with the real world. Some, like Chyna and Tammy, had so much success so early in their careers that they never learned to adjust to the good life in the first place. And when it was yanked from underneath them by the fickle nature of the fans, they couldn't adjust. And some like Hogan just keep getting offers to come back. Some like Ric Flair have never let go or been able to so much as retire from the ring gracefully. And some, like the Rock, have successfully left the business and become a bigger star for it. But he's the exception. Most who escape successfully do so under the guise of finding Jesus, like Ted Dibiase, Sting, and Nikita Koloff, and end up better people, if not always better financially. It's not the has beens embarrassing them-selves while struggling for one last hit of media atten-tion who really make me sad, but those who were great once and hang on for one match too long, or get out alive and then end up dead through no fault of their own, who really make it tough to be a fan sometimes.

Maybe I'll retire and become a motivational speaker.

3. Posted on www.pwinsider.com.

## ★ ★ NEW YEAR'S REVOLUTION (RAW) ★ ★

FROM: San Juan, PR
DATE: January 9, 2005
ATTENDANCE: 13,700
BUYRATE: 375,000 buys
ADVERTISED MAIN EVENT: HHH v. Batista v. Randy Orton v.
Chris Jericho v. Chris Benoit v. Edge

### RESULTS:

RAW World tag team champions Eugene & William Regal
d. Christian & Tyson Tomko (12:21, ★★½)

WWE Women's champion Trish Stratus d. Lita (3:45, DUD)

Intercontinental champion Shelton Benjamin d. Maven (6:06, DUD)

Muhammad Hassan d. Jerry Lawler (10:50, -☆½)

Kane d. Gene Snitsky (11:45, ½★)

RAW World champion HHH d. Edge, Chris Benoit,
Chris Jericho, Batista, & Randy Orton (34:57, ★★★★)

**HAPPY NEW YEAR! 2005** began with the ascension of Batista to something much more than anyone but Jim Cornette ever expected, and where it ends up is anyone's guess.

But first, let's do some housecleaning and count down my top ten matches for the year that was 2004:

10. Smackdown, March 18—Eddie Guerrero v. Rey Mysterio 17:53, rollup ⟶ pin, ★★★★¼). Kind of a forgotten classic to start the list off, as the newly crowned champion Eddie Guerrero defended against Rey Mysterio after a gauntlet-type series on Smackdown, and the result was one of the best matches on free TV this year. Not quite the equal of their MOTYC[1] in 1997, but still a damn fine TV match and the match that should have kicked off a great reign for Eddie, showcasing a new kind of main event style.

1. MOTYC: "Match of the Year Candidate"

9. Wrestlemania XX—The Rock and Mick Foley v. Evolution (17:02, Orton RKO ➞ pin Foley, ★★★★¼). Call me crazy, but this had three of my favorite wrestlers in it, out there having more fun than any human being should be having in a match that was supposed to be a blood feud between Foley and Orton. But considering how depressing the year would get, can you blame me for wanting a little fun now and then? Rock is the king, case closed.

8. RAW, May 3—Chris Benoit v. Shawn Michaels (28:28, HHH Pedigree ➞ Benoit pins Shawn, ★★★★¼). This was actually a very disappointing finish for a match that was supposed to be an all-time classic. We were basically promised that it was going to be one leading up to it, and while it was fantastic for a TV match, it was lacking a real finish and never paid off the promise that a Benoit-Michaels feud had been promised for nearly a decade. Well, Benoit could still get the title back, and god knows Shawn will get title shots until he's dead, so maybe they can have the PPV classic yet. For now, there was the Showdown in the Desert.

7. Backlash—Randy Orton v. Mick Foley (23:04, RKO ➞ pin, ★★★★). Although I rated it a bit lower initially, I'd have to rate it higher here because it had more overall impact and made Orton

into a superstar, and that's kind of the point. Plus, I was there live, and anything that makes Shane McMahon mark out deserves at least #7.

6. No Way Out—Eddie Guerrero v. Brock Lesnar (30:06, frog splash ⟶ pin, ✶✶✶✶1/2). Sadly not the rocket into the stratosphere that we all thought it would be for Eddie, this is still an awesome big v. little match, although one that I don't love as much as others seem to. For sheer emotion from Eddie and heat from the crowd, it's great, but there were better matches. Still, everything from here on is ✶✶✶✶½ or better, so this is the elite level now.

5. Wrestlemania XX—Eddie Guerrero v. Kurt Angle (21:32, rollup ⟶ pin, ✶✶✶✶½). Speaking of Eddie, he managed to follow up his title win with a match at Wrestlemania that would have been a MO-TYC in any other year, but wasn't even the match of the *show* at XX. That's pretty scary, actually. And in one of the nicest continuity touches in recent memory, the

**RIGHT: Rey Mysterio and Chavo Guerrero**

finish of this match was actually mirrored by their Summerslam rematch. That ain't bad.

4. Backlash—Chris Benoit v. HHH v. Shawn Michaels (30:09, Sharpshooter ⟶ submission, ✶✶✶✶¾). Well, the sequel hardly ever lives up to the original, but they sure gave it their best go with this one. Sure, my being there live might have clouded my judgment, but that's my prerogative. Plus, I got to see Shawn Michaels tap to the Sharpshooter, so huzzah. Not as great as Wrestlemania, but then not much is. Whether or not Benoit is "for real" in the long term, however, who knows.

3. TNA Turning Point—AMW v. XXX (21:02, Harris powerbomb ⟶ pin Skipper, ✶✶✶✶½). Yup, the TNA

barges into the WWE's exclusive party again this year, stealing the show with what would have been my MOTYC in any other year. After redefining the cage match in 2003 and nearly topping *that* list, they tangle again on the TNA's second three-hour PPV and damn if they don't make me all happy to be a wrestling fan yet again. Nothing like a little crazy violence to keep me satisfied.

2. Royal Rumble 2004—Royal Rumble match (61:37, Benoit eliminates Big Show, ★★★★★). The Rumble is really tough to screw up, but this one was even more awesome than usual. Plus, Benoit won, which was one of the rare occasions where the WWE didn't tease us and then screw us over in the end. Even if he hadn't won the title at Wrestlemania, I'd always have this. But he did, so this gets #2. Did I overrate it? Possibly. Do I care? If you have to ask . . .

1. Wrestlemania XX—HHH v. Shawn Michaels v. Chris Benoit (24:46, crossface → submission, ★★★★★). Like you even needed to ask. What is probably now my favorite moment in all of my wrestling fandom, and one of my favorite matches ever, sees Chris Benoit finally paying off years of jobbing and suffering due to politics and height dis-

advantage. People always said that he was too small to be a main eventer and he'd never be World champion in the WWE, but guess what? He *could* be champion, and he was for six months, and I'll always have that. This also showed that HHH could still turn it up if need be, and stands as probably the greatest three-way match in the history of wrestling. And probably the greatest Wrestlemania main event in history. That's a great match, y'all.

You'll note that among the usual names on these kinds of lists, like Shawn Michaels and Chris Benoit, there was an appearance by Batista there for the Wrestlemania tag team match. Indeed, as 2005 was starting Batista was without a doubt the hottest act on the RAW side of things and getting hotter by the day. Not only was his silent-but-deadly routine catching on with fans but also he was drawing big reactions for his entrances and mannerisms. Plus, he was truly developing into an organic babyface, while still playing a heel. By that I mean the fans *wanted* to see him turn on HHH and give him what he deserved, as opposed to being told by the promotion that this was the guy they should cheer. As January began, plans for Orton v. HHH at Wrestlemania were all but dead barring a miracle, and Batista v. HHH was penciled in.

That organic turn was best summed up by a night on RAW called "Beat the Clock," which was part of the excellent buildup to the New Year's Revolution show in January. In November, HHH had been stripped of the RAW World title because of a screwy finish to a three-way match with Benoit and Edge, and indeed all three of those contenders, along with Batista, Chris Jericho, and Randy Orton, were put into an Elimination Chamber match to settle the question of who the champion was. Ironically, the buildup of the show took all the focus off of Edge and Benoit, the two guys who actually had reason to claim ownership of the World title, but that's part of the reason why Edge was such a good heel at that point—it just gave him something else to whine about.

Anyway, Beat the Clock night was a really cool concept that gave some depth to what would normally be a plodding show filled with main eventers squashing lower-card guys. The deal was simple: Since the rules of the Elimination Chamber favor whoever actually enters the match last (much like the Royal Rumble), all six contenders would wrestle singles matches on that episode of RAW, and whoever won their match fastest, entered last. This was an amazing twist of writing logic, because it actually gave *drama* to the matches and made the audience care about the outcomes of meaningless drek like Randy Orton v. Maven or Batista v. Rhyno. In fact, Batista destroyed Rhyno so fast (in a little over three minutes) that HHH was then forced to beat Intercontinental champion Shelton Benjamin in less than that time, or forfeit the final spot. And since anyone who lost on the night would be replaced in the PPV match by the person who beat him, there was additional drama added by the fact that Benjamin had beaten HHH three times previously and was unbeaten against him. Of course, HHH won, but not fast enough to knock off Batista's mark, and suddenly there was more friction between the Evolution members. And why? Because Batista was being booked to look better than HHH and constantly show him up, something that no one else had been even close to doing. The match itself, which I thought they might give to Batista just to shake things up, was actually the best of the three Elimination Chamber matches and saw HHH very subtly betraying good friend Batista by not saving him from Randy Orton's RKO finisher when he had the chance. HHH then finished off Orton with the Pedigree to regain the World title, which ended up surprising exactly no one. This actually marked HHH's tenth World title, and it's well-known that he won't stop until he's reached Ric Flair's record of sixteen World title reigns. In fact, Flair's reigns can be stretched to twenty-one with some creative math, so there's a lot of HHH winning titles still to come in the future, I'm afraid.

That show, which was a smash hit with 375,000 buys, really showed the potential drawing power of Batista and also showed that actually taking the time to properly build up an important match could pay off with more money being made for the promotion. Crazy concept, I know. The show also marked the effective end of Maven's career, as he was given an effective heel turn a month earlier and was programmed against Intercontinental champion Shelton Benjamin in an important feud for him. However, the resulting match on the PPV was such a disappointment, with Maven stalling endlessly before falling victim to a quick pin, that he was immediately depushed again and punished with job after job, until finally getting the ax in July of that year. That cut actually showed the shockingly ineffective success rate of the Tough Enough program, as there was almost no one from the shows left on the roster as of 2005. The victims to date:

- Tough Enough #1 winners Maven and Nidia both made it to the main roster fairly quickly, but Maven suffered from a series of

BELOW: Al Snow

injuries and Nidia got shafted with a bad trade to RAW after a hot start as Jamie Noble's on-screen girlfriend on Smackdown. Nidia's reinvention in 2004 as a "spitfire" (according to Jim Ross) who was a spunky babyface wrestler bored the shit out of the fans, and she was fired soon after. Maven was fired in the next round of cuts. Additionally, runner-up Chris "Harvard" Nowinski had a promising start as a cocky heel on RAW, but a series of concussions left him on the shelf for more than a year, and he never returned, as they forced him into retirement at a very young age. And people actually accused him of milking the injury before that happened. Oddly enough, the only signee out of the group to actually survive the cuts was Josh "Matthews" Lumburger, who dropped his wrestling career altogether and became a B-show announcer for the WWE instead.

- Tough Enough #2 winners Jackie Gayda and Linda Miles were both briefly used as in-ring performers, but both were moved to valet roles instead. Jackie married Charlie Haas in 2005 and both were fired as a honeymoon present, while Linda Miles was axed for speaking too highly of herself well before then. Matt Morgan, who quit the show due to injuries but was signed quickly after that because of his size, was given multiple shots at a push and was fired in the bloodletting of 2005 when he too failed to get over.

- Tough Enough #3 winners Matt Cappotelli and John Hennigan have yet to be fired, and in fact Hennigan went on to be half of the Smackdown tag team champions as Johnny Nitro of MNM. Who knows if and when Capotelli will show his face on TV again—possibly after Bob Holly retires, I'd imagine. He was originally supposed to win the Cruiserweight title from Chavo Guerrero in early 2004 as his big debut, but another injury suffered at the hands of Bob Holly took care of that plan, and woman's wrestler Jacqueline was used instead. No, I don't know how that works, either.

- Tough Enough #4 winner Daniel Puder has yet to debut on TV yet, but contestant Marty Wright debuted in July 2005 as "The Boogeyman," and certainly time will tell with *that* one. I'm gonna go out on a limb and say it'll bomb.

Puder was actually the subject of a bit of controversy early in his run for the Tough Enough title, as the contestants competed on Smackdown instead of a separate TV show like the first three groups had, and one of the ridiculous goals for the group was taking Kurt Angle down and pinning him in a short amateur

ABOVE: Al Snow

wrestling match. Puder was trained in mixed martial arts, however, and decided to make things a lot more interesting than they had been to that point, not only attempting to take Angle down but also locking him in a front chokehold and nearly making Angle tap out to stop the pain. It was all done within a few seconds and only mixed martial arts fans knew what to look for, but suddenly everyone backstage was squawking about how unprofessional Puder was being, and fans who were into the more realistic Ultimate Fighting Championship style of fighting were eating up the rookie Puder, and the WWE had a potentially big angle dropped right into their laps. Their response: They completely ignored it and continued booking the contenders in ridiculous challenges like seducing Bob Holly while wearing dresses, and in a notably bad moment at the Armageddon PPV, boxing each other to determine who is more skilled at a sport that has nothing to do with what they're supposed to be training for. Puder actually coasted on the controversy from the Angle situation and won the competition, but mysteriously has yet to show up on WWE TV since then. Long-term training or conspiracy? You decide.

Of course, January would not be January for wrestling fans without the Royal Rumble, and although the previous year's effort would be nigh impossible to top, there was certainly a lot more uncertainty about the possible winners of 2005's version. Well, "uncertainty" probably isn't a great choice of words, as there was a fifty-fifty shot of either Batista or John Cena winning the match and very little chance of anyone else doing so, but no one had any clue who would be booked as the winner out of the two. And wouldn't you know, it came down to RAW's hottest act, Batista, against Smackdown's hottest act, John Cena. The finish was seriously botched, as it was supposed to see Batista clothesline Cena out and hang on for the win, but he gave himself too much momentum and hit the floor at the same time, thus necessitating Vince McMahon calling an audible by running out and restarting the match. Vince's run-in was actually an amazing thing later on, because when he slid into the ring and stood up, he tore both quad muscles on his legs and was rushed to hospital after the show. Doctors thought he would remain in a wheelchair for months and could possibly walk again by Christmas, which would match the amazing progress made by HHH after his similar injury in 2001. Vince, who is clearly an alien sent from planet Steroid to destroy us all, was out of the wheelchair in weeks and strutting again by Wrestlemania, looking no worse for wear. I only hope that when I turn 150 like Vince, I'm half as spry as he is.

Anyway, Batista's win cemented him as a main eventer and essentially finished off his face turn, as he was clearly favored by the fans now, despite his continued association with HHH. This led to HHH making an obvious and hamfisted attempt to "secretly" implicated JBL in a plot to send Batista to Smackdown and thus keep him away from the RAW World title match at Wrestlemania, and that marked the point where the effectiveness of the character started to wane for me a bit. Really, the appeal of the guy was that he was always one step ahead of HHH, but now he was several behind. Even worse, they could have redeemed the whole thing by having Batista reveal that he knew all along, but instead chose to have HHH and Flair discussing their plot openly, like drunken Bond villains after a night on the town, while Batista listened from another room. I mean, even the little kids watching had the plot figured out by that point, and to make Batista look like such an idiot that he needed HHH to explain the plot step by step for the audience was not only insulting the intelligence of Batista but of the audience as well.

For his part, HHH defended the title against Randy Orton at the Rumble, in a match that marked the effective end of Orton's interminable babyface push, putting him away cleanly with the Pedigree after Orton suffered a "concussion" during the match. This would prove to be Orton's last shot at the title, and he left for Smackdown having completely failed in every aspect of his feud with HHH—he got turfed out of Evolution for winning the World title when he was only supposed to "soften up" Benoit for the boss, then lost the title to HHH only a month later, swore revenge for that, and failed to beat him when left one on one at the end of New Year's Revolution, and finally choked in his last shot at the belt at the Rumble. Truly, his babyface run from September to January is one of the most spectacular failures, in story line terms and in box office terms, since the glory days of Lex Luger doing the same stuff in the '80s. Orton's character went a little crazy leading up to Wrestlemania, turning heel and challenging the Undertaker in a desperate attempt to rekindle his Legend Killer moniker and end Undertaker's Wrestlemania winning streak.

But before that, there's still the matter of what happened to John Cena after the Rumble . . .

## ★ ★ NO WAY OUT (SMACKDOWN BRAND) ★ ★

DATE: February 20, 2005
LOCATION: Pittsburgh, PA
ATTENDANCE: 8,000
BUYRATE: 240,000 buys

### RESULTS:

Rey Mysterio & Eddie Guerrero
d. Smackdown tag team champions The Basham Brothers (14:47, ★★½)

Booker T. d. John Heidenreich (6:49, DQ, ½★)

Chavo Guerrero d. WWE Cruiserweight champion
Funaki, Paul London, Shannon Moore, Spike Dudley,
and Akio (9:47, ★½)

Undertaker d. Luther Reigns (11:42, ★)

John Cena d. Kurt Angle (19:20, ★★★¾)

Smackdown World champion JBL
d. Big Show in a barbed wire cage match (14:50, ★★¼)

**SO IN THE SPIRIT** of doing things a bit differently for this month's recap, I present an exclusive, never-before-seen PPV rant in its entirety. A word of explanation: When this show originally aired in February 2005, I was busy preparing for my nuptials the following week, and was busy getting drunk, tattooed, and hanging out at strip clubs the weekend of the show. And then came my bachelor party! Thank you, I'm here until Thursday, try the veal. Anyway, since I had more important things to do than write a rant on the show at that point, I left it on the "to do" pile for months, until I figured that since people had waited this long for the rant anyway, waiting a little longer and spending a few bucks to buy the book wouldn't kill them, either. While normally I have included snippets of the PPV rants in the form of specific match recaps in my past books, this marks the first time that I'm giving you an entire PPV rant, uncut, and entirely unpublished before now.

*The SmarK Rant for WWE No Way Out 2005*
    —*Live from Pittsburgh, PA*
    —*Your hosts are Michael Cole and Tazz*
    —*Opening match, Smackdown tag team titles:*
*The Basham Brothers v. Eddie Guerrero and Rey*
*Mysterio.* This is one of those backward-booking
deals, where they knew they wanted Eddie v. Rey
at Wrestlemania and needed a way to get there,
so the natural first step was to have them team up
and challenge the tag champions. Kind of sad
that Eddie would go from main eventing the previous year's version of this show and winning the
World title, to opening the show. This was set
up, story line–wise, by Rob Van Dam suffering
an injury (a real one) and thus not being able to
wrestle here in a rematch for the titles. The
Bashams, desperately needing any kind of career
boost to give them personality, had just recently
joined JBL's "Cabinet" as secretaries of defense,
to go along with the prestigious appointment of
Buckwheat lookalike jobber Orlando Jordan.

Eddie starts out with Danny and they do some
trash talking, but Eddie grabs a headlock right
away and takes him down by the leg. Rey comes
in and nails him in the corner, and follows with
a legdrop for two. Rey gets caught in the heel
corner and double-teamed briefly, but comes
back with an armdrag on Doug and it's back to
the challengers again. Eddie works him over in
the corner and snaps off a rana, but it's more
double teaming from the Bashams. Danny uses a

straitjacket choke on Eddie to slow him down,
but gets caught with a backdrop suplex to break
that up. Doug cuts off any potential tag and elbows him down for two, but walks into a boot.
Doug comes back with a powerslam for two, but
Eddie tags Rey back in, and he's the proverbial
house of fire. Crossbody gets two on Doug, and
the Rube Goldberg bulldog (called a DDT by
Michael Cole) gets two. However, the Bashams
do the old switcheroo and take over, as Rey is
*your* face-in-peril. I always thought that the
Bashams should do the switching gimmick with
S&M masks, ala the Killer Bees, but sadly that
gimmick was dropped early in 2004.

Danny puts Rey in a full nelson for the big
sympathy spot and beats on him in the corner,
and it's more heel shenanigans as Eddie gets involved with the referee. The Bashams drop Rey
on the top rope for two. The match really grinds
to a halt as Danny chokes away and cuts off a tag,
allowing Doug to come back in and follow up
with a backdrop superplex attempt. Rey fights
out of it and comes down with a moonsault press
for two. Then it's back to the restholds, as Danny
clamps on a chinlock to prevent Rey from tag-
ging again. Yeah, it's old school babyface heat
stuff, but I like a more energetic approach to
beating on a babyface for sympathy. The
Bashams hit Rey with a double inverted powerbomb, but Eddie breaks up the count at two.

Rey keeps fighting, dodging the Bashams, and

making the hot tag to Eddie, and he's all over them. Backdrops for everyone and he dropkicks Doug, then takes them both down with a flying headscissors that gets two on Danny. The Bashams hit Eddie with a sloppy double chokeslam and that gets two for Danny. Another double team backfires, as they try a double suplex and Rey spears Danny into a cradle from Eddie for two. Eddie stops and grabs one of the tag belts, hoping to cheat and thus win, but the Bashams do a switch while Rey tries to argue some morality into him. Back in, Eddie misses the frog splash and recovers, but then plays dead to trick Doug into thinking he splatted. That bit of chicanery gets two off a rollup. Danny tosses the belt into the ring and the ref takes it away, but Rey tosses the other belt to Eddie and he hits Doug with it for the pin and the titles at 14:47. That ending looked all kinds of messed up, as the timing was way off, and Rey using the belt after yelling at Eddie about breaking the rules earlier in the match didn't make sense. ✶✶½

—Next up, the "Rookie Diva Talent Competition," aka "Time to fast forward." They all ended up fired by the middle of year, if you care, including color commentator Dawn Marie.

—*John Heidenreich v. Booker T.* This was the ugly period for Heidenreich in between his endless feud with the Undertaker and his idiotic face turn. The poem he reads before the match was pretty good, though. Booker powers him into the corner to start, but gets clubbed down with the clubbing forearms that club. Clothesline gets two for Heidenreich. Thank god for auto-complete when Heidenreich is wrestling, otherwise his matches would take me another ten minutes each while I spell check. Booker slugs back and runs into an elbow, which allows him to roll out and take a breather. They brawl outside and Booker gains control, as I ponder exactly what Heidenreich is supposed to be doing while "selling." Seriously, the guy is *awful* at it, making goofy faces and veering wildly between being totally in control and looking out of it.

Heidenreich comes back with a clothesline (yes, another one) and stomps away on him, then sends him into the post. That allows Heidenreich to work on the arm, really picking up the frenetic pace of the match, but Booker fights out of the wristlock. Heidenreich elbows him down again, really showing his range in the ring tonight, and goes back to that wristlock. Booker fights back with a spinebuster and the sidekick. Heidenreich sells it like he's dead, because he has no in-between shades of selling, and Booker goes for the finish with the axe kick, but misses. Heidenreich also blocks the Bookend, but clotheslines Heidenreich to the floor. They fight over to the announce table and Heidenreich grabs a chair for the DQ at 6:49. The crowd boos the crap out of that finish, rightfully so. This was quite terrible and they tried to drag the feud longer before turning Heidenreich face a few weeks later. ½✦

—WWE Cruiserweight Title: *Funaki v. Spike Dudley v. Paul London v. Chavo Guerrero v. Shannon Moore v. Akio.* We start with Paul London against fluke Cruiserweight champion Funaki. Funaki, used mainly as an announcer for years, was given the title in December to show how little they cared about the belt at that point. London overpowers him to start and gets an armdrag. He dives on Funaki out of the corner, but misses a charge and gets bulldogged for two. Funaki tries to finish, with whatever his finisher is, but Spike Dudley trips him up and London rolls him up for the pin at 1:39. Next up, Spike Dudley v. Paul London. Spike works him over in the corner, but Funaki trips up Spike to give London the pin at 1:59.

**ABOVE: Funaki, Spike Dudley and Chavo Guerrero**

Next up, Paul London v. Shannon Moore. Moore comes in and gets two on London, and a rollup for two. Backslide gets two. He grabs a headlock, but London rolls him up for two. Moore whips London into the corner a few times and goes up, but misses a moonsault and London finishes him with the 450 splash at 3:37. So now it's Akio v. Paul London, the main event of many Velocity shows throughout 2004. Akio kicks him down for two right away, then brings him into the corner for a version of Tajiri's Tarantula. That gets two. Akio hits the chinlock and follows with an enzuigiri for two. He keeps stomping away and chops London in the corner, but Paul comes back with a neckbreaker off the top rope to put them both down for the count. London makes it back up first to break the count, but Akio stays down and he's gone at 7:05. Stupid finish.

**BELOW: Spike Dudley, Funaki and Chavo Guerrero**

So that leaves Chavo v. London for the title. Chavo pounds on the tired London (although the match has only gone seven minutes thus far) and works a cover for several two counts. This brings up the unique physics of wrestling, where time elapsed is a subjective matter and people can act like they've exerted twenty minutes' worth of energy in a two-minute TV match. I think it has something to do with Einstein's theory of relativity. Not to be confused with HHH's theory of relatives, which is how he has stayed on top for five years. London reverses a slam into a cradle for two, but Chavo pounds him down again. London comes back with a Northern Lights suplex for two and makes the comeback, firing away with forearms and a backdrop. Rollup gets two, but Chavo reverses and holds the

ropes for the pin and the title at 9:47. Cheap finish, incredibly rushed match that meant nothing. Chavo would suffer an injury and lose the title to London a month after this, and pretty much everyone else involved in the match would be fired in the bloodletting of 2005. ½✶

—After fast forwarding through more crap from the Divas, we head back to JBL, who delivers a variation of his famous "I am a wrestling god" interview from Royal Rumble. JBL actually became one of the best talkers in the business by the end of his seemingly never ending title reign, but unfortunately couldn't back it up in the ring outside of garbage matches.

—*Undertaker v. Luther Reigns.* This was the last-ditch effort to get anything out of Reigns, as they pushed him against Undertaker in hopes of getting him some heel heat. It didn't work.

Reigns slugs away to start, but runs into a big boot that gets two for Undertaker. Taker works the arm and it's the Ropewalk of Doom, with a foot of space between Taker's arm and Luther's head, and he gets two off a Downward Spiral. Taker chokes away and goes after the ref with some harsh words, and that allows Reigns to undo the turnbuckle. They fight over that and slug it out in the corner, and that drags on for a while. They seriously just keep punching each other for like two minutes, and then awkwardly work into a spot where Reigns gets whipped into his own exposed turnbuckle. Irony can truly be a fickle mistress.

Taker pulls the prone Reigns out to the apron and elbows him in the throat, which is apparently "vintage Undertaker" according to Michael Cole. Man, no need to verbally blow the guy every time he does a simple move. Back into the ring, Undertaker now tastes the bitter cold steel of the exposed turnbuckle, and I bet it doesn't taste good! Reigns stomps away on him and whips him into the corners, not thinking about, say, whipping him back into the exposed turn-buckle corner instead, and gets a suplex for two. The crowd is deathly silent as Reigns's dull offensive series continues and he pounds away on the back and drops an elbow for two. This sets up a half crab from Reigns out of a lame kneebar and Undertaker slugs out. Michael Cole calls that "throwing hands," which makes me want to "throw hands" right in his face to shut him up.

Taker throws hands and gets two on Reigns. Undertaker tries a comeback, but no, the boring Reigns's offense continues, as he spears Taker and gets two. Another elbow gets two. This match is going *nowhere*. And not even nowhere fast, nowhere *slow*. Reigns tries for the Test Drive neckbreaker, but Undertaker fights out and gets some clothesline in the corner. He tries Snake Eyes, but Reigns seems unaware of what was being tried and doesn't sell properly, so Taker boots him down and drops the leg for two. Chokeslam sets up the tombstone, but Reigns escapes and gets an inverted DDT. Cole interprets this as a swinging neckbreaker, which is interesting because it was neither a neckbreaker nor swinging, and then proceeds to say "swinging neckbreaker" about eighteen times until I want to "throw hands" at him again. Reigns tries it again, prompting Cole to say it again, but Undertaker reverses to a DDT and finishes this boring-ass crapfest with the tombstone piledriver at 11:42. Thank god. ✶

—#1 Contender tournament final: *Kurt Angle v. John Cena.* This was the finals of yet another derivative tournament to determine who gets a title shot, which was seen in various forms seemingly millions of times through 2004 and then again multiple times in 2005. John Cena was still the U.S. champion at this point, and consensus was that Cena needed to go over big time and in dominating fashion to get him ready to co-headline Wrestlemania against JBL and carry the World title.

Angle takes him down with a headlock to start and hangs onto that, preventing Cena from escaping a couple of times. Cena finally brings him into the corner to force a break, and then tries his own headlock. Angle quickly schools him by reversing to his own facelock on the mat, but Cena fights out of it. Angle gets clotheslined to the floor and they brawl onto the announce table, where Cena shows good fire and hammers away on Angle. Back in, Cena gets two. He pounds away in the corner and catches Angle with a clothesline out of the corner, setting up the F-U. Angle wriggles free from that and bails out of the ring. Back in, Cena stomps away in the corner, but Angle cuts him off and reverses another attempt at the clothesline out of the corner, turning it into a german suplex into the turnbuckles. Ouch, man.

Angle goes right after the neck now, hitting a snap suplex for two and grinding his arm into the neck on the mat. Backbreaker gets two. Angle stomps away and takes him down with a bodyscissors. Cena fights up out of that and elbows Angle down, but gets caught with another german suplex, which turns into the rolling germans. That gets two. Cena comes back with a flying shoulder tackle, which Cole refers to as his

"pound and ground" offense. Notwithstanding that the proper term is "ground and pound," as taken from the Ultimate Fighting Championship, I fail to see how jumping in the air fits the definition of "ground" in the first place.

Angle goes to the eyes, but Cena hits him with a spinebuster for two. Angle comes back with the german suplexes again, but Cena catches him with a backdrop suplex into a powerbomb for two. Another try at the F-U is reversed by Angle into a sunset flip for two, and Angle snaps off an overhead suplex to put Cena down again. This allows Angle to hit Cena with an Angle Slam, but Cena reverses out and DDTs him for two. Another try at the F-U, but Angle reverses that into the anklelock. Cena kicks him out of the ring to escape, however. Cena actually goes up and guillotines Angle with a legdrop as he's coming back in, and gets two. Nice bit of thinking on his feet there. He charges into the corner and hits boot, but recovers with the F-U and gets two. This marked one of the few times someone kicked out of the F-U, in fact.

Cena stops to celebrate prematurely, and Angle kicks him in the knee and goes to work on the ankle, getting ready to go for the kill with the anklelock again. He rams Cena's ankle into the post, and he's just an absolute master of drawing sympathy heat for Cena, as he applies a leg lock to Cena and forces him to get to the ropes. He keeps stomping the ankle and softens him up with the Angle Slam, leading to the anklelock. Normally, this is certain death for any babyface caught in the move, but Cena is the Chosen One and so he gets to fight to the ropes, forcing Angle to switch to the unbreakable heel hook. Cena makes the ropes, however, and the ref gets caught in the middle and knocked out. First ref bump on the night, actually, which is rare for them.

ABOVE: Big Show

Angle goes for Cena's chain, but gets speared into the corner while thinking it over, and Cena finishes with the F-U at 19:20 to earn the Wrestlemania title shot. Real good effort from Cena here, as Angle always brings out the best in him. Not as technically good as a lot of Angle's stuff, but the point was to make Cena look like a world-beater, and that's exactly what it accomplished, as he survived all of Angle's crazy counters and fought out of the unbreakable heel hook to get the clean pinfall. ✶✶✶¾

—Smackdown World Title, *Barbed-Wire Cage Match: JBL v. Big Show.* As usual, the rules are the standard pin, submission, or escape. This was set up by a three-way title defense at Royal Rumble, where JBL beat both Big Show and Kurt Angle in a better-than-average match, but screwed over Big Show to do so. So this is the re-

match, in a cage designed to cash in on the ECW craze of 2005. Odd that they'd choose to cash in on that craze by sticking two of the guys most hated by ECW fans into this kind of match. Although the match was sold on the barbed-wire aspect as though it was covering the cage, the wire was only at the very top of the cage and would never be used in the entire match.

Show slugs JBL down to start and pounds him in the corner, but JBL shoulderblocks him down. Neckbreaker allows JBL to climb the cage, but he balks at the barbed wire on top of it and changes his mind. He opts for a crossbody attempt instead, but Show slams him for two. Show keeps pounding him in the corner, but JBL climbs again. He stops at the wire again and tries another shoulderblock instead, but Show simply stands there and knocks him down, then suplexes him. JBL comes back and sends him into the cage to take over. Show starts bleeding, so JBL hits him with a flying shoulderblock and starts chopping. Show goes down and JBL boots him in the head and drops an elbow for two. He undoes one of the leftover tag ropes and chokes Show down, squeezing more blood out of him, and clubs him down with the clubbing forearms.

Show fights back with a big boot and a power-bomb, looking awkward while doing so, and now it's JBL's time to bleed. He's a hell of a bleeder, I'll give him that. Show sends him into the cage to work on the cut, but now JBL's flunkies run out and try to get into the cage with a pair of bolt cutters. General Manager Teddy Long boots them all out of the arena again, but Orlando Jordan gives JBL the bolt cutters before he goes, and JBL slugs him down and adds the Clothesline from Hell, which looks to finish but only gets two. This match is totally heatless, as the fans don't even pop for that near-fall.

Another go at the clothesline is blocked by Show, who chokeslams JBL for two. JBL goes low, however, and another clothesline gets two. This one is not quite from hell, merely from a close substitute, like New Jersey. They fight up to the top and slug it out on the top rope in a spot that means nothing toward the match and is only there to set up the big special effect for the match: Big Show chokeslamming JBL to the mat and right through it, creating a giant hole in the

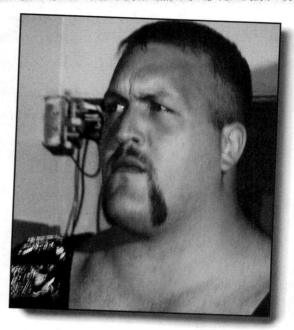

**ABOVE: Big Show**

ring. Show casually walks to the door and escapes from the cage, but *wait* . . . it turns out that JBL actually crawled right out via the hole created by his fall, and thus wins the match.

This was not made clear by the camera angles in the least, as they opted for going for the surprise finish by not focusing on JBL's escape and instead following Show out of the ring. This left the crowd totally deflated and confused, much like this match made me feel while I was watching it. Sometimes "creative" is not necessarily "good." This would prove to be the final "skin of his teeth" title defense for JBL, however, as his luck (and eight-month title reign) came to an end at Wrestlemania 21. ✶✶¼

The Bottom Line: Although as of this writing we're only about seven PPVs into 2005, this one easily ranks as the worst of the year thus far, totally eclipsed by the Wrestlemania show that followed it, even more eclipsed by the next Smackdown show (Judgment Day), which redeemed JBL somewhat as a worker, and blown away by all three RAW PPVs that surrounded it, not to mention the ECW PPV in June. I'm sure the WWE has it in them to do something worse, more than likely at the Great American Bash in July, but I don't see how. Strong recommendation to avoid.

# MARCH 2005 AND BEYOND

## ★ ★ ★ ★ WRESTLEMANIA 21 ★ ★ ★ ★ ★

FROM: Los Angeles, CA
DATE: April 3, 2005
ATTENDANCE: 20,193
BUYRATE: 950,000 buys
ADVERTISED MAIN EVENT: HHH v. Batista

### RESULTS:

Rey Mysterio d. Eddie Guerrero (12:37, ★★★¼)

Edge d. Chris Benoit, Chris Jericho, Shelton Benjamin, Christian, & Kane (15:22, ★★★★¾)

Undertaker d. Randy Orton (14:11, ★★¾)

WWE Women's champion Trish Stratus d. Christy Hemme (4:41, DUD)

Kurt Angle d. Shawn Michaels (26;14, ★★★★¾)

Akebono d. Big Show in a sumo match (no rating)

John Cena d. Smackdown World champion JBL (11:25, ★¼)

Batista d. RAW World champion HHH (21:34, ★★¾)

**AND SO AFTER** two years of trying new stars and re-pushing the old ones, we end up at Wrestlemania XXI in Los Angeles, dubbed "Wrestlemania goes Hollywood" by the marketing machine, despite the show not being in Hollywood and the people involved all being lousy actors. But semantics like the truth have never stopped the WWE before, and why would they let it get in the way of a good show?

The promotional build for the show was actually quite interesting from a marketing standpoint, as they chose to focus more on the "Hollywood" atmosphere of the show rather than building up strong, money-drawing matches. Linda McMahon boldly claimed in an investor's conference before the show that they were shooting for 1,000,000 buys as a number. That sentence is more effective if you read that like Dr. Evil, by the way. Point being, this seemed like an excessively large number for a show that seemed to be more in the 650,000 buy range as far as the card went. However, the WWE seemed to have the last laugh when initial estimates came in close to that goal. Later, it was learned that in fact that number was higher because the show was available in more countries, so the actual North American tally was in fact closer to 650,000, but either way a buck is a buck and it was a nice chunk of change. Still, it hammered home the point that without the international market, the WWE would be in serious trouble in 2005.

As for Wrestlemania . . .

*Rey Mysterio v. Eddie Guerrero* This was set up when Rey and Eddie won the tag team titles at the No Way Out show in February, although as mentioned it was mainly backward booking to set up this feud. That is to say, they came up with the idea of Rey v. Eddie at Wrestlemania to appeal to the Latino crowd, which would make up a significant portion of the crowd, and to get there they went with the "First time that tag team champions are wrestling each other at Wrestlemania" story line. In a more general sense the story line was that Eddie was frustrated by Rey's success, as opposed to his losing streak leading up to the show. Really, however, the point of the match was to see if they could top themselves and deliver a better match than their legendary showdown at the WCW's Halloween Havoc in 1997. Eddie in particular felt pressured, mainly by himself, to snap himself out of the in-ring funk he had been in since the previous summer and do something memorable to open the show. Sadly, that pressure seemed to show on both of them, as Rey got a rare case of nerves and blew several trademark spots, seemingly more absorbed by the minutia of trying to

keep his mask straight than thinking about the match. Eddie tried to compensate, but given the shortened time of the match compared to what they were needing, it just never clicked. Rey won the match with a surprise rollup at 12:37, setting up a heel turn for Eddie later in the spring, and setting up a feud between them that lasted well into the summer.

"Money in the Bank" Ladder Match *Edge v. Chris Benoit v. Chris Jericho v. Shelton Benjamin v. Christian v. Kane* First, the inclusion of Kane in this seemed like an odd choice, given the contrast in styles that it would produce, and second because it seemed like the perfect place to bring Matt Hardy (who was ready to return from knee surgery) back into the fold. At any rate, this was set up by the most ham-fisted type of buildup possible, as the story line essentially had Chris Jericho campaigning for a big Wrestlemania match that people would remember. The result was the "Everyone not doing anything better" crew getting rounded up and stuck in here, with the prize being an open contract for the winner to face the World champion, whoever he may be, whenever the winner wanted, for a period up to one year from this match. However, it was kind of sad that the Intercontinental champion, Shelton Benjamin, was put into this situation. You'd think that the secondary champion should already be the #1 contender in theory, so that was bad enough, plus the title meant so little that it wasn't even being defended at the biggest show of the year (for the second year in a row, by the way). However, great wrestling makes me forgive lots of stupid stuff, and this was no exception.

In the tradition of the "TLC" ladder matches of the past few years, a genre that had become burned out, the six competitors once again reinvented the ladder match. The result was a major coming-out performance by Shelton Benjamin, as he seemingly defied gravity at points. More importantly, all the big "holy shit" spots in the match were established in a manner that was intelligent and didn't make the audience groan five minutes in advance of them happening. I mean, when someone is setting up six different ladders and there's six guys in the match, there's not much surprise when all of them climb up the ladders and do big moves off them. However, in this case things were done seemingly without reason (like one ladder falling onto another at an angle), which then become something else entirely (like Shelton Benjamin running up those ladders like they were a ramp and launching himself off them). Those are the best kind of spots, I think. Also, given the people involved, all of them were smart enough by this point in their careers not to do the annoying "slow climb" spots that have plagued ladder matches in the past. "Slow climbing," as the name implies, is the act of taking far too much time in walking up the rungs of the ladder far slower than any human being without

severe vertigo would be capable of doing. The goal is to build drama by allowing the other guy more time to make the "unexpected" save, but really when the guy is stopping on the third rung to order a pizza, it's time to speed things up. Thankfully, this was not the case here, as people sprung up and down the ladders at warp speed and there was always someone handy to believably make the save. And finally, Chris Benoit was the other star of the match, although not in the same fashion as Benjamin's flashy spots, by doing something really rare for a ladder match: Consistently selling injuries from start to finish and building up drama for the audience the old-fashioned way, by getting his ass whopped for ten minutes. The result of all of this was probably one of the best ladder matches in recent history, as all the factors came together when a series of crazy spots left everyone incapacitated and Edge took advantage of the injured Benoit, hitting him with a chair and climbing the ladder to win the contract at 15:22. This match nearly justified purchase of the show by itself, and at ✮✮✮✮¾ ranks highly on my top ten matches of 2005 list.

As a "cool down" segment for the fans, a skit with Eugene making his return and getting assaulted by Muhammad Hassan was put after the Money in the Bank match, but even that had a surprise ending. Yes, Hulk Hogan had another project to shill, so he made another return to the WWE after vowing never to deal with Vince

McMahon again the last time he did so. In this case, his new reality show *Hogan Knows Best* was the subject of his self-promotional tour. This had actually been easy to predict, because he was inducted into the WWE Hall of Fame a few nights before and had received a standing ovation from the fans, the length of which magically increases each time Hogan tells the story. The last version he was sharing had the ovation at twenty minutes, but that's actually a mild exaggeration compared to the whoppers that Hogan usually gives the mainstream media with regards to his career. Try reading his book sometime if you want several examples. Anyway, since Hogan had to defend America against the free speech being spewed by Muhammad Hassan, he hulked up and chased off the evil Americans of foreign heritage, and a match was set up for the next PPV, Backlash. This rationale actually reminded me of the classic xenophobic moron character portrayed by Hacksaw Jim Duggan, as he would prevent Nikolai Volkoff from singing his Russian national anthem, because America is the home of the free! At any rate, the silliness here didn't end with Hogan's confrontation with Hassan, as Shawn Michaels also ran into Hassan in the days following Wrestlemania. In a classic bit of mind-boggling lack of continuity, Shawn was upset at losing a fluke match to Hassan's manager Daivari on RAW, so he demanded a handicap match against Hassan and Daivari at Backlash. How-

ever, he was "forced" to find a partner by Eric Bischoff, for concerns of his safety, despite the fact that Bischoff was involved in a million lame story lines where he booked babyfaces in handicap matches just to be a jerk. In fact, he did a few more times after Shawn was refused his request. The result of all this was Hogan making his big return to wrestling, with Shawn as a partner, as they squashed Hassan and Daivari at Backlash. Hassan still wasn't getting over and could now add "Can't draw heat by beating on Shawn Michaels and Hulk Hogan" to his impressive resume of failures to that point. The all-American lovey-dovey crap spewed by both Hogan and Shawn, complete with tag team posing routines, just about had me retching up my lunch, until Shawn redeemed it all by turning on Hogan and going heel again later in the summer. Really, rather than the blowoff match between them, I think a more entertaining use of my money as a consumer would be filming the discussion backstage where they try to come up with the most creative excuse to avoid doing a job to the other guy.

*Undertaker v. Randy Orton* Okay, so I got a little off-track there. Anyway, next up was the match that hopefully put Randy Orton back on track toward being a superstar again. Hopefully, my bile toward Orton isn't misinterpreted as a result of this book, because I've been pretty harsh on him throughout. In fact, I think his heel persona is perfectly entertaining and he's a drastically improved wrestler since his rookie days, maybe one of the most improved in the shortest period of time ever. However, the babyface turn and resulting feud with HHH really rubbed me and others who enjoyed him as a heel the wrong way. By March, his character was going in kind of a strange meta textual direction, as he basically came to the realization that his career was stagnating as a face, and he decided to challenge the Undertaker at Wrestlemania and thus end the 12-0 winning streak accumulated by him. After turning on new on-screen girlfriend Stacy Keibler to really hammer home how bad of a person he was, and reuniting with permanent heel father Bob Orton Jr. to hammer home that he was *genetically* evil, he was ready to take the next step and end Undertaker's streak at twelve. However, besides the evil gene, he also had the injury-prone gene (hell, his dad wore a cast on his arm for like ten years) and suffered yet another shoulder injury a week before the show. Thus, instead of the logical finish of Orton killing the legend of Undertaker, it was Orton trying a tombstone piledriver and having it reversed by Undertaker at 14:11 for the pin. Really, having Orton win the match and then disappear for surgery for months afterward wouldn't have made sense, but it was probably the worst-timed injury possible for Orton, who was really heating up as a heel again because of the story line with Undertaker.

He was drafted to Smackdown in the spring and looked to resume the Undertaker feud once he recovered, although whether that will carry him to the top, as the WWE seems to want it to, remains to be seen.

WWE Women's Title: *Trish Stratus v. Christy Hemme* Yes, after investing $250,000 in Hemme, you had to know that she'd become involved as a wrestler at some point, although debuting her at Wrestlemania against the best female wrestler ever is something of a serious miscalculation on their part, I'd think, and shows how weak the division had become by that point. Trish of course easily dispatched Hemme in 4:41 with a kick. As a sidenote, Hemme was "trained" by Lita in the story line to build up the match. Having Lita, one of the sloppiest and most injury-prone women's wrestlers of the modern era, train anyone is like getting singing lessons from Vanilla Ice. Hemme's acting range is about as impressive as his, too. Sadly, following this match Trish began complaining of neck problems and didn't defend the title for months afterwards. Not that there's anyone left to defend against anyway.

*Kurt Angle v. Shawn Michaels* This was more of an old-fashioned grudge match, my favorite kind. Angle, who by now pretty much does what he wants story line–wise, wanted a Wrestlemania dream match with Shawn Michaels just to see if they could pull off a ✷✷✷✷✷ classic, and by god they came close. The buildup was pretty fantastic, too, with the surprise appearances of Shawn on Smackdown and Angle on RAW for the standard sneak attacks. Thankfully, they had completely backed off on having people cross brand lines in recent months, so when someone showed up on the other show, it was quite unexpected instead of cliché. The really cool build for the match came when the WWE called Shawn's former partner, Marty Jannetty, back into the fold for a two-show shot—one on RAW, one on Smackdown. Shawn and Marty did a nostalgia reunion on RAW against La Resistance (and looked better than every tag team currently working in the WWE, and how scary is *that*?), and with Marty's nostalgia built up, Kurt Angle destroyed him on Smackdown to really stick it to Shawn's fanbase. The Angle v. Jannetty TV match was actually quite fabulous, clocking in at around ✦✦✦✦¼ by my watch and really showing that Marty could still hang with all the kids called up by the WWE. In fact, he was given a contract as a result of his performances that week, but never showed up on TV. We later found out that this was due to an arrest for DUI, which violated his probation for a previous domestic violence charge, and thus he was in jail again. Unlike Steve Austin, who was an established star and used to make money for the company, all it earned Marty was another pink slip, instead of media attention and a spot on the show as "co-general manager." This is more like Hollywood than the WWE will ever admit. Vince always wants to be compared to movies rather than sports, but some comparisons are probably not what he wants to hear.

Back to the match again, as Michaels and Angle truly set the bar high for themselves and everyone else on the show, with each playing exactly to their strengths. Angle got to use lots of crazy counters, and Michaels had the living shit beaten out of him for twenty minutes. That, my friends, is the formula for a great match. The only true weakness with the match came at the finish, as Angle locked in his deadly submission move, the heel hook, and Shawn spent a superhuman amount of time in the move compared to everyone else in the business before tapping out like a man at 26:14. This flaw was *almost* redeemed by a bit earlier in the match where Kurt Angle pulled down the straps of his singlet to demonstrate his intensity, then pulled them back up again later so he could pull them down again. Almost, but not quite. Still, the match was ✦✦✦✦¾ according to me and many others, some of whom had it at the full ✦✦✦✦✦ (which I wouldn't argue with very strenuously at all) and essentially rocked my world and didn't even need to call me back the next day.

Sumo Match: *Akebono v. Big Show* This was set up because, uh, they wanted a sumo match between Big Show and Japanese sumo legend Akebono. Akebono won. That's pretty much it.

Smackdown World Title Match: *JBL v. John Cena* So as expected, John Cena's big babyface push to the top culminated here, in a match against a guy who had been World champion of Smackdown for longer than any human being should have to sit through. I mean, seriously, it was nearing a year as champion for JBL at that point—I think us fans who signed that petition had learned our lesson by then. The buildup for the match was once again "Stodgy old-school conservative battles loose cannon who plays by his own rules," and while both Cena and JBL were fantastic talkers by Wrestlemania XXI and really hammered home that JBL was desperate to keep the belt and Cena was desperate to prove himself and win the belt . . . well, the match just didn't deliver.

Cena had already been cost the U.S. title to JBL's main monkey boy Orlando Jordan, jobber among jobbers, and Cena was supposed to be pissed about that and a zillion other things, but when it came to the actual match, it was just, I dunno, two guys wrestling a match. And not a very good one at that, as most of the offense belonged to JBL and it was all "I punch you, you punch me" type of stuff that

**RIGHT: A-Train and John Cena**

never left the realm of the mundane. Even the finish, built up for a whole year, was anticlimactic, as Cena reversed the Clothesline from Hell into the F-U and got the pin out of nowhere at 11:25 to win the title. The crowd, accustomed to a series of near falls leading into the big finish, didn't even believe that particular near fall was *the* finish to the match, and barely popped for it, more shocked than elated.

Thankfully, they would have a rematch at the Judgment Day PPV in May that more than lived up to the expectations set by the build for their Wrestlemania match, wrestling exactly the kind of violent, bloody, over-the-top garbage brawl that they should have done at Wrestlemania. As a wrestling fan, I almost felt sorry for JBL, because he actually deserved to lose his title in a more dramatic and satisfying way than he did. Had they reversed the matches, with Cena beating a bloodied and cowered JBL into submission (as he did in the rematch), thus forcing the immensely proud champion to yield his life's obsession away, this would have been a fantastic end to the show. However, the other problem with the match then comes up, as the creative team constantly treated Smackdown like the B-show, despite it having more viewers than RAW when the numbers are translated to reality. Fans were so well trained by the WWE that they considered the Cena-JBL match a joke, something secondary to the *real* main event, which of course must always involve HHH. Cena, however, was becoming such a phenomenon with TV ratings and merchandise that he was moved to RAW, with his newly won (and pimped out) title, in the draft lottery of 2005.

RAW World Title: *HHH v. Batista* This was of course the "real" main event, as HHH finally defended against hot new babyface Batista. Sadly, the buildup to the match was far better than the feud that followed it, as Batista's turn resulted in him powerbombing HHH through a table to set up the actual match. Everything that followed was exponentially more dull, and the proverbial wad had been shot before they even stepped into

the ring together for the first time. The match itself was far too much of HHH forcing the unstoppable monster to stop and sell, and the crowd reactions were rather scary for the future of Batista. The crowd was more concerned about HHH not winning than they were about Batista losing, which shows how focused the promotion truly was toward HHH and making sure he was the only star worth investing emotions in. Batista was exposed completely here, with a long match and too much selling, but came back well to score a rare clean pinfall victory over HHH at 21:34, and thus win the RAW World title in the process.

In the aftermath of the show, much like the previous year, we had two brand new champions, untested with the titles. In 2004 it was Eddie Guerrero and Chris Benoit, in 2005 it was Batista and John Cena. I have no doubt that the titles will be off both guys by Wrestlemania XXII as they continue to recycle the same formula in hopes of finding their new can't-miss superstars, and I have no doubt that HHH will be involved again. Still, as long as they keep trying, I'll keep hoping for the best.

# BONUS CHAPTER JUNE 2005

*The SmarK Rant for WWE Vengeance 2005*

—*Live from Las Vegas, NV*

—*Your hosts are JR, King, and the Coach*

—Opening Match, Intercontinental Title: *Carlito v. Shelton Benjamin.* Carlito was only a week off winning the belt from Benjamin on RAW at this point, having jumped from Smackdown in the draft lottery of 2005, ending Shelton's eight-month reign as champion. They fight over a lockup to start and Shelton takes him down with a fireman's carry for two. Carlito takes him to the mat with a headscissors, but Shelton escapes and we're back to square one. Carlito pounds on the back, but Shelton slugs back and hits him with a knee to the gut for two. Carlito tries another headlock and gets nowhere, so he takes a break outside and decides to walk out on the match. Benjamin catches up to him and sends him back into the ring, where a snap suplex gets two. Carlito tries the old thumb to the eye, but Shelton pops up to the top and hits him with a flying clothesline for two. Carlito uses another cheapshot to gain control, and then chokes him down and out of the ring. Back in, that gets two. He hits a couple of slams while the crowd actually turns on Shelton, chanting "Shelton sucks" and cheering for Carlito. Weird.

And now it's chinlock time, as Carlito gets two off that. Shelton snaps back with a rollup for two, and the crowd boos him. Back to the chinlock goes Carlito. Shelton comes back with a back elbow, and the crowd boos him for that, too. Shelton makes the comeback with a samoan drop and gets two, selling an injury that prevents him from bounding around the ring like normal. They slug it out and Shelton wins that, then backdrops him into the neckbreaker for two. They fight up to the top and Shelton necksnaps him to bring him down, then springs in from the apron with a bulldog for two. Shelton goes for a german suplex, but Carlito grabs the ropes to block and undoes the turnbuckle pad in the corner. He hits Shelton with a bad looking powerbomb variation and Shelton comes back with the dragon whip kick, which sets up the stinger splash. Carlito moves, Shelton hits steel, and it's good night Irene at 12:49, as Carlito retains. I found this sluggish and awkward. ✶✶

—*Victoria v. Christy Hemme.* Victoria debuts her newer, more evil entrance music here and Xena leather outfit. This was set up by Victoria attacking a bunch of divas after a swimsuit competition, thus drawing a face pop, but it supposedly turned her heel. Hemme tackles her slugs away on the mat, then screeches a lot and chokes away in the corner. Her offensive output is stopped by Victoria, who hotshots her to take over and hangs her by the hair over her shoulder. Choking in the corner follows and Victoria grabs a chinlock. Hemme fights back as the announcers say "spitfire" about nineteen times in reference to her, but Victoria slugs her down again and goes for the Widow's Peak. Hemme reverses out of it, so Victoria beats on her in the corner. She goes up to try a moonsault, but misses, and Hemme comes back with the usual clichéd hairtosses that all bad women's wrestlers do. A DDT gets two. A sunset flip out of the corner, however, is blocked by Victoria for the pin at 5:06. Total waste of PPV time, as the feud was never followed up on TV. ¼✶

—*Kane v. Edge.* Kane beats on him in the corner to start and slugs away, then backdrops him. More punching in the corner and the crowd wants Matt. Kane clotheslines him out and goes after ex-wife Lita, then stomps Edge a little bit more back in the ring. The crowd lets us know that Lita is a crack whore as Kane drops an elbow and chokes away. Edge bails to the apron and Kane hammers him to the floor, but gets speared while going after him. Edge stomps away back in the ring as he takes over, and spears him into the corner. All this kick and punch offense is gonna put me to sleep. More choking, to really pick up the pace. Edge slugs away and Kane no-sells it and punches him right back. Edge hits him with the Edge-o-Matic, but Kane does the zombie situp and thus panics Edge. Kane comes back with, you guessed it, more punches, and drops Edge in the corner with Snake Eyes to set up a clothesline for two. The usual cut-and-paste offense from Kane continues with a sideslam and flying clothesline, but Edge blocks that clothesline with a dropkick. Kane no-sells, but Snitsky runs in, as does Lita. She does the old fake seduction trick, but Kane, role model to kids everywhere, chokes her down and grabs a chair. This allows Snitsky to boot him down, and Edge gets two. Kane keeps no-selling, blocking a DDT from Edge, and getting rid of Snitsky. Chokeslam finishes for Kane at 11:11. Incredibly boring match that triggered *two* rematches on RAW before they gave up on trying to get this stupid feud over. ✶½

—*Shawn Michaels v. Kurt Angle.* Yup, it's the rematch from Wrestlemania, which was basically set up with one show by Shawn saying "Um, you want a rematch" and Angle being all "Uh, yeah" and that was pretty much it. Angle was essentially moved from Smackdown for this rematch, and because he's Kurt Angle and can do whatever he wants at this point. They fight over a lockup to start and Angle takes him down to the mat, but Shawn quickly escapes to the ropes. Shawn grabs a headlock, but Angle counters him with a single-leg takedown, and they both back off. Angle goes back to the headlock, but Shawn hiptosses out and grabs an armbar. Angle escapes by going after Shawn's arm in turn, and Shawn bails and recovers outside. Back in, Shawn starts throwing chops, so Angle backs off. Angle gets another takedown, so Shawn backs off. Angle tries the takedown again and starts fighting for the anklelock, but Shawn fights him off and he has to settle for a half-crab instead. Shawn quickly makes the ropes. Shawn goes back to the chops in the corner and goes up with a sunset flip for one, but Angle quickly reverses to the anklelock. Nice sequence! Shawn makes the ropes and pushes Angle out of the ring as a result.

They head outside and Angle tries to Angle Slam Shawn into the post in a repeat of the Wrestlemania spot, but Shawn escapes from that. Angle makes the most of the situation and german suplexes him headfirst into the table instead. Dear god, that was nasty. Back in, Angle gets two off that. Angle, Mr. Intensity, yanks him up by the ponytail and knees him in the face, then a neckbreaker gets two. Another great thing about Angle—he varies up his offense, throwing in stuff like neckbreakers that you don't expect from him. Angle chokes him in the corner and

stomps away, which pretty much negates any cheers he might have been getting, and he goes about the task of beating the hell out of Shawn Michaels, another guaranteed heel heat response. Shawn tries fighting back, but Angle powerbombs him into the turnbuckles, and gets two. Talk about abusing the guy's neck. See what I mean about mixing up the offense, though?

Angle drops some elbows and fires off a suplex for two. He goes to a chinlock, which does fit with the psychology of the neck injury at least. Shawn fights up, so Angle flattens him with a german suplex for two. Shawn is taking the beating of a lifetime here. I love it. Angle Slam is reversed to an armdrag by Shawn, but Angle clotheslines him down again for two. They head up to the top and Angle tries a superplex, but Shawn slugs him down to block it. However, he jumps off and lands into a belly-to-belly suplex from Angle, which gets two. Angle grabs a sleeperhold and holds Shawn on the mat for a few near falls. Shawn fights up again and escapes with a backdrop suplex, and it's a double KO. They slug it out and Shawn makes the comeback with the kip up and the inverted atomic drop. He goes up and drops the flying elbow, and just when it's time for the superkick, Angle pops up and clotheslines him with *mustard*. Well, so much for that comeback.

Angle Slam is reversed to a DDT by Shawn, however, and that gets two. Shawn stays on top, however, and makes Angle keep kicking out of it. Shawn tries a suplex, but Angle reverses right into the rolling germans and the Angle Slam out of that. That gets two. Angle goes for the anklelock, but Shawn cradles for two, and then Angle just hangs on and applies the move. Shawn reverses Angle into the ref, however, and it's ref bump time. Shawn charges and gets dumped to the floor (as sensitive fans in the front row yell "C'mon Shawn, shake it off!") but he hurts his knee. Angle is all over it, of course, and pulls down the straps to really emphasize his intensity. It's anklelock time, although really that doesn't do much against Shawn's bad knee. Shawn manages to kick away from the move, but Angle hangs on viciously, much like Wrestlemania XXI. Shawn tries to make the ropes, but gets pulled back into the middle of the ring again and looks ready to tap. One more reversal sends Angle into the corner, however, and breaks the hold. Angle charges in to finish, but Shawn superkicks him absolutely out of nowhere and both guys are out again. Shawn rolls over and gets two. Angle, completely out of it, tries to go up to the top, but Shawn superkicks him on the way down to finish at 26:09. Well, you knew that Shawn was going to get his win back sooner or later. I don't think it was as purely epic and dramatic as their first match at Wrestlemania, with more slow spots in the middle and a weaker finish, but it was still in the same percentile, so to speak. ★★★★½

—And now, for our designated nacho break segment, ring announcer Lillian Garcia reveals her true love for Viscera and asks him to marry her. Sadly, the answer is interrupted by the return of the Godfather, who runs a strip club in Vegas and thus was available for the show tonight. Long story short, Viscera decides to once again embrace his inner pimp, and he leaves Lillian all alone. Well, you live, you learn.

—Smackdown World Title: *John Cena v. Chris Jericho v. Christian.* Cena was drafted to RAW with his title, basically rendering the belt totally meaningless since it no longer represented the show that he won it on. This is kind of a sad blowoff for a feud between Christian and Cena that had been building (albeit in one-sided fashion from Christian) for months leading up to this, before Jericho turned on Cena in a tag team match to interject himself into the feud and thus render Christian's involvement rather pointless. Christian's involvement was rendered more pointless when Christian was shipped off to Smackdown in the draft lottery. Cena tackles Jericho to start and Christian attacks both of them. Jericho and Christian argue over who gets to choke Cena down, and then decide to take turns beating on him. See, there's a good message for kids here.

Jericho quickly turns on Christian and drops an elbow on him, but Tyson Tomko gets involved and drops Jericho on the railing to get rid of him temporarily. That allows Christian and Cena to do their thing, as Cena hiptosses him and stomps a mudhole in the corner. However, he does not walk it dry, and that fatal error allows Tomko to nail him, too. So the ref ejects Tomko from ringside as a result. Christian gets distracted by that and Cena pancakes him and tries the F-U, then simply dumps him to the floor instead. Jericho pops in with a flying elbow from the top for two on Cena. Suplex and seated dropkick follow, and they slug it out. Cena boots him while he tries a charge into the corner and pounds him down in the other corner. Jericho comes back with the bulldog, but misses the Lionsault. He recovers with a baseball slide that puts Cena on the floor, and they do some brawling out there.

Jericho preps the Spanish table and tries to suplex Cena onto it, but Cena reverses to a DDT on the floor. And now Christian has recovered enough to get back into the match, so he attacks Cena and gets two on him in the ring, while Jericho sells the injury on the floor for a while. Christian hits the chinlock, but runs into a clothesline and flying shoulderblock from Cena. Cena comes back on him with the backdrop powerbomb and he tries the Five-Knuckle Shuffle, but Jericho yanks him out of the ring and sends him into the stairs. Christian, however, baseball slides both the ref and Jericho at the same time, leaving us with Jericho and Christian in the ring while Cena lays around outside.

Jericho tries the Walls of Jericho, but Christian

cradles for two. Christian goes up and Jericho slugs it out with him up there, but Cena catches both of them with a powerbomb and everyone is out. Cena tries covering both guys, but only gets two each time. Cena and Jericho slug it out and Cena makes the big superman comeback, clotheslining everything that moves and taking Christian down into Jericho's head. A double Five-Knuckle Shuffle follows and he rolls up Jericho for two, but Christian rolls up Cena for two. Jericho rolls them both up at the same time for two. Well, that's unique. Everyone collides and it's a triple KO. Jericho climbs and Cena shoves Christian into him, knocking him to the floor, but he can't get the F-U on Christian. Christian escapes and gets the inverted DDT for two on Cena. Christian gets frustrated and grabs the belt, while Tomko returns from exile and lays out Cena with a clothesline, thus allowing Christian to get two. Nice use of ref distraction there.

Cena backdrops Christian onto the floor, but Jericho catches him from behind and applies the Walls of Jericho. He releases and dropkicks Christian off the apron, but goes right back to it again, forcing Christian to break the move by rolling up Jericho for two. Jericho tries to bulldog him, but gets reversed into the Unprettier, which Jericho reverses by shoving Christian into Cena. Cena then picks Christian up on his shoulders, uses his legs to knock Jericho out of the ring, and he finishes Christian with the F-U at

15:20. Super-hot three-way match, which was looking like standard RAW fare for a while with the "I'm knocked out now you two wrestle" stuff at the beginning, but the last five minutes was some superbly choreographed stuff. ✦✦✦✦

—Hell in a Cell, RAW World Title: *Batista v. HHH.* Batista is decked out in the badass white tights and pads tonight. HHH attacks to start and Batista recovers outside. Back in, they fight over a lockup and Batista overpowers him and adds a clothesline in the corner, and dumps HHH with a clothesline. They brawl outside and HHH gets rammed into the cage a few times, but recovers and sends Batista into the post. HHH adds a necksnap as Batista tries to head back into the ring, then pinballs him into the cage for a wicked bump from Batista. HHH takes over and pulls out his trusty toolbox, finding a chain there. Now what would a chain be doing in a toolbox? I'm tempted to deduct ¼✦ for that.

Anyway, HHH beats the hell out of Batista with it and hangs him on the top rope with it, forcing Batista to necksnap out of it. With that accomplished, he proceeds to whipping HHH like the proverbial dog with the chain. Sadly, the moment is ruined somewhat by HHH blatantly telling Batista "now post me" while on camera, which sets up Batista ramming his back into the post and cage in succession. This draws blood on HHH, who responds by coming back with a spinebuster. JR's analysis of the situation: "He may be able to capitalize, but maybe not." How truly insightful. HHH does, however, capitalize, by grabbing a steel chair wrapped in barbed wire. JR declares that this is why he's called the Cerebral Assassin. Because he can hit a guy with a chair? I mean, sure, it would hurt, but it doesn't take Einstein to figure that out.

Batista absorbs some nasty shots with that weapon, and then comes back with a lariat and grabs the chair himself, continuing the theme of the match thus far. He absolutely lays into HHH's face with it, which is pretty cool. Then we get the classic "grinding the barbed wire into his face" spot, followed by the equally classic "cheese grater on the cage" spot. Batista adds a javelin into the cage as HHH bleeds buckets all over the place. Back into the ring, although with Batista's luck out there tonight I'm not sure why he'd want to head back in, Batista pounds away in the corner. And indeed, he misses a charge and hits the post, allowing HHH to take over again. Shoulda stayed on the floor, Dave.

HHH tries Kick Wham Pedigree on the chair, but only gets as far as Kick Wham before Dave backdrops out of it. They slug it out and Batista powerslams him on the barbed-wire chair, and that gets two. JR gives him a nice backhanded compliment by noting that "he may be a no good bastard, but that was a hell of a kick out." Not the kind of thing you can have printed on a Xmas card, but good enough. Batista grabs the chain and goes for the kill, but HHH DDTs him on the chair and Dave starts his own river of crimson. They brawl outside as JR notes that HHH needs to pin him in the ring, but not so: In 2002, HHH pinned Chris Jericho in a Hell in a Cell match on *top* of the cage. And now, because *you* demanded it, HHH pulls a sledgehammer out from under the ring. What all is *under* there? JR of course notes that it's as legal as a wristlock. I'd like to see a weapons match where everything is legal *but* wristlocks, just to hear what his analogy would be.

They slug it out and Batista goes for the demon bomb, but HHH backdrops out of that and then does his usual Evil Plan Culmination: He hits Batista with the sledgehammer, but Batista hits him right in *his* sledgehammer, if you know what I mean. And again, Batista uses the "anything you can do" mentality and gets the hammer for himself, but runs into a chain-assisted punch from HHH. That gets two. However, when HHH tries to come off the top with the chain, Batista holds up the hammer and HHH lands on it. Well, they're 1–1 now, I guess. Normally, I hate that spot because it involves holding up a boot to block a move that couldn't conceivably do any damage even if it wasn't blocked. However, seeing HHH spit out blood on impact made it pretty cool.

Batista gives him a ride to the floor, via the top rope and Utica, and adds a shot to the stairs for good measure. Then in case HHH didn't quite get enough, he grabs the stairs and rams them into HHH's head. I was hoping for something more visually dramatic like *throwing* them at HHH's face, but that might be a bit too dangerous. Into the ring, and now the base of the stairs gets set up in the corner, and HHH meets it head on a few times. Luckily, his Neanderthal forehead gives him a few inches of extra padding. With HHH dead to the world, Batista gives him the thumbs down and goes for the powerbomb, but HHH goes low and a Kick Wham Pedigree follows. That gets two, as someone actually gets to kick out of the deadliest move in wrestling. They actually shouldn't have Batista do the "thumbs down" signal unless the move is gonna hit.

HHH goes for another Pedigree on the stairs, but Batista counters with a *nasty* spinebuster on them instead. That's gonna hurt in the morning, man. He tries to finish with the powerbomb, as HHH grabs the sledgehammer in an effort to counter the move, but he can't swing it in time and Batista finishes him at 26:57 to retain the title. This was HHH's first singles loss in the Hell in a Cell match, and Batista's last match on the RAW brand, as he moved to Smackdown in the draft lottery on the very next episode. Simply brutal and hellaciously violent, it ruled not only because of all the crazy violence but also because both guys exchanged stuff rather than one guy taking a beating (i.e., Batista) for twenty minutes and then making a comeback. It was about Batista beating HHH at his own game (pardon the pun), and it was probably Batista's best singles match, well, ever. ✶✶✶✶¼

The Bottom Line: With three matches at ✶✶✶✶ or better, all in a row, that puts Vengeance into some pretty elite company as far as PPVs go. I wasn't expecting a lot out of this one coming in, and it didn't have the epic feel or long-term ramifications of something like a Wrestlemania, but it's well worth tracking down the DVD and watching HHH get beaten to a pulp. Highest recommendation.

# EPILOGUE

**BUT BEFORE WE WRAP UP,** there's one last thing that needs to be discussed, and that's the bizarre saga of Matt Hardy.

As noted earlier, Matt's career had been on a downswing since 2003 and his ill-fated move to RAW, as he wanted to be closer to real-life girlfriend Amy "Lita" Dumas. Although he got screwed over in the story line bigtime by Kane, it was actually knee surgery that put him on the shelf for a long time in the summer of 2004 and most figured that he would return with a newer and more edgy gimmick to exact his revenge around Wrestlemania time. He even posted examples of it to his Web site, as he apparently had come up with his own new look as the "Angelic Diablo," a goth-looking Raven wannabe who lived life on the edge or something. By January 2005, however, it was apparent that something strange was happening to his personal life.

The first indications came when rumors swirled that John Laurinaitis had to take someone aside backstage and give them a talk about being more discreet with their love life, especially where married people are involved. People filed that one under "amusing side-notes" and forgot about it for months, until shortly after Wrestlemania (where Matt Hardy had been ru-

mored to appear and make his return), when Matt seemingly went crazy on his Web site and started taking down all pictures of Lita that used to be there. He also started posting cryptic messages about how she ruined his life and generally slagging her. Apparently, the party was over for them, but then it got weirder. He also started making not-so-veiled swipes at Adam "Edge" Copeland ("Adam Copeland is feces" for instance), and suddenly everyone put two and two together and remembered the anecdote about the indiscreet wrestler having an affair behind his wife's back, and the shit really hit the fan. Edge and Lita were screwing around, as Edge's wife, Lisa, discovered when she checked his cell phone records and found him calling Lita dozens of times over a short period. Lisa even posted an impassioned and nearly incoherent rant on Matt's Web site, calling Lita a bitch and saying she looked like a man.

To say Matt didn't take it well is quite the understatement, as he seemingly fell into a depressed state and posted increasingly bizarre rants on his Web site. Finally, in May 2005, the WWE fired him because of repeated requests to stop posting about the situation, requests that he ignored. The fans quickly picked up on the firing and rallied behind Matt, turning him into something of a cult hero, and started hitting Edge with smarmy chants of "You screwed Matt," which the announcers were unable to play into the story line because Matt Hardy was now persona non grata as far as the WWE was concerned. It got worse when ultra-cynical (and very much "hip to the room") East Coast crowds further turned their venom on Lita, who was supposed to be a virtuous babyface. Giving her the dreaded "slut" chant and treating her worse than any heel they had on the roster, the crowds were so mean to her that when story line husband Kane was attacked by aimless roster waste Viscera, the crowds actually sided with the heel Viscera and booed supposedly sympathetic babyface Kane.

The creative team was now in the desperate situation of having to get the heat off of fired Matt Hardy and onto employed Kane, so they ran (what else), another tournament for the #1 contender spot. This whole mechanism was designed to get the finals down to Edge v. Kane, so that Lita could turn on her "husband" and join up with Edge. And now they had a very hot heel couple, who honestly were ready for a main event slot as packaged. So the next week new champion Batista squashed Edge like a bug and that was that. However, the heat was still on Matt Hardy, who the crowds wouldn't shut up about, and Kane was dismissed with boos whenever they tried to make him seem like the victim. In fact, the more they tried to make the "monster" look sympathetic, the more jaded crowds turned on him, because wrestlers are supposed to be tough guys, not wusses who cry when their hearts are broken.

So where else could this go, but a hurried wrestling wedding between Edge and Lita. The usual silliness applied, but when it came time for someone to object, Matt Hardy's music and video played, and everyone was shocked, to say the least. However, Edge played it off as a joke. This would have been the dumbest move in a long time on the WWE's part had things not played out as they did. Building up someone as a working-class hero and promising an appearance, which is then yanked away, is a bad thing to attempt unless you have that person already under contract. Even the writers were convinced that this wasn't so, and that viewpoint was reinforced by Matt Hardy's increasingly bizarre behavior on his Web site, like creating a homemade reality show where he shot at pictures of Lita and then ran them over with his car.

By July, Matt's ninety-day no-compete clause was to be up and it was assumed he would show up in the TNA, but the week before the TNA July PPV, Matt suddenly showed up on RAW, playing a role not unlike that of the late Brian Pillman's "Loose Cannon" character, as he attacked Edge and was "arrested" by security for trespassing in the WWE's arena. Although the camera being on Matt for the whole time ruined the "shoot" aspect for most people, the appearance and realistic emotions behind the whole feud left it as one of the most effective and powerful angles they had come up with in years.

And that's exactly the kind of thing that the promotion needed all along. Not more muscleheads being called up every week like Chris Masters or the Boogeyman, but story lines that offer a real emotional connection for the viewer and allow even the most jaded fans to wonder to themselves if something was real or fake. I want to be fooled as a fan. Not just "worked" by lying promoters out for a buck any way they can, but actually sucked into a story line and then genuinely surprised at the turns that the plot takes. For all the TV writers they hire, not a lot of them actually appear to have watched much TV. Instead of taking stupid sitcom plots from *Everybody Loves Raymond* or whatever show is at the top of the heap at that moment, the writers should be sticking within the genres that fans relate to. *24* is written and plotted as episodic action-adventure television, and that's exactly what the WWE is constantly aspiring to be, and probably should be. *Oz*, the long-running prison drama on HBO, is exactly the kind of gritty male soap opera that men could watch without being embarrassed about doing so. The twists and turns on both shows were both gripping and yet believable within the realities created by their universes, and that's the important thing. If you want to be outrageous and shocking, fine, but at least be internally consistent and find ways to make characters that people *care* about. All the repackaging in the world couldn't get Kane heat from the fans, but Matt Hardy became a sympathy case for millions because he was very publicly cuckolded by a scheming girlfriend. Who can't relate to that? Millions of guys have been dumped by their girlfriend for some smarmy asshole like Edge, so why not capitalize on that like every prime-time soap opera from *The OC* to *Beverly Hills 90210* has done?

I think that's where I'd go if confined to the notion of "soap opera for men" like the WWE seems to be. Because really, if you look at the track record for all the new guys I've mentioned thus far, who actually managed to survive the numerous cuts? John Cena and Batista are the two biggest examples of success, but they were bred for superstardom from day one. But both also got over because of characters that fans could invest in, not because of hackneyed sitcom writers getting them to do comedy skits with "ass cream" or whatever inane notions they came up with on a napkin the night before. Randy Orton, also on their short list of guys for the future, got over because fans saw a guy working his way to the top, not because of the millions of cheap tricks they tried once he turned babyface.

Now more importantly, let's look at who didn't get over. Guys like Mordecai and Kenzo Suzuki and Muhammad Hassan were given elaborate vignettes and characters that could be summed up with one or two characteristics, but none of them were real people and they all failed because once in the ring, they were exposed for what they were. Guys like Matt Morgan and Nathan Jones were pushed because of size, but again, were exposed once in the ring and given nothing that fans could care about outside of it. The company constantly preaches that the best characters come from taking the person and "turning it up to eleven," with Steve Austin being the prime example of that, but they still insist on falling back on tired gimmicks and the same tired mind-set of what a wrestler must look like. Is Marty Wright *really* the "Boogeyman" deep down? Does John Heidenreich *really* enjoy writing poetry and making friends with underage girls? Actually, I don't want to know the answer to the second one. But I think my point stands. And I think George Burns said it best with regards to their problems building characters that people care about: "Acting is all about honesty. If you can fake that, you've got it made."

# LAST WORD

*In the months between my initial writing of the book (July 2005) and this writing (February 2006), lots of things in the wrestling world and my relation to that world have changed, and I thought I'd slip in a few words to cover them.*

**FIRST AND FOREMOST,** one of the main themes of this book is the struggle of Eddie Guerrero to overcome his demons and rise up the ladder of the WWE, which he managed to accomplish once in 2004. 2005 saw him nearly do the same thing again, finding his groove as a villain in a silly storyline with Rey Mysterio about Rey's son and who the father really was. While it didn't win any awards for the acting, it did make Eddie into a hot enough commodity again that when Dave Batista suffered a serious muscle tear in October of 2005, he was going to be given the Smackdown World title for the second time. Sadly, that was not to be. In November of 2005, Eddie Guerrero died of heart failure, directly caused by a congenital defect, but helped along by years of drug and steroid abuse. Unfortunately, there would be no happy ending to his story, although there rarely seems to be in wrestling anyway. The WWE was nice enough to wait a couple of months before exploiting his death for every cent it was worth, and I doubt that anyone was surprised by that. The result was a vigorous series of press releases declaring newer and tougher drug tests and regulations, with stiff penalties up and down the promotion for anyone caught using anything. In a shocking turn of events, no one in the promotion tested positive for anything, and in fact Vince McMahon himself appeared on the cover of a bodybuilding magazine showing off his insanely chiseled features, no doubt accomplished entirely through genetics and training. I know that I for one slept better knowing Vince was on the case when it came to preventing further tragedies from drugs.

As for me, well, I just stopped watching entirely around the time that they finally forced Jim Ross off the air and replaced him with former ECW shill Joey Styles to coincide with RAW's return to the USA Network. I have nothing against Joey personally, but the common feeling from other announcers is that he is totally lacking in his own opinions and will mindlessly recite anything fed to him in his earpiece, and is thus helpless without it. Most count that as a criticism of his abilities, while I count it as lifetime job security in the WWE. At any rate, the decline in quality with John Cena on top of the promotion just got to be too much for me, and I no longer had the desire or the time to devote two hours of my life to a show I actively disliked as much as Monday Night RAW. Eddie's death didn't help bring me back, either. I still watch the occasional PPV and follow enough of the storylines and backstage gossip to know what's going on, but the last few years have really ground me down as a fan, and considering how long I've been watching, that's saying something. And I know that I'm not alone in my feelings—although the foreign markets are still booming, the WWE has been relying on them more than ever with dwindling attendance in North America, as well as seeking out new sources of revenue. One example is the 24/7 "on demand" cable channel that they launched in 2005, which finally showcases the potential of their giant library of wrestling.

No doubt technology and inertia will keep the WWE alive for as long as Vince is also alive, but there has long been so much potential in the new crops of people developed by their systems, which unfortunately has been wasted for the most part. Maybe competition from the UFC and TNA will wake up the sleeping giant, or maybe HHH will inherit the business from his father-in-law and drive it into the ground even further, I don't know. But either way, I've got better things to do with my time and money than waiting around to find out, and that makes me even sadder than the events of this book do.

Scott Keith
February 8, 2006

# INDEX

# ABOUT THE AUTHOR

**SCOTT KEITH** is the fiercely Canadian (except when it comes to Toronto) author of three other books about the wacky world of professional wrestling: *Tonight . . . in This Very Ring* (Citadel Press), *Wrestling's One-Ring Circus* (also Citadel), and *The Buzz on Professional Wrestling* (Lebhar-Friedman Books). Best known for his extremely opinionated and often controversial rants about this so-called sport, Scott is often loved or hated but rarely ignored by his readership. Scott began writing about wrestling in 1996 for an Internet discussion group and from there graduated to the well-loved Wrestlemaniacs Web site. When that site was bought out by CBS *Sportsline* in 1999, he moved with it, turning his PPV reviews and snarling recaps of the WCW and WWF TV programming into cult sensations along the way. After years of maintaining his own Web sites (the dearly departed Rantsylvania.com and TheSmarks.com), Scott shifted his focus to writing for the biggest remaining independent wrestling Web site, 411 wrestling.com. And when their focus shifted to pop culture, Scott shifted with them, beginning extensive DVD reviews for the newly renamed 411mania.com as well. Scott's wrestling rants also appear on www.insidepulse.com. And he now has his own weblog, which has brought in a whole new fanbase because it's not only about wrestling but also about pop culture as well. It's called "Scott's Blog of Doom" and the link is: rspwfaq.livejournal.com. For those who ask, Scott's all-time favorite wrestlers are Ric Flair and Chris Benoit, and yes, he did once say that "HHH is God," although he regretted it years afterward, as HHH also seemed to develop the same opinion of himself. It should be noted that Scott doesn't directly blame himself for that development, although others do. Scott lives in Saskatoon, Saskatchewan, Canada.